Enjoy The Journey

And

Take Along What Really Matters

By Dr. Nancy T. Burk, MscD.

Enjoy The Journey And Take Along What Really Matters
By Dr. Nancy T. Burk, MscD.
Copyright © 2008 Wellness Information Network™

Wellness Information Network™ 10672 Gabacho Drive
San Diego, Ca. 92124.
nttburk@earthlink.net

ISBN: 978-0-692-00051-9

TABLE OF CONTENTS

Universe, Earth, Nature, Pets

PREFACE

Life is a journey. It starts with God. Even though we may not know Him, He knows us. Then it continues with our family...our parents, their parents and their faith, beliefs, traditions and ways of living, acting and being. Along the way, we experience many things...things that happen because of our heritage, genes, upbringing and parenting.

As we grow and "spread our wings", we become responsible for the things that happen to us. We find ourselves enrolled in "The School of Life". How well we learn our lessons depends on what we believe and the choices we make. What and who has formed our beliefs? Have we read the right guidelines for living? Some choices we make are good and some are not so good. However, by asking God to help us, we learn to make better choices.

How we act, react and adapt to life's changes makes the difference between having an optimistic or a pessimistic view of life. I believe it is not what happens to us but how we handle the situation. If life is full of lemons, make lemonade!! We learn to make lemonade by finding out what really matters and taking that along with us, leaving behind things in the past that are traumatic, hurtful and hinder our progress.

Sometimes we can carry around bundles of garbage from past hurts, etc. that can plague us all our lives. We are responsible for discarding faulty programming and negative thinking that we have collected, so we can really enjoy life. That is what this book is about...*ENJOY THE JOURNEY AND TAKE ALONG WHAT REALLY MATTERS.* Another way of putting it is, "In joy (enjoy) our journey with God and take along what really matters" or "By rejoicing in the Lord as we go on our journey, we take along what really matters." "Rejoice in the Lord always, again I say Rejoice." (Phil 4:4)

INTRODUCTION

Friends have been asking me for years, "Nancy, when are you going to write a book about how you have been able to overcome all the challenges you have had in your life?" Three years ago I actually wrote six chapters but never finished. I sent off proposals to three different publishers but received only rejections. I decided that maybe I would start with small magazine articles, but after three or four rejections or no responses, I stopped and decided it was not the right time.

I am including the above because I want people to know that just because a rejection is received, a temporary setback occurs in life, or a prayer isn't immediately answered, it doesn't mean one gives up. It may be disappointing, but there could be many reasons why things don't turn out the way we want them to. It may be that in the big picture, what we want is not in our highest and best interests (God has a better and different plan for us), it may be that some unfinished business needs to be taken care of, more lessons need to be learned, more insight or awareness needs to be gained or it is just not the right time.

For in the final analysis of things, WHAT REALLY MATTERS? What is it in life that is most important? Is it success, and by the way, what is success? Is it making "it" in the world.... and what is "it"? Is it accumulating vast amounts of money, having a big house, becoming famous, having "power"...and what is "power"?

In September 2003, my high school graduating class had our 50th Reunion Party. I remember some classmates and I discussing this question of WHAT REALLY MATTERS after fifty years of life's experiences. In high school, there is such emphasis on appearances, popularity, one's family or background or where one lived. After high school, life steps in and is no respecter of background, appearance or popularity.

WHAT REALLY MATTERS is HOW one has lived his/her life. How have we treated people? What kind of relationships have we had? How have we handled disappointments, illness, stress, and loss? What has motivated us? Who and what have we believed in? Have we been an example of love, honesty, and courage? In Ephesians 4:1-2, Paul calls us, "...to live a life worthy of the calling you have received. Be completely humble and gentle; be patient, bearing with one another in love."

I am writing this book so that every reader can analyze his/her life and see if in your heart you have lived according to WHAT REALLY MATTERS and only each person can answer that question for himself/herself.

What I write about in the ensuing chapters is WHAT REALLY MATTERS to me, and how I have been able to meet the challenges of life. I hope no one gets the idea that I am portraying myself as the ideal person because I have made my share of mistakes, but where I have made mistakes, I hope I have learned from them and hope others learn from my mistakes as I share them. I am not perfect and do not pretend to be better than anyone else, as I am not. Where I have fallen short, God's grace has been sufficient to lift me up. I believe God wants our heart and intent to always be in the right place, even though things do not always turn out, as He or we would like.

This book shows how I have experienced God in my life. Some of you will have different beliefs, perceptions, and definitions or will not agree with some things in the book and that is okay. I recognize others have had different experiences in their lives and it is helpful when we can share and learn from each other's experiences. If each reader can pick up one beneficial idea or learn one thing new, that is my goal.

In Chapter 1, my family background, childhood, teenage years and the beginning of my journey is described.

In Chapter 2, I talk about the importance of faith, describe how blessed I was to grow up in Christian family, and share the beliefs that have sustained me throughout my life.

Chapter 3 provides information on hope and what part it plays in helping a person to keep going when there are setbacks and discouragements.

Chapter 4 shows the importance of learning, not only our formal education and training, but learning the "lessons of life".

Chapter 5 talks about how important prayer is in our journey. Communion with God provides direction and wisdom along our way as well as a way to worship our Creator and express thanks for all He gives us. It provides a channel to express our deepest needs, desires and dreams. We also need to listen to what God says to us through our "inner self" and meditation.

Chapter 6 is about self-discovery, self-knowledge, "stretching our wings", becoming independent and taking responsibility for our choices in life.

The subject of Chapter 7 is about using our talents, contributing to society in the form of work, career, raising a family and volunteering.

Chapter 8 shows how love is the "greatest of these", explains the different kinds of love and how these kinds of love have been manifested in my life, including my marriage to a wonderful man.

In Chapter 9, I show how important it is to use our minds to help build clarity, strength and purpose in our lives, to help change faulty and negative programming to positive messages, and to help improve our relationships. Through the use of Hypnotherapy, we can access the subconscious to help us get well and maintain our bodies in a state of well-being.

Chapter 10 deals with health and healing...physical, mental, emotional and spiritual. It shows how important it is to take responsibility for one's health and provides techniques and methods for healing naturally, and chronicles my health history, showing how God's amazing grace has pulled me through a multitude of health challenges.

Chapter 11 talks about my miracle recovery through "God's Amazing Grace", from the Flesh-Eating Bacteria.

Chapter 12 describes the importance of relationships and explains the role of love and forgiveness.

In Chapter 13, I describe the importance of caretaking (self, children, family and the universe) and how this has been a part of my life.

Chapter 14 describes the "Fruits of the Spirit" and invites us to manifest these virtues in our daily life.

The subject of Chapter 15 is peace and how each of us needs to focus on peace every day for our lives and for the world.

Chapter 16 talks about celebrating life regardless of the challenges facing us on a continuing basis, and how Tom and I have celebrated life in our marriage.

Chapter 17 summarizes what I feel is the answer to WHAT REALLY MATTERS. "Make me a Blessing." I show how God has provided me many opportunities to share my faith and life with others as an example of His miracles and answers to prayer in my life.

Chapter 18 Takes us to all the States that we needed to complete our tour of the United States of America. This was a 40 State, 18,000 miles, in 7 months in which we framed the U.S. in 2005. In 2006 and 2007 Nancy's last trips to our property in Oregon and seeing her Sisters, as well as her medical history from 2005 - 2007

In each chapter I name a hymn or hymns that mean a lot to me having to do with the subject and provide quotations from either the New King James Version or the New International Version of the Bible. These verses have helped me not only meet the challenges of my life but to live an abundant and blessed life under circumstances that some would call frustrating, painful and discouraging. God has given me a strong Spirit to make the most out of a body that almost gave out three times and each time came back as a witness to show "How Great God Is".

Chapter titles are not sequential in order of importance but according to how they fit into my life's experiences.

CHAPTER 1

BEGINNINGS MATTER
JOURNEYS MATTER

Hymn: Child of Promise, Child of Blessing

Scripture: "Train a child in the way he should go, and when
he is old, he will not turn from it."
(Proverbs 22:6)

THE START OF MY JOURNEY

Beginnings are important throughout life. The Bible says, "In
the beginning God..." (Gen 1:1). Every beginning starts with God
and each day can be a new beginning with Christ. If we start down
the wrong road, we can always turn back and/or take another one...a
new beginning. We have a plaque on our wall that says, "This is the
first day of the rest of my life". Journeys are important as well. We
start out on our life's journey when we are born and how we are
raised helps to determine what we take along. Our faith, growth, and
what we learn determines what we leave behind.

I was blessed to have been raised in a Christian family. My
parents gave me the faith, hope and love I needed to sustain me on
my challenging journey as I learned to take along what really
matters.

FAMILY BACKGROUND

MY FATHER

My father (we always called him "daddy"), John Troendly,
was the son of an educator who served as the Colorado State
Superintendent of Schools. As well as owning a farm, but my father
was the one who took care of the farm, with the help of his mother.

1

He never had any formal education himself, but was extremely self-educated. He was always a Jack-of-All-Trades. He could do anything he set his mind to do. (A good role model for me in my career and life). In his lifetime, he was a farmer, motel administrator, helped to build airplanes during the war, insurance salesman, Real Estate Broker, apartment manager, made his own blueprints, designed and built houses (mastering every job involved from carpentry, painting, electrical wiring to roofing and concrete work). We lived in the bottom story of a duplex my dad built while he finished building our two-story home that he designed with my mother after the war. Later on, when my dad was in his late 60's he built their retirement cabin in the San Diego Mountains with the help from my mother and brother-in-laws. He loved to talk to people and people were drawn to him.

He finally retired from State Farm Insurance and sold his business. To this day we have insurance with the same office and one of the lady staff members told me they still have people come in talking about "John Troendly" and what an interesting person he was. When I was a college major in business, I loved discussing different business law cases with him. Because he was in so many businesses himself, he provided valuable insight.

He had a wonderful sense of humor and when he was telling a "story" or "joshing", as he called it, his eyes would twinkle and you knew he was embellishing it, because the crow's-feet by his eyes would give him away. He lost a thumb when he had the farm in Idaho because a neighbor called out to him for help with her washing machine ringers. In the process of helping, his own thumb got caught and it was cut off at the joint. He put pressure on it with a rag and drove himself into town. Since there was no doctor in the small town, he went to the barber who poured alcohol over the stub and sewed it up (a great lesson in courage and transcending pain). He always joked that he lost it sucking his thumb. That sure stopped any of us kids or grandkids from sucking our thumbs! His favorite expression was "By George".

We went to church every Sunday and my father often taught Sunday school class, mostly for boys of my age group. My mother played the piano for Sunday school. My father always said grace before meals. We were taught to be thankful for whatever we had and to share it with others - that included our faith!

2

When I was sick my dad helped my mother take care of me and he was the one who gave me my shots. He was a wonderful husband to my mother and a wonderful father to us six girls. In his later years he contacted Emphysema and suffered a great deal. My parents were able to celebrate 50 years of marriage before my dad passed on at the age of 72.

MY MOTHER

My mother (we all called her mama), Edna, was the daughter of a street corner preacher, who was also an architect and carpenter. Her birth mother passed with tuberculosis when my mother was just seven years old. My grandfather (Sydney W. Motley) read everything from Karl Marx to Das Capital, and ran for the Governor of Idaho on the Socialist Ticket. Everything that he advocated was put into practice by FDR. He knew the Bible inside and out. When I was a little girl in Idaho, before we came to San Diego, he lived with us and used to hold me in his lap, telling me all the Bible stories by heart.

My mother was extremely intelligent and went to a two-year Teacher's College. She was interviewed and hired by the Idaho State Board of Education to be a schoolteacher, and began teaching grades one through twelve in a country schoolhouse.

As you may remember, my father was the son of an educator and served on the Board of Education in Idaho, which hired my mother. It didn't take long before he was attracted to the very pretty new school marm. He courted her and before long asked to marry her. However, she kept him waiting two years before she said "yes".

My mother's father was living in Missouri, at the time, which was my mother's place of birth. When she wrote him that she was considering a marriage proposal, his first inclination was to remind her that she had a lot of potential and was intelligent enough to become principal of a school if she continued to pursue her teaching. With regret, he told her that if she really loved John, it was her choice to make. However, he said to be cautious and told her that since John was a farmer to watch how he treated his stock and if he treated the farm animals in a kindly way, he would be more apt to care for a wife in a kindly and caring way.

3

My mother made the choice to leave her teaching and became a farmer's wife. It was a hard life, feeding hired hands, doing farm work and raising five children. I was the only one not born on the farm and the last of six girls (Charlotte, 17 years older; Ruth, 15 years older; Edith, 13 years older; Mary, 11 years older; and Carol, 6 years older).

My mother had an extremely strong faith and spirit. She lived the path of her faith, although my father was sometimes impatient with others, particularly when he ordered something and didn't get it. They both taught us moral values and gave us high principles and guidelines to live by. My mother's favorite expression was "My Stars!"

There was never any cursing or taking God's name in vain. My mother always said that swearing or using vulgar language to express yourself was a sign that you lacked respect for yourself and for God and were not taught any better. She said, "I want my children to learn a higher way of life." When we did not follow her instructions we got a spanking, but we knew what it was for and that we deserved it. She was always full of love and forgiveness, while stressing the importance of learning from your mistakes and correcting the negative behavior.

My mother had a kind heart, and as I said before, even during rationing, shared whatever we had with others. She always welcomed our school friends to our home and seemed to have "home made cookies" ready all the time. When I grew older, as a member of youth or college church groups, my mother always made it known that she was willing to host any gatherings at our home. However, everyone knew and understood there was never any smoking or alcohol in our home.

She passed on June 1975 after five years of continuing heart attacks and bad health at the age of 76. I will have much more to say about this wonderful woman and the spiritual foundation for my life's journey that she and my father gave me.

MY CHILDHOOD

I was born in Jerome, Idaho, on September 4, 1935. My father delivered me since the doctor could not get there in time. I have fond memories of our life in Idaho. Grandpa Motley, (my mother's father), Uncle Lawrence, (my mother's brother), and my father built our home in Jerome As I said earlier, my Grandpa Motley lived with us and I used to sit on his lap while he told me Bible stories. He knew the Bible by heart, and so I had an early introduction to the life of Jesus Christ and His great love for all of us. He called me "his little red dear" as I had a red snowsuit and several red dresses.

My parents loved to fish and camp. I loved camping too - the beauty of the outdoors has always fascinated me. When I was small I used to sleep in the car with Carol, my sister closest to me in age, while my parents and older sisters slept in the big tent. I will never forget my last vision before closing my eyelids - the vast sky with beautiful twinkling stars!

SAN DIEGO

When we first came to San Diego in 1940, we lived at the Sunset Auto and Trailer Court that my Uncle Dan (my father's sister's husband) owned. My father helped my Uncle manage the court. When my father started working for Convair to help build airplanes, we moved into our own home in Pt. Loma.

WORLD WAR II-BEGINNING

I was six years old when World War II broke out. On December 7, 1941, my parents, one of my sisters and I were having a fun day at the San Diego Zoo. I remember very vividly. A loudspeaker repeatedly booming, "All military personnel report to your duty stations at once. The Japanese have just bombed Pearl Harbor".

All at once everyone started running towards the exits. My parents grabbed me and my sister's hands as we rushed along with the rest of the crowd. I was frightened, as everyone seemed to be in a panic. We finally reached our car and started towards our home. On the way my mother turned to my father and asked him, "What is going to happen now, John? What are we going to do?" He replied, "I don't know Edna, I don't know". Well. If your parents don't know what to do in an emergency, it is pretty scary. We lived two blocks from the Naval Training Station and the San Diego bay. There was even the talk of the Japanese bombing San Diego or sending a submarine over here. In my six year old mind Pearl Harbor seemed as close as Idaho and for all I knew we could be bombed within the next week. It seemed like my carefree childlike world had come to an end. We heard President Roosevelt's speech of "a day that will live in infamy" over and over on the radio as everyone gathered around and wondered what would happen next.

Every day the conversation centered around the war, the different battles and how many were being killed. Then came the reports of the Nazi atrocities against the Jews, the prison camps, gas chambers, people being starved and buried alive. I cried a lot in those days. It was hard for me to believe that people could be so cruel and inhumane to one another. Little did I understand what effect this kind of conflict would have on my health later on.

DAILY LIFE

There were many good memories as well. In hard times one learns to appreciate all things that are good. We went to church every Sunday as a family. I sang in the Jr. Choir and my father and mother both helped out in Sunday school, while my sister and I both attended Sunday school class with our age group.

Up to about the time I was nine years old, I had Sunday school books, which told about the Bible stories and the life of Jesus. Then I entered Communicant's Class, learning of the history of the church, learning what it meant to have a personal relationship with Jesus Christ as my Savior and what it meant to be a member of the church. I learned the books of the Bible, memorized my favorite verses and shared in class what they meant to me. Upon completing the class, we were baptized in church and received our very own Bibles in front of the congregation.

Our family gatherings were full of great times. My mother made the best home-made noodles, fried chicken, mashed potatoes and gravy, stuffing, parker house rolls, fruit salad, bean salad, applesauce cake, banana bread, cookies (filled with raisins and chopped nuts, chocolate with icing, oatmeal, chocolate chip), coconut, devil's food and angel food cake with 7 minute frosting,

6

apple pie (cinnamon pies in jar lids made from leftover crust) and I could go on and on. While the meal was being prepared, my father entertained everyone with his "stories'. My mother had a beautiful oak upright piano and after we ate, she always played the piano while we gathered around and sang. The Holidays were especially fun, with the singing of Christmas carols. We always opened our packages Christmas Eve and then went to the eleven P.M. church service.

During the war we would either take short afternoon Sunday drives, or go to the zoo or the beach, either with my older sisters, friends or parents. On our drives, we often went someplace for a picnic. My mother always had good sandwiches, lemonade and home made cookies.

One day at the beach, as I was in the water, I felt a sharp pain in my ankle and yelled out to my sister. She helped me on shore and my ankle was bleeding profusely. Thank God my parents were there, because they had plenty of clean towels, which they used to wrap my ankle. We got home and tried to get a doctor but couldn't find any available on a weekend (in those days you didn't have E.R.) My older sister called a friend who was a lifeguard. He came over, looked at my wound, said it was from a stingray and told my dad to get iodine to pour in the wound. It took four people to hold my legs and arms while my dad gave me the iodine. Two days later it was healed and we were told that because I bled so much, the bleeding took the toxins out of my system. What an experience to share at school!

My parents never gave expensive gifts for Birthdays or Christmas because we didn't have a lot of money but my mother always had a home made Birthday cake and ice cream and my friends were always invited. We always got some gift though, mostly clothes. My mother was a beautiful seamstress, and she could make anything, from pajamas to coats. She made and cut her own patterns and designed and made the clothes we wore. When I was about 8 years old, I had a red and white checked dress with a ruffle on the bottom that I just loved. As I got older, whenever I saw a dress style I wanted in an ad, catalog or store, I would show it to her. We would pick out the material at the fabric store. She would make the pattern and before I knew it, I had a beautiful new dress.

The seams on the clothes never came out and every dress was individually lined with a built-in slip.

My sister, Edith, who had a job, was the one who gave me the few toys I had, including stuffed animals and my only pretty doll with hair. I learned to make my own toys and found I could be quite creative. My doll buggy was a cardboard box with a hole in the front that my father made and tied a rope to it so I could pull it along. Cardboard boxes came in handy and I used one to make my own miniature dollhouse, cutting up another box to make the upstairs and different rooms. I used wallpaper catalogs to wallpaper the rooms and made my own stick furniture from pieces of tree branches. I used to mix flour and water together for paste. I cut my own paper dolls out of the Sunday funnies and even made some myself as well as their clothes. Looking back on those days, I think I learned some valuable lessons about appreciating the things I had, taking good care of them, and learning ways to adapt different materials to make what I wanted.

As I found out later with the Arthritis, being able to adapt to a different way of doing things was a positive behavior pattern that turned out to be very beneficial for me. I found out that there was very little I could not do in life. I just did it a little differently than other people.

WW II IN DEPTH

We would go to the nearest movie theater and see "The Eyes and Ears of the World". My sister Edith had married a man in the Fourth Marine Division and he was in the famous battles, Roi-Namur, Siapan, Tinian, and Iwo Jima. We searched the movie pictures for glimpses of his face or other young men my sisters had known from school in Idaho who were now all overseas. The servicemen who were wounded would return to San Diego and visit us first. My father worked swing shift in the defense plant and often we would stay up late listening to a serviceman who had just returned. My bed was the living room couch and so I couldn't go to sleep until everyone else did. Many times I would lay outstretched on the couch with my head in my mother's lap and my father holding my legs while the war stories, which sometimes included buddies bleeding to death, arms and legs being shot off or scattered on the battlefield, were retold. We had bunk beds in our garage and we never knew when we awoke who would come out of the garage. We deliberately left the garage door unlocked and the word spread fast that any returning serviceman was welcome at the Troendly's. We practically ran a U.S.O. out of our home. The rationing caused my mother to be short of certain ingredients for cooking, but she was very creative and served delicious meals. Whatever we had we shared with the servicemen.

Until the war ended we lived a different life. At school we had Air Raid drills where we would climb under our desks until we had places to go for bomb shelters. Even bubble gum was a black-market item. My favorite hike was in the hills above our home where I used to gather wildflowers but now it was full of foxholes where servicemen from the Naval Training Center would train. I even tried to do my part for the war effort by serving lemonade to the troops as they would march by our house but the Chief told me that I had to stop because the purpose was to toughen up the men for battle and such kindness would not exist over there. "War is Hell," I was told.

When the war came to an end, there was great joy and dancing in the streets of San Diego. Since our home was only two blocks from the Naval Training Center and the bay, the street in front of our home overflowed with servicemen and there was lots of hugging, kissing and honking of horns.

AFTER THE WAR

However, everything changed during the Post War period that followed. Some of the wounded servicemen found that trying to make a living was quite difficult. Romances and quick marriages had not lasted. Moving from a wartime economy to a peacetime economy was not easy.

Change was going on in my body as well. Gradually, I began having pains in my fingers. My parents thought I had injured them playing jacks or other games and took me to a doctor. He diagnosed it as "growing pains" since I was entering puberty and said it would go away. Within six months, the middle finger of my right hand became swollen and inflamed. Several other fingers became stiff and my parents knew something was wrong.

9

RHEUMATOID ARTHRITIS

My parents took me to another doctor and he diagnosed it as Rheumatoid Arthritis but said he did not know what to do for it except take large doses of aspirin. That helped some, but not a whole lot. Again, this was very frightening to me. At ten years old, I was beginning to develop and becoming quite conscious of my body. At school some of the kids stared at the "girl with red, swollen fingers". Just the weight of a sheet on my body was enough to cause me to cry out with excruciating pain. However, my mother had the gift to be able to hold me without causing pain. She would cradle me in her arms, pray with me and tell me that "there was always hope for a better tomorrow".

EFFECTS OF WAR STRESS ON HEALTH

When the war ended in 1945, is it any wonder that I developed Rheumatoid Arthritis, an immune system related disease? It is well known now that continued stress and trauma over a number of years can cause severe damage to the immune system. I was continually caught between the "fight or flight syndrome" during the war years, wondering if we would be invaded by enemies or if we would be able to escape. Would we live or die? I continually thought about man's inhumanity to man. Why do people kill each other? Why do we have to have wars? Then when the Rheumatoid Arthritis (R.A.) became so painful with my inflamed and swollen joints, I began to wonder, "Why do I have to suffer?" Where does the suffering in the world come from? Why would a loving God permit such cruelty and suffering? However, these questions of doubt faded away as my faith took over.

I was blessed with parents who continuously searched for the best doctors and treatment for me. Without their faith, hope, love and support, I never would have lived past the age of 18. One of the things that helped was my parents arranging for me to have piano lessons. I took lessons for several years and kept practicing even when I had finger pain. The doctors have often said that playing the piano kept my fingers from getting worse. It also gave me a sense of accomplishment and joy. I have always loved music anyway.

SEARCHING FOR THE ANSWER

My parents took me to one doctor and then another one, looking for some hope and treatment that would help. Finally, we found one who gave me shots that really seemed to help. His office was located at one side of his home and he made some "Hungarian goulash" for me to take home as well as giving my mother the recipe saying it had all the ingredients for proper nutrition. He also taught us to heat paraffin on the stove and using a fine paintbrush, to cover both my hands with hot paraffin. I was to keep the paraffin on for several hours until my hands sweat out the toxins in my fingers. By then the paraffin was cool and we slipped out my hands like they were in a glove.

I was always amazed at the perfect mold the paraffin made of my hands! I was doing well under his care, until he started "getting sick". More often than not, he was unable to see me and had a nurse take over. Finally, we were told he was in a hospital in another state. Apparently, he had been experimenting on his own body with different medications and had become addicted.

Well, the search for a doctor to help me began again. My parents found a doctor who said gold shots were the answer, so I began gold treatment until my kidneys were in danger and became damaged. That doctor didn't know what else to do, so we began searching again. My parents had heard of a place in Wheeler, Oregon called the Rinehart Clinic where they were treating Rheumatoid Arthritis. Not sparing any cost, my parents made an appointment and took me to the clinic where I underwent a complete medical exam, had every test in the book, and had "bee venom" shots. After a series of these treatments, lasting about a month during one summer, we came back home.

I am grateful to my sisters for helping out. My sister, Mary, gave my folks some money for the trip to Oregon, while my sister, Edith, took care of our roomers and boarders. I was doing well for about six months, when the pain came back very strong again. So the search began again.

11

The cost of all the previous "searching" (doctor, drugs and transportation) was really beginning to pile up. My mother tried to find a job teaching, but the California School System required a four year degree and my mother had gone to a two year teacher's college, because that was all that was required in 1917. This was 33 years later and requirements had changed. My mother had kept an avid interest in the schooling of all of us and she spent many hours after school "tutoring" us whenever we were weak in a subject. Any school would have been lucky to have had a teacher like her. It broke my heart when she had to take a job at the school cafeteria to help pay my medical bills. However, my parents were determined to give me the care that I needed, no matter what they had to do.

The next doctor tried a drug called "meprolone", as I remember. I think it was a predecessor to some of the steroids. It seemed to help for a while, but then made me very sick, so I had to stop it. At that time, the doctor tried to get my parents to put me in a Crippled Children's Home and Hospital. However, my parents were not willing to "give me away" to an outside institution. That same doctor was treating some male twins who had Rheumatoid Arthritis and the disease was progressing about the same as in my body. The doctor told the parents of those twin boys the same thing - to place their sons in this Crippled Children's Home. They followed his advice. I happened to remember their names, and later in life after telling one of my friends, who was a physical therapist, about this story, said that she had worked with these twins at the hospital but that the doctors had kept them in bed for so long that the muscles atrophied and they were totally bedridden. One of them finally died and the other one became trained as a ham operator from his bed using special equipment. That was the last I heard about them.

Thank God my parents kept searching and never gave up! They held out hope that somewhere, somehow there was an answer. The disease had progressed so much that I could hardly walk. I had to quit my junior year of High School and have a home tutor, which enabled me to keep up with my class. One doctor told me that he might be able to give me some powerful drug to temporarily help me "hobble up and get my High School Diploma" but that the effects would be so bad that I would be bedridden after that. He said my prognosis was so poor that I would never be able to finish school, get a job, get married or be able to live a normal life.

12

Spending most of my life in bed that year gave me plenty of time to think. Bed rest did not take away the pain, and in fact, made me worse, since I became weaker. So I made a decision that I would do whatever it took to stay out of bed during the day. No matter how much pain I had, I was determined to walk and keep on. I was not going to have some doctor sentence me to a life of "nothingness"!

My oldest sister, Charlotte lived in Los Angeles with her husband and two children. Her doctor had attended a medical seminar with another Doctor of Internal Medicine who was treating Rheumatoid Arthritis with cortisone, which was supposed to be the "wonder drug of the century". My sister's doctor contacted this Internist and he agreed to take on my case. The first appointment was in my sister's home in L.A. He seemed genuinely interested in helping me, so the summer of 1952, I was placed in the Los Angeles hospital where this doctor practiced and for a week received I.V. treatments of this drug. After that, I was given an oral maintenance dose of cortisone and we stayed at my sister's house in L.A. until the doctor was assured that the dosage was correct. I had immediate relief. It was like a new life had been given to me and when we got back in San Diego, I called all my friends to tell them.

However, the doctor had said that certain side effects may gradually appear and we had to schedule monthly appointments to see him. My sister, Carol, drove my mother and me to Los Angeles for each appointment, which was on a Saturday, while my father held down his business in San Diego. I was able to go back to school and finish my senior year with my class, went to football games, participated in "Senior Ditch Day" at the beach and even went to the Senior Prom and graduated in June 1953.

MY FIRST NEAR DEATH EXPERIENCE

Towards the end of the school year, the adverse reactions of the cortisone began appearing. My body swelled up like a balloon, extreme fatigue set in and I had the "moon face" and acne that is common to this drug. The doctor gave me other drugs to try to combat the reactions of cortisone. That summer I was taking 60 pills a day along with the cortisone. As time passed, I couldn't remember things and every little noise would set me crying. I couldn't stand any light in my eyes and wore a blindfold in the day to protect me from eye pain.

From this point on, I will relate what my mother told me about my condition, because my mind is blank concerning this period. I started having hallucinations and thought I was "Lucille Ball". I threw things and said terrible things. At this point, the doctor told my mother to bring me up to the L.A. hospital to be taken off cortisone. He told my mother it was extremely serious for my body to be jerked off this kind of drug immediately as there was danger of imminent death; but that under the circumstances, he had no choice.

My mother stayed in my hospital room around the clock to watch over me. As all the drugs, including cortisone, were released from my body, my vital signs became weaker and weaker. The monitor showed almost a flat line. The doctor told my mother to prepare for the worst and to contact a mortician and he then left the room for a short time. My mother said she prayed one last time. Suddenly, without warning, the doctor rushed into the room and said my vital signs were coming back. Gradually, they became stronger and stronger until I regained consciousness.

After I was released from the hospital, I stayed at my sister's again until I was strong enough to go back to San Diego with my mother. Little did I realize I had just survived my first near death experience and that I would have two more later in my life. It took six months recuperation at home and then the doctor placed me on ACTH, another steroid, which was reported to have less severe side effects. The ACTH was given by intramusculature injection and my father practiced with an orange so he could give me an effective shot. This treatment allowed me to live a fairly normal life for a little over twenty years, but on the inside of my body, it was taking its toll. My health challenges continue in other chapters.

CHAPTER 2

FAITH MATTERS

Hymn: Faith of our Fathers, I Know That My Redeemer
      Liveth

Scripture: "...............If you have faith as small as a
               mustard seed, you can say to this mountain,
               'Move from here to there' and it will move.
               Nothing will be impossible for you." (Mt
               17:20)
               ".... I no longer live, but Christ lives in me.
               The life I live in the body, I live by faith in
               the Son of God, who loved me and gave
               Himself for me." (Gal 2:20)

WHAT IS FAITH?

Faith is being sure of what you hope for and certain of things even if you can't see them.

Faith is the essence of things hoped for, the absence of things not seen.

A living faith is applying what you believe in and putting your trust in your faith so much that you are willing to surrender your life to it. When a person faces rough roads or stormy seas along the journey of life, faith is the courage to trust and "Let go and let God", knowing you are in the secure hands of the Lord, that whatever happens will be for the best because God loves you and will take care of you.

TAKING ALONG FAITH ON OUR JOURNEY

Our faith begins with God and is an extension of who we are. If we are Christians we will be living a Christ centered life, and

15

others will see us applying His teachings as we travel along on our life's journey. We are confronted by so many challenges and choices nowadays, that each day, we need to ask ourselves, "What would Jesus do?".

Jesus has provided us with the imprint and model of how to live our life. God has provided us with the power to carry out this kind of life in the midst of the most difficult of circumstances. He doesn't promise a smooth journey but always promises to be there with us to give us the strength, comfort and love as we follow His path.

WHAT I BELIEVE

I believe God is the Creator and center of all creation and we are all interconnected through Him. I believe we are all God's children, even those who do not acknowledge Him. He is the source of my being. I see Him in nature and all creation and am called to be a steward and caretaker of all. I believe He came to earth in human form as Jesus Christ who taught us how to live in a Godly way, loving God with "all our heart, mind and soul" and loving others as we love ourselves, forgiving and releasing all judgment. Because we choose to live in ungodly ways, it was necessary for Christ to redeem us by dying on the cross and being resurrected to give us new life and a new beginning. "For God so loved the world that He gave His only begotten son, that whosoever believeth in Him, should not perish but have everlasting life." (John 3:16)

By repenting and admitting our mistakes, the grace of God allows us to become whole so that we can claim this new beginning and grow spiritually which is a life long process. Christ sent us the Holy Spirit to teach us and comfort us as we grow along the way, so that we might be reconciled with God and others. We are assured of eternal life through this process. However, for me, it is more important to live in the "here and now", so that my faith is a living faith and everything that I believe is being carried out in my thoughts, words and actions every day of my life.

I believe God loves and forgives all humankind and calls us to do the same. I believe I become rich by understanding the beliefs, culture, traditions, music, art, etc. of all peoples and treating them with kindness and love.

I believe peace begins with me, that I am to serve as an Instrument of Peace in being a part of the solution for world peace and calling others to do the same.

I believe in miracles, angels, the mysteries of life, the power of prayer, and meditation and trust God to guide me and help me seek to do His will, always out of love and living my faith in the service of love for the good of all.

I believe in the hereafter, or in a "life after life", but as long as I still have God's work to do in this life, my main focus is on living a life "worthy of His calling".

FOUNDATION OF MY BELIEF

I was blessed to have been raised by parents who taught me how to overcome with faith, hope and love. Having lived through World War II as a child, I had a lot of trauma rooted in man's cruelty to man, It raised questions about my faith, but love from my parents and God saw me through. For part of my life, it was more of an intellectual faith. In my college years, it became more of an emotional faith, but it wasn't until I really began searching in the 1970's to find out the reason for my Arthritis and pain that I really began to understand the "big picture". I started in with the physical and found out how our body/mind/spirit is all intertwined.

One is not healed in the body alone; the mind, emotions and spirit are all involved. Doctors are channels or helpers. God is the source of all healing. From this foundation, I have learned how to take responsibility for my health, emotions, and actions by reading and becoming consciously aware. I learned how to listen to my body, so that I knew what to do to about my limitations and expand my options while maximizing my strengths. My faith kept me strong when doubts would creep in.

My marriage to Tom was a real gift from God and we have both grown in faith through our journey together. My parents, family, husband and experiences have taught me that one can indeed have a life full of challenges and still enjoy the journey by taking along what really matters. In the process I am being transformed and reconnected to God. I have experienced in Christ the truly Amazing Grace of a Great God, who cares about each one of us in a very personal way.

17

MY LIFE IS LIVED BY STEPS OF FAITH

Every step I take is a step of faith. I live my life, especially now, one day at a time and one step at a time. I have had to learn to walk over again so many times after breaking bones, after so many surgeries or hospitalizations that I know I would not be walking today if I hadn't used the phrase, "I can do all things through Christ who strengthens me.", KJV (Phil: 4:13) with every step that I took to relearn how to walk again. I literally pushed excruciating pain out of my mind and body with that phrase. It shows how faithful God is to us. When I was in college I used to go to a church college age group whose favorite phrase was, "I know not what the future holds, but I know Who holds the future." I have no fear of death, after facing it three times and still God pulled me through. My time will come to go home when I have accomplished His purpose for my life. Until then, I say with Paul, "...I no longer live but Christ lives in me. The life I live in the body, I live by faith in the Son of God, who loved me and gave himself for me."(Gal 2:20) and " For to me to live is Christ and to die is gain" (Phil 1:21)

HOW TO HAVE MORE FAITH

1. Pray...Lord help me to have more faith.
2. Read the Bible, positive books and true stories of people who have overcome life's adversities and challenges through faith.
3. Review your own experiences of success and overcoming through faith

CHAPTER 3

HOPE MATTERS

Hymn: Blessed Assurance
My Hope is Built

Scripture: "...tribulation produces perseverance, and
perseverance, character, and character, hope. Now
hope does not disappoint, because the love of God
has been poured out in our hearts by the Holy Spirit
who was given to us." (Rom 5:3-5)

WHAT IS HOPE?

Hope comes from having purpose and meaning on our
journey. It is the feeling that whatever is wanted will happen; the
feeling of expectation, of optimism. It is the opposite of despair and
depression. It is an "inner knowing" and security that God holds the
key to our future, and He will never let us down It is the substance
of dreams...and if you dream it and believe it, you can expect it, and
you can achieve it.

It all begins in the mind with God as the provider. I think
when the seed of hope is implanted in our consciousness, it produces
a positive effect that sets the wheels in motion to activate certain
energy vibrations that bring about the results that we want and
expect. On the other hand, if we allow despair to take over, it leaves
no room for hope and simply sets up a negative cycle until we
consciously make a decision or effort to change our state of mind. If
we do not make a decision to change our state of mind, we set up a
self-defeating path for our life that is miserable and full of negative
events.

THE POWER OF CHOICE

Every minute of every day we make choices. Every choice has a consequence, either positive or negative. If our choices are based on the direction God provides us, with hope and optimism, they will be life affirming and be translated into moving us into a direction of achieving our most deepest desires and goals which set a course for our future that is full of abundance, fun and joy. Then when life presents us with challenges, we will be able to overcome them with a strong spirit.

HOW TO INCREASE HOPE

1. Pray. Ask God to help you make a conscious decision to move from despair to hope and to give you more hope, more optimism, more motivation.

2. Read the Bible, positive books and stories about people who have overcome adversities and challenges.

3. Listen to a motivational speaker on tape or in person.

4. Listen to upbeat music.

5. Exercise. Some doctors are actually prescribing exercise, instead of anti-depressants for depression as it stimulates the endorphins (feel good chemicals) in the brain.

6. Visualize what you want, how it will come to you and then imagine receiving it. Expect results.

TAKING HOPE ALONG ON MY JOURNEY

When I was having a lot of pain as a child, my mother always told me there was hope for a better day. She said new techniques for dealing with pain and Rheumatoid Arthritis were going to be part of the future and to just have faith for today and live to the best of my ability and God would take care of tomorrow. And she was so right! She said that around 1949, and in 1976, when my first knee gave out on me, they had just invented the artificial knee joint implant and I received one of the first in this country.

Hope is what has kept me going when the "going was tough". It has helped me make lemonade out of lemons and to be more optimistic even in the darkest of circumstances. My mother used to sing the songs, "Whispering Hope"..."making the faithful rejoice", and "Look for the Silver Lining" to me, which I have internalized in my thoughts.

However, there are times when I have a bad night and day with no letup from excruciating pain, and I allow despair to take over. It is then that I admit to myself that I am getting "stuck" in negativity, which I know can only cause more pain, so I ask God to help me make a conscious decision to get back on the right track with hope.

JOB'S DAUGHTERS

Being a member of Job's Daughters and holding several different offices during my teenage years reinforced the message of hope within me. I had to memorize many passages from the book of Job in the Bible about how Job was steadfast in his faith, despite the trials and tribulations he went through. It helped me understand my disappointments and pain as I related to Job's pain when he cried out, "What is man that you make so much of him, that you give him so much attention, that you examine him every morning and test him every moment? (Job 7:17, 18) Then later on, even in despair, Job declares his faith by saying, "I know that my Redeemer lives" (Job 19:25) Because of Job's faith and hope, God rewarded him greatly. I learned that regardless of one's challenges, God is faithful.

HOPE AND HEALING

Larry Dossey, M.D., in his book, *Prayer is Good Medicine,* says, "Hope heals. Faith mobilizes a person's defense and assists in getting well, and optimism leads generally to better outcomes." This is borne out by case studies. On the other hand, hopelessness kills.

Dr. Dossey says, "Many studies show that people can die as a result of dire beliefs and a sense of overwhelming futility." Concerning the controversy of giving verbal hope to a person that is diagnosed with a terminal illness, Dr. Dossey believes that there is always the possibility that things may turn out better than predicted and that believing in a good outcome may tilt the chances for making that come true. Other doctors believe that is unethical. However, Dr. Dossey solves the dilemma by the use of love. The sick person needs love, not chatter.... love, like hope, heals...it is the very foundation of prayer, he says.

THE GREATEST HOPE

My greatest hope lies in the fact that Jesus Christ is my Lord and Savior and comes from the belief that our life does not end with this life. Life goes on in the form of the Soul and one day we will all be united as one with God.

CHAPTER 4

LEARNING AND KNOWLEDGE MATTERS

Hymn: Wonderful Words of Life

Scripture: "In the beginning was the Word and the Word was with God, and the Word was God." (John 1:1)

TAKING ALONG THE BIBLE ON OUR JOURNEY

The Bible is the most important book in the world. It is the most read and the greatest, as it contains the Words of Life. It is the story of man's experiences with God throughout the ages. We find the guidelines for living and understanding our lessons in the school of life, through the life and words of Jesus Christ. It is not necessarily an easy book to read, as sometimes the truth is hard to perceive. But each one of us must say and pray, "Open my eyes that I might see, glimpses of truth Thou hast for me; Open my heart, illumine me, Spirit Divine." This means we must not only read the Bible, but also understand it and apply the teachings of Christ in our daily lives.

LEARNING

Scripture: "The mind of him who has understanding seeks knowledge, but the mouths of fools feed on folly. "(Prov.15: 14)

MY THOUGHTS ON LEARNING

Learning is more than reading or obtaining an education. For real learning to take place, there has to be an understanding and an ability to apply what has been learned. Knowledge for knowledge's sake is just a collection of trivia.

I've always felt that it was important to use words in conversation or writing that everyone can understand. That's why I always have a Dictionary near to help me choose the right word when I am writing. I was taught to read books and things on all subjects and viewpoints even if one does not agree with them. My Grandpa Motley was very strong in his Christian beliefs and yet he read things that were antagonistic to his beliefs. He told me, "If your faith is strong, you can read anything and not be afraid. It is important to be well informed on all views...be open to searching and analyzing, you might learn something new."

FREEDOM TO CHOOSE

We base our decisions and choices from our learning and knowledge. However, many times our ego takes over and the freedom to choose is translated into a license to do what we want, regardless of the consequences. Are we hurting other people in this process? This is at the core of one of the greatest spiritual lessons. God gave us one of the greatest gifts by giving us the freedom of choice. It is up to us to take personal responsibility for our choices. Are we seeking to do what we want or are we honestly searching for God's will for our life? Prayer and meditation are the greatest avenues one has for discerning that our choices are in accordance with God's will for our lives.

I have always cherished my freedom to choose and pray for God's will in discerning the right choice. Sometimes peers want to sway us and at other times, those in authority want to tell us what is best for our lives. As we are growing up, we need to learn from our parents, but at a certain age, we need to start thinking for ourselves by studying and analyzing the issues to ascertain what is in our highest and best interest with God's help. I have made some life changing decisions, particularly when I was sixteen, as I laid in bed for six months after the doctor told me I would never be able to walk again. I was determined that no doctor's words would control my destiny and I vowed with God's help that I would walk again, as I have learned to do many times after injuries, falls and surgeries since then.

VOTING

My parents always stressed the importance of voting and the idea that our right to vote could be lost if we became apathetic and didn't vote. They taught by example to study and do research. Then we sat around discussing the pros and cons of each issue as well as the candidates. They said that it was important for me to vote my conscience and that it was OK to disagree but be able to explain the reason. I registered when I was twenty-one, voted in my first election right after that (1956) and have voted in every election since then.

LEARNING FROM MY PARENTS

Besides teaching me moral lessons on behavior and citizenship, my parents have always been interested in my education, both at church and school.

My mother first taught me phonics before I even went to school by making up rhymes or from familiar songs; i.e., "By the light of the silvery moon, I used to spoon with my honey and croon loves tunes...." The sound of words fascinated me. Then I had to find out the meanings, so I started reading the dictionary, when I was very young (about 6 or 7). When I was baptized around nine years old, I received my very own first Bible. I had already memorized the books of the Bible and knew important Scripture verses. My parents bought me many books, including one that had a great deal of influence on my life. It was. *"The Little Engine That Could"* ("I think I can, I think I can, I know I can, I know I can, I KNOW I CAN.") The phrase from the Bible, "I can do all things in him (through Christ) who strengthens me." (Phil 4:13) has helped me recover from many a surgery or accident.

THE POWER OF WORDS

I began to understand the power in words when I was small. At about the same time, my sister loved to show me how much smarter she was because she was older, and knew more. I decided to show her I knew as much or more, so I read the dictionary, until I found the right word, "addlepated" (showing a muddled or confused mind; stupid) and used it to get her attention. It worked! Those familiar with sibling rivalry will understand the delight I received from this "gotcha". I found out words could be used in a positive way or a negative way to hurt people or make them angry.

One of my behaviors that I have had to continuously work on is in my choice of words when I am hurt or angry. It is easy to lash out at those who try to manipulate and tell you what to do with your life, especially when the tone is very demanding ("you should", "you shouldn't"). I learned from the Bible that it is much better to respond with love and understanding, which gives us an opportunity to grow as well as provide an example to people that there is a better way. .

These are the lessons of life that we are all here to learn. I used to think that when my formal education ended, that was the end of school. Instead, I found out that we are all in the "school of life" to learn lessons for our soul growth. Before words are spoken, they are thoughts. I have done a lot of studying in my life about the effects of thoughts, words and self-talk or what we tell ourselves about situations and people. Negative thinking and self-talk over a period of time can cause illness. On the other hand, positive thinking (attitude) and self-talk or changing one's perception can help people heal. I will talk more about this in a later chapter.

MY EDUCATION

I did well in elementary school, especially in spelling and writing. When I went to school, we had to copy down math problems from the chalkboard. When I turned in my paper, the teacher found that I had all the wrong answers, because I had copied the wrong numbers from the board (3's were 8's, and I had other numbers mixed up).

The teacher consulted with my mother and that led me to getting glasses at an early age. However, it took awhile for the teacher to figure out what the problem was, and in the meantime, I received poor grades in Math. I was sure happy when that was rectified!

We had a Spanish teacher come in once a week when I was in the 5th and 6th grades to teach us numbers, simple phrases, items of clothing, names of animals, fruits and vegetables and songs in Spanish. We would play "Yo Tengo" (I have it) or "Bingo" as the teacher would call off the Spanish names and we would have bingo cards with pictures of fruits, vegetables or clothing. We had lots of fun with Spanish!

JUNIOR HIGH SCHOOL

Junior High School was fun because there were more classes with different teachers and more friends to make. Our Spanish class was full of a variety of experiences, not only more in-depth study of the language, but also learning of the culture. We learned to do Spanish dances and were featured in auditorium concerts. I found diagramming sentences in English class quite interesting and Social Studies helped me see people in a new way. There was even a special time for Study Hall. I loved the music classes and became a member of the choir and joined a sextet that sang at various functions inside and outside the school. Girls and boys were socializing more and despite some limitations with the Arthritis, I participated as much as I could. The School Camp at Palomar was lots of fun and made me feel like I "belonged".

ORGANIZATIONS

CAMP FIRE

Throughout Junior and Senior High School most of my activities were through organizations (church youth group, Job's Daughters, Camp Fire Horizon Group and Hi-Debber's). I have described some of these groups in other chapters. I began my involvement with the Camp Fire Organization in elementary school when I was a member of the Blue Birds, continued it in Junior High, in a Camp Fire Group sponsored by Jean Kenneally. It was during this time that I yearned to go to the Camp Fire Girls summer camp in the Cuyamaca Mountains. It was called Camp WOLAHI (for work, love and health). However, my folks did not have the money to pay for the camp, but one could "earn" their way by selling 200 dozen doughnuts. I don't know how I did it, (I do remember the blisters I had on my feet from walking so far) but for two years straight, I solicited orders for and my mother helped me deliver 200 dozen doughnuts so I could go to the camp for one week for the two years. The hikes, swimming pool, crafts, nature lore, K.P., and evening campfires with songs were all fun and made me feel like I was part of a "special group". My friend Sheila went with me the second year. I had my first trip to Knot's Berry Farm and other places with our Camp Fire group.

"Miss Jean's" leadership continued with the Rosettes, the Horizon Club or Camp Fire Group for Senior High. My activities with this group are discussed during my High School years.

JR HIGH AND HI-DEBBER'S

The Jr-High and Hi-Debber's, a club for teenage girls, was sponsored by the Walker-Scott Department Store in San Diego. We had monthly Saturday meetings at a downtown theatre with showings of films of our movie idols (Elizabeth Taylor, Debbie Reynolds, Jane Powell, Roddy McDowell, Eddie Fischer, Tab Hunter, Pat Boone, Sandra Dee, Bobby Darin, etc.) and sometimes they would appear in person. There were fashion shows and they held drawings to give away merchandise. One time my number was called and I was thrilled to win a white blouse. It was a good marketing tool for the department store as we all bought our clothes from them. They also sponsored a talent show that was broadcast over the radio and unknown to me (as a joke, I think), my sister turned in my name to play the piano. When they called my mother to set a date, we were all surprised to say the least! I was excited and scared at the same time, but I practised and practised and got through it.

28

With the graduation from Junior High School, my friends and I were looking forward to going to High School with great anticipation. That summer there were try-outs for the Drill Team and Band. Quite a few of my close friends were trying out and I thought I like to try out as well, since the Arthritis was not bothering me at that time. Robert Browning said, "Your reach should always exceed your grasp, or what is there a heaven for!" I talked to my mother and she said, "Well, if you think you can do it without hurting your legs or health, it's OK, but promise me if the pain gets too much or you think it will cause a flare-up, that you will drop out".

I was elated! However, the second day of try-outs, the pain started up and I found I couldn't keep up with the rest of the team. I told our teacher that it was too much for me and she was already aware that I was having trouble, so we agreed that I would drop out voluntarily. When I told my mother what had happened, she said, "Well I knew if I told you, 'no', that you would be upset, and I figured you wouldn't be satisfied until you found out the answer by yourself." (Today, this is known as experiential learning). What a wise woman my mother was! My parents brought us up and taught us well, giving us a good foundation of values and morals but from that point on, didn't tell us what we should or shouldn't do. They made it known that they would always be there to support and love us and if we wanted guidance or advice, all we had to do was ask. However, we were always encouraged to search for and find our own answers as well as live up to our potential. One day I was writing a paper for school and I wanted to know how to spell a word, but I was lazy so I asked my mother. She said, "there's the dictionary, look it up for yourself...I won't always be around to help you." The minute she said it, I knew she was right.

HIGH SCHOOL

High School was everything we dreamed about and more! We had our school colors, our school song and everything. I was assigned to a class called "Adaptive Physical Education", where we did exercises on a mat in the gym to help our special physical condition. I made it through my sophomore year but had to drop out for my junior year and have a home tutor, because of the increase in pain and I was not able to do the walking required to go from class to class. Being able to go back for my senior year, participating in all the activities and graduating with my class meant so much to me. At graduation, my parents were proud of my recognition as a CSF (California Scholarship Federation) member because of my grade point average. I found it rewarding as well, but my greatest delight was going to the Senior Prom. To think that the year before I had to have a home tutor because I couldn't walk, and now going to the Prom and dancing was like a dream come true! That year, our football team even won games over rival schools that always beat us.

I have always loved school. I had my favorite subjects though. English (writing and spelling), Psychology, Social Studies, Literature, Civics, Spanish, History, Sociology, etc. were my favorites. Math and I never did get along too well. I never got interested in Science until later on in life. I think if the method of teaching Math and Science when I went to school was the same as it is today, where the teachers make the subject come alive, it probably would have caught my interest. I did have a Biology teacher in High School though, who assigned us projects that were fun and educational at the same time.

What attracted me about education is that it takes one into unknown worlds that are really fascinating. Especially, when I had to deal with the pain of the Arthritis, I found that if I focused on a particular subject, it took my attention off the pain for a while. I could lose myself in a book, or whatever I was involved in.

I really enjoyed English Literature and giving book reports on the classics. I had a wonderful History teacher who made the subject come alive! We had a lot of fun in my Conversational Spanish class. Even those who were late for class, had to give their reason in Spanish too. Most latecomers weren't quite sure of how to put their excuse into Spanish words, and the outcome proved to be quite funny. Needless to say, most everyone rushed to get to that class on time! In my Civics class, the teachers had speakers representing various careers come in and speak before our class.

My father was invited to speak about the Real Estate and Insurance professions. My father was always a good public speaker and I was so proud of his presentation. As a class project in Civics, our teacher asked us to write an essay about the role that Public Schools played in building good citizens. The top three essays in the class were then entered in a contest for all countywide High School Seniors. I won first prize of a $50.00 Bond and was interviewed on a TV. Program. It made me thankful that I had paid so much attention to the power of words and writing. I realized that education and learning provided the key to getting what you wanted in life.

MY CLOSEST HIGH SCHOOL FRIENDS

My closest bonds during this age came from my friends in the Rosettes Horizon Club (sponsored by Jean Kenneally). We had meetings over at "Miss Jean's" and enjoyed many delicious treats such as the orange scones that she made. She was President of the Rose Society and had a rose garden that was beautiful beyond words. At the end of our meetings we would walk through the rose garden and she would cut our favorite rose and give it to each of us. At our meetings we planned work projects, outings and other activities to earn our beads and badges for learning outdoor skills or helping other people. It was a process of learning values and how to contribute to society or become better citizens.

Miss Jean took our group "under her wing" and gave us a place to go where we could be ourselves, outside of our families. She had no children of her own and was like a second mother to us. She had a cabin in the Cuyamaca Mountains that we went to on weekend overnighters. We loved our campfire times, cookouts, "Come as you are Breakfast", initiations and projects. Dedi, especially, had such a creative mind and always came up with such adventuresome ideas for activities. One time when we had an overnight sleepover at a home, we blindfolded the new members while they walked on raw eggs, eggshells and grapes. Then we took turns reading Edger Allen Poe with a flashlight in the dark. Another time we went to the La Jolla Caves at night and walked down the dark stairs with flashlights until we came out onto the rocks where Dedi did a modern dance on a big rock in the moonlight, to the sound of the waves. It really was quite beautiful.

During my Sophomore and Senior year I was active in the Rosettes group, but since I had to drop out of school during my Junior year due to my Arthritis, my friends came over to see me at home. Shirley Horton (now Roth), who lived fairly close to our

31

house came to see me almost every day and fill me in on the latest news at school.

My other friends in the group came often. They are: Shirley Batt (now Mann), Shirley Bamford (now Minor), Cordelia (we call her Dedi) Wedgewood (now Ridenouer), Sheila Berthiaume (now Dallenbach), Ives Wooley (now Ort), Barbara (we call her Chu-Teh) Killion (now Germaine), Pat Curtis (now McGregor), Lydia Satzchko (now Norman), Barbara Davis (now Cazes), Mary Ward (now Booth), Bobbie Stone (now Kelley), Lua Beyer (Foster, now Hooper), Betty Frank (now Adams), Sally Bonham Clark Mozingo (dec), Mary Klein Wade (dec.). This group of friends has always been like a family to me. We still get together with "Miss Jean" and have had "Celebrations of life" for the two members who have passed on (Mary Wade and Sally Mozingo.).

PEOPLE WITH DISABILITIES

Now, discussions are held on how to treat people who are disabled. Back in the 1950's, people, especially teenagers, didn't know what to do when they saw a person who had a disease; all they knew is that the person was "different". Before I left school to have a home tutor my limp was quite severe and many of my other classmates looked by me as if I was invisible, because they didn't know how to deal with the situation. Many have since apologized but I really understand now, even though it hurt at the time. I have been told by my friends that the leader of our Rosette group, "Miss Jean" discussed me with my friends at their meetings. She told them the best thing they could do was just to love me and accept me for who I am; to visit, talk, or listen to me, or just come and sit with me. Is it any wonder that we all love her so much? She taught us all so much about the things that really mattered.

PLANS FOR COLLEGE DELAYED

In my senior year of High School, I had taken the college entry tests and planned to go to San Diego State that fall, but the adverse effects of my medication and near-death experience made that impossible.

BEGINNING COLLEGE

After I recovered, my parents and I discussed the matter, and I decided to enter a two-year community college instead of a big four-year college where I would have to do so much more walking. I took general education courses, which could be transferred to a four-year college later on. Again, I loved all my classes and did well. The class I took in "Public Speaking" turned out to be a real opportunity for me. Getting up to give a presentation in front of classmates whose job it is to critique you is an eye-opening experience. It is said that Public Speaking is the number one fear, even before death, which is second. Well, before we finished that class, we all had to conquer that fear. As a result, I learned how to correct everything I was doing wrong. This proved to be a real asset later on in my career, as I was required to speak before many audiences as a part of my job. I would recommend a class in "Public Speaking" to everyone! General Psychology, Social Psychology and Anthropology were all so intriguing. One of my professors was blind, but he knew who you were by the sound of your footsteps and voice. It was a good lesson for me to see someone who was physically challenged, doing so well in holding down a responsible position. After graduating, I still wasn't sure of what subject I wanted to major in, so I decided to work for while.

MORE COLLEGE

After working for five years as a Clerk-Typist, I decided to go back to college and investigated the possibility of financial help with a small private Methodist-affiliated college near-by. I was able to have part of my tuition paid by a scholarship, due to my grades, and applied for a loan to pay the rest.

I loved California Western University! The campus overlooked the ocean on Point Loma and sitting on the lawn writing reports and doing homework was so inspirational! I made many friends in my graduating class and most of us still keep in contact.

I was able to complete my Upper Division work in a year and a half, by going to summer school as well. I graduated with a

BBA (Bachelor of Business Administration) with a minor in Psychology. In those days (1963) there was only one other female besides myself in the school of business. My Industrial Psychology professor had everyone in class submit an essay on the future role of the Personnel Department in Business. She felt my essay was good enough to submit for a national competition sponsored by the American Society of Personnel Administration for college business majors. As it turned out I won first place (an award of $250.00) and an invitation to have my flight paid for to be keynote speaker at the 1963 convention banquet in Cincinnati, Ohio.

It was quite an adventure and honor for me. My essay was also published in the quarterly journal of the organization. My education was really paying off for me.

It was 1969 before I went back to get my Master's Degree but knew it would help me get promoted in my career with the Government. This time, I worked during the day and went to United States International University at night, majoring in Human Behavior and Psychology. Often I would not get home until 11:30 P.M., and would be at work the next morning at 7:30 A.M.

In a course entitled, "Conflict Management", I had a professor who bragged that he would never give a woman an "A" in his class, because, "women did not know how to deal with conflict". I knew that subject had emotional overtones for me, but I was determined to meet his challenge and accept this opportunity.

The professor gave me a very hard time, but I worked equally hard to do a good job in every assignment. I worked especially hard on our class project. After the final exam was graded, he admitted in class that for the first time he was giving an "A" to a woman, and he called my name out. I had met the challenge!

I had completed all the other course work for my Master's Degree when I got married in May 1970, and all that was left was my thesis. We first had to take a class on the proper way a thesis should be written (setting forth several hypotheses, using standardized measurement instruments to test the hypotheses, and after obtaining the results, to mathematically define the results by the Standard Deviation, the Mean and the Mode, to evaluate the hypotheses, and finally come to some conclusion.) This class included, choosing our subject title, submitting our proposal, Table

34

of Contents, and being assigned to our Thesis Committee (Chair and three committee members). This Committee determined when your thesis was acceptable and gave the approval for you to graduate. Every chapter had to be turned in and each committee member would go through it, making suggestions and redlining all parts that needed to be redone and corrected.

One of the members of my committee wanted me to use the Standardized Instruments he had developed when he obtained his doctorate. I had made a study of Standardized Instruments and had already decided I wanted to use the Ohio Leadership Questionnaires for my thesis because I felt the Instruments he suggested were not appropriate for the hypotheses I wanted to test. This committee member was very intimidating but I had the courage to politely let him know what I wanted to do. He was very upset but the Committee Chair upheld my decision. However, this one committee member redlined every single chapter I turned in and I had to redo each chapter approximately ten times!

I spent four weeks of my vacation from my job working on that thesis, from 7:00 A. M. to 11 P.M. I don't know how many times I was in tears about to give up when Tom would hug me and give me encouragement to keep on going. He often said, "You've completed all the course work and have gone this far on your thesis, don't turn your power over to that professor."

Well, I finally finished and my thesis entitled, "The Leadership Qualities of Women Supervisors as Perceived by their Superiors and Subordinates" was finally approved! I graduated in 1971 and have often said Tom deserves half of the credit, because of his support.

TRAINING AND SELF-EDUCATION

From 1971 to 1978 I was preoccupied with my marriage and job but took night classes which helped me learn new skills, abilities and knowledge or help me fine tune those I already had which would enhance my chances for promotion or qualify me for different jobs.

Tom and I were both active in the local chapter of the International Transactional Analysis Association (ITAA) and took training and classes through them, which gave us a lot of insight into our own thoughts and behavior and our interactions with others. We also became qualified to lead therapy groups and we did so in our home.

I had to tape them and the tapes were reviewed and critiqued by a professional therapist. I learned a lot, not only in working with others but for my own life. We were also active in the American Society for Training Directors (ASTD), which provided a lot of training that helped our career prospects.

Then I met Dr. Norman Shealy through a two-week course at U.C.S.D. in 1978. He encouraged me to do a lot of self-education and reading on natural health and healing. I studied herbs, nutritional supplements and homeopathy as well as joining the National Center for Homeopathy. It included journaling (self-exploration into my feelings about a variety of subjects and issues) and writing them down in a journal.

It has been said, "The pen is mightier than the sword." The power of words and writing can never be underestimated, both as a tool to understand oneself and to persuade others. Journaling provided a lot of personal growth for me as well as the knowledge that in order to understand one part of ourselves; we have to understand all parts (physical, mental, emotional and spiritual). That started an in-depth spiritual journey and has continued through this day. As long as I am on this earth, I will continue to study and learn the lessons of life.

MY DOCTORATE

In 1989 I started my formal education once again, with the International University of Metaphysics and the goal of obtaining a doctorate. However, that required going through another Bachelor's and Master's Program in Metaphysical Sciences. I again had to do a Master's Thesis (this time I did not have the obstacles that I had before) and my work and dissertation for my doctorate was completed in 1992.

MORE TRAINING IN HEALING METHODS

In 1990 I became interested in flower essence therapy and Tom and I attended the International Flower Essence Convention in Australia. I knew then that I wanted to become a Flower Essence Practitioner. I took intensive training with the Flower Essence Society in Nevada City, CA in 1993 and became a Certified Practitioner in 1994. It was wonderful to see the results on myself and others as the flower essences took us to a deeper place within to help us heal physically, mentally, emotionally and spiritually.

I was fascinated by the mind-body-spirit connection and felt led to explore it further by taking training and becoming certified in 1994 as a Clinical Hypnotherapist through the American Institute of Hypnotherapy. Tom obtained his certification as a Clinical Hypnotherapist in 1995. I also took training and became certified as a Clinical Hypno-anesthesia Therapist as well as a Regression Therapist. Combining Hypnotherapy with Flower Essence Therapy empowered me to help myself and others understand the past and release old trauma so that we can live a more effective life today. In 1997 Tom and I became Time Line Therapists as well. We continue our learning and studying every day and by attending scheduled conferences, classes and training each year to stay current in our subjects. The school of life always provides a wonderful opportunity to learn and be a blessing to someone each day

FINAL THOUGHTS ON LEARNING

As one can see, learning is not only with the mind but involves skills as well. Because of my physical challenges, I have often had to learn to do things a different way. When I was younger, I used to cry because of the things I couldn't do. I have learned to say, "How can I do this?", rather than "I can't do this". I think of alternate ways of doing the task, try each one and see what works best for me. At times we need to relearn skills, such as walking, because we were unable to use them during periods of sickness, and muscles became weak or atrophied. That is where the strength that comes from faith really helps out.

Sometimes we need to "unlearn" bad habits we have picked up, information that is out of date or negative ways of thinking, feeling or acting. It is good to review and analyze our thought patterns and behavior on a regular basis to determine if we need to discard any of these as "extra baggage" that is not productive or fruitful to our journey, as they could hinder our effectiveness, take away our energy and render our joy incomplete.

HELPS IN LEARNING

1. Read the Bible everyday, comparing the language in different versions and using handbooks and other sources to increase our understanding and gain new insights,

2. Read the Dictionary as often as possible to increase our vocabulary and improve our spelling,

3. Read positive magazines and books to increase our knowledge on different subjects.

4. Books and classes open doors to opportunity for our futures.

5. Obtain as much education as possible and learn to apply it with understanding and compassion.

6. Learn something new every day from books, other people and the school of life. Every person we meet has something to teach us...listen!

CHAPTER 5

PRAYER AND MEDITATION MATTER

Hymn: Sweet Hour of Prayer
    Take it to the Lord in Prayer
Scripture: "Pray without ceasing." (1 Thes 5:17)
    "Be anxious for nothing, but in everything by prayer
    and supplication, with thanksgiving, let your requests
    be made known to God..."(Phil 4:6)

TAKING ALONG PRAYER AND MEDITATION ON OUR JOURNEY

I would not be alive today if it wasn't for the power of prayer.
However, we cannot expect to just sit back, pray, do nothing to help
ourselves and ask God to answer all our prayers. Life requires action
and we are called to help ourselves as much as we can, but I obtain
my strength for action living through prayer and meditation.
Someone once said, "Do not pray for easy lives. Pray to be stronger
persons. Do not pray for tasks equal to your powers. Pray for powers
equal to your tasks."

If you don't know how to pray, a way to begin is to go into a
quiet place and just say, "God, teach me to pray." Prayer begins by
acknowledging our Creator and praising Him for His greatness. We
thank God for His goodness and request sustenance for the day,
asking forgiveness and confessing our sins, also asking God to help
us forgive others.

We request deliverance from evil and from our willful self or
ego. We pray for comfort and healing for ourselves and others
(petition); for guidance in our life and in the life of our nation and
the world (intercession); we pray for God's protection, love and
light, that His presence in our lives will be a beacon of love and light
to others in their journey.

GOD'S WILL

I pray specifically for my needs and desires; however in the same breath I also ask God what His Will is for me for the same thing. This is what Christ did in the Garden of Gethsemane, "O My Father, if it be possible, let this cup pass from me: "Nevertheless, not as I will, but as Thou wilt" (Matt 26:36-39) and again "...if this cup may not pass from me, except I drink it, Thy Will Be Done. " (Matt 26:42)

It is important that we not get our ego involved in our prayer so that we seem to be asking God to bend to our will. The serenity prayer is helpful here. "God grant me the serenity to accept the things I can not change; Courage to change the things I can; and the wisdom to know the difference."

SCRIPTURE PRAYERS

Christ continually prayed and gives us the best example through the Lord's Prayer.

The Psalms serve as prayers of worship or thanksgiving. "The Lord is my shepherd, I shall not want..." (Psalm 23) "I will lift up mine eyes unto the hills from whence cometh my help..." (Psalm 121)

BREATH PRAYERS

Since I believe in praying throughout the day as well as at special times, I use "breath prayers". Certain phrases that are meaningful to me are practiced often enough so that they become almost automatic and are as natural to me as breathing. I might take them from a favorite hymn (Breathe on me breath of God...fill me with life anew. That I may live as you did live and do what you did do) and (Open my eyes that I may see the truth...Open my heart illumine me...Open my ears that I may hear). Or I might take them from scripture, "I can do all things through Christ who strengthens me". "The Lord is my strength and my fortress, of whom shall I be afraid", or from some saying I have heard, such as, "The Love of God enfolds me"

PRAYERS SENT BY INTERNET

This is the Five Finger Reminder about Prayer

1. Your thumb is nearest to you. So begin your prayers by praying for those closest to you. They are the easiest to remember. To pray for our loved ones is, as C. S. Lewis once said, a "sweet duty."

2. The next finger is the pointing finger. Pray for those who teach, instruct and heal. This includes teachers, doctors, and ministers. They need support and wisdom in pointing others in the right direction. Keep them in your prayers.

3. The next finger is the tallest finger. It reminds us of our leaders. Pray for the president, leaders in business and industry, and administrators. These people shape our nation and guide public opinion. They need God's guidance.

4. The fourth finger is our ring finger. Surprising to many is the fact that this is our weakest finger, as any piano teacher will testify. It should remind us to pray for those who are weak, in trouble or in pain. They need your prayers day and night. You cannot pray too much for them.
5. And lastly comes our little finger, the smallest finger of all. Which is where we should place ourselves in relation to God and others. As the Bible says, "The least shall be the greatest among you." Your pinkie should remind you to pray for yourself. By the time you have prayed for the other four groups, your own needs will be put in proper perspective and you can pray for yourself more effectively.

Jesus said, "Love your neighbor as yourself." How can we love our neighbor if we don't love ourselves first? If we love ourselves (not in an egotistical way but like the way God loves us in an unconditional way), we will have the energy to not only love others unconditionally but also live our faith by helping others.

MY PRAYER LIFE

My parents also set an example of prayer for me. So many times when I was in pain, especially as a child, my mother would hold me and she would pray with me. For me, prayer is a necessary part of life. There have been times in my life when literally every breath was a prayer.

SHORT PRAYER TO BEGIN DAY

Oh God, help us today to face life rather than retreat from it. Let us live by our faith rather than our fears. Give us courage to live abundantly by plunging into life rather than withdrawing. In Jesus Name, Amen

From the moment I awake in the morning until I go to sleep at night I find myself in prayer. It is an experience of communion with my Creator. I feel so safe and so loved. I can talk about anything and know I am being listened to and understood without judgment. It includes my deepest thoughts, concerns, sorrows, plans, joys, and dreams. I worship, give thanks, confess my weaknesses and sins, ask for forgiveness and ask for guidance according to God's will. I pray for others and myself, for health and being whole in Christ. I ask for an understanding or making sense of what goes on in life, especially when it involves violence or so many people being hurt. There are so many challenges that confront us all...physical, mental, emotional, spiritual. It is so comforting to lay all our cares before one who can release all our burdens. I constantly pray for peace and that I might be an instrument for peace. I pray for discernment for making right choices and for opportunities to be a blessing to others. At night I gives thanks for the blessings I have received during the day.

WHERE I PRAY

I believe anyplace and anytime is the right time for prayer. My ideal is to have a Sacred Spot where it is quiet or with spiritual music in the background. For years I chose a favorite chair and had prayer at approximately the same time every day, right after breakfast. The sun came shining in the window at my back and it was as if God's light was shining on me. I have always found nature to be an ideal spot for prayer. That's one of the reasons we love motor homing so much because we can find these beautiful spots in nature where we feel so close to our Creator. When my dad passed away, I was single and just had a small apartment. A friend came by and took me to the Rose Garden in Balboa Park. Neither one of us spoke out loud, but I was able to go within myself, talk to God and found peace. My dad had been suffering from Emphysema and I was comforted knowing he was out of his pain.

Several years ago, we were redoing our backyard and had a Japanese sun house constructed with glass windows or doors on three sides. It opens up to a deck with our spa on one side, a Japanese garden in the center with our patio beyond and the other side has several tall trees with lots of ferns, red berries and greenery, that we call "our Oregon side". We put several chairs inside with a recliner, the CD player and a bookshelf with my spiritual books and several Bibles. A Cross-with a dove is on the top of the bookshelf as well as two angel figures and a candle. When I am stressed out, have heard too much "negative media", or just want to commune with God, I go out to my sun house "Sacred Spot" and find instant solace. I do my scripture reading, my Bible Study Class lessons and read my spiritual books out there. As I am reading, I look up and see the beauty of the colors of the flowers in the garden and it provides a wonderful place for sharing with Jesus. It reminds me of the hymn, "I Come to the Garden Alone".

WHEN TO PRAY

For me, the answer to that is anytime and all the time. If we have a need for guidance, help or want to thank God at a specific moment, then that moment is the opportune time to contact God. When Christ said to go into a closet and pray in secret, I believe He meant to go into our "inner self". It takes practice to be able to go into your inner self in the midst of chaos, noise or other people all around, but the Creator hears our deepest longing and listens to us. Deep breathing helps start the process of going to the center or core of our being.

PRAYER IS THE ANSWER

I remember a time when I was working and on my way home in heavy rain. I was driving up Grape Street Hill to catch the freeway in my little Datsun. Well, water got in the distributor and the car just stopped. I was able to guide it over to the side and saw a young man with an umbrella motion to me. He came over to the car and I rolled down the window. He said he would push the car around the corner where it was level and the water could drain out. Then he offered to take me to his apartment where I could use the phone. I may have been naive in those days, but I didn't know what else to do.

He looked under the hood and felt that when the rain stopped it would be OK for me to drive again. The young man's apartment was right across the street and his buddy was waiting for him as he had gone to a nearby 7-11 market to pick up an item.

It was good to be out of the rain, but I realized that I might have put myself in a precarious situation. I tried to call Tom but there was no answer, and then it dawned on me that he said he would be working late that night, although I didn't want to say anything.

The doorbell rang and two girlfriends came in so I felt a little more at ease. We talked and in an attempt to be pleasant, I remarked about the green plants growing in all the pots. Then I remembered when I worked at NAS Miramar that the Security Officer had shown us what marijuana looked like and these plants looked very similar. I really began to feel nervous when they offered me some tea, but I politely said, "No, thank you". I sent up a flash prayer to God that the rain would stop very soon and that my car would start. Well, in about five minutes, the young man looked out the window and said the rain had stopped, so we went outside. I got in my car and it started up. I thanked the young man and was on my way home. All the way home I thanked God for keeping me safe in an uncomfortable and somewhat scary situation.

THE EFFECTIVENESS OF PRAYER

The National Institutes of Health (NIH) is funding a study at Johns Hopkins of a group of women with breast cancer who say a meditative prayer twice daily. The University of Pennsylvania and Duke University, as well as Georgetown University and others, are all studying the effects of prayer. The consensus is that prayer unequivocally works and has a definite positive effect on one's health and healing. Findings included lowering of high blood pressure, healthier immune systems, prayer boosted morale, lowered agitation, loneliness and life dissatisfaction, enabled people to cope better, stay healthier in all ways and live longer. Larry Dossey, M.D, has written a book, *Prayer is Good Medicine*, (Harper Collins), citing many cases and studies which showed that prayer works. How prayer works is a matter of speculation. Some think prayer fosters a calm and state of peace within that leads to beneficial changes in the cardiovascular and immune system.

In a study using brain-imaging techniques at the University of Pennsylvania, documentation shows changes in blood flow in particular regions of the brain during prayer and meditation. For me, all I need is my own experience of surviving so many health challenges, including the flesh-eating bacteria. Prayer is the reason I am still alive.

SITUATIONS IN MY LIFE WHERE PRAYER WAS ESPECIALLY VITAL

MY HEALTH

Prayer has been the rock that I have held onto throughout all my health challenges. I will cite some of the most important. When I first was diagnosed with Rheumatoid Arthritis and the excruciating pain was so great that I could not bear the weight of a sheet on my body, my mother had the gift of cradling me with love and praying so that the pain subsided.

The countless hours I have spent in hospitals for joint implant surgeries and the ensuing recovery periods, including the

45

many times I had to learn how to walk over again, was only accomplished through prayer, faith and the strength God gave me. Prayer was the basis for my survival of three near death experiences In 1998 when I had the Flesh-Eating Bacteria, Tom requested prayers from everyone and we believe that is what brought me through a disease that most people never survive at all or survive only with the aid of amputation. Most people die within 24 hours. It was 96 hours before I even was taken to ER due to a faulty first diagnosis.

The recovery period of almost two years was almost as difficult a challenge as surviving the disease itself. The hours of excruciating pain when the bandages were taken off raw skin and redressed, not only my arms but also my thighs from which the skin grafts were taken, were only tolerable through prayer, love from Tom and others, and by the grace of God.

The recovery from my broken right pelvis in 2002 was particularly a challenge because the sciatic nerve was affected which would not allow me to sit, stand or lie down without excruciating pain for almost three months. Prayer, faith, love and strength from God were again what allowed me to make a comeback.

However, every physical setback (particularly accidents and injuries) has an emotional impact, usually fear. Since I broke my pelvis as I was standing on the second step of our motor home, trying to unlatch a stuck screen door, Tom did not want me to get in and out of the motor home without him helping me, for fear that I would again fall and hurt myself. He was down fishing when the fall occurred and has not gone fishing again without me being in the motor home and staying there until he returned. I have been wanting to be able to show him I could again get in and out of the motor home safely so I could be more independent and he wouldn't have to help me so much. So, for a year and a half I have prayed that the right time would come when he would be open to working with me to "stand by" while I did it myself and assure him that I would be safe. That time finally came in 2004, at Detroit Lake, Oregon, in August, after our Alaska trip when we were both relaxed and had four days to just take our time. I suggested it as we had come to Detroit Lake so Tom could get in some fishing. He seemed willing to help work out some blocks encountered getting up and down the stairs and getting the screen door open without the possibility of it getting stuck again. After overcoming a few challenges, it worked and what a sweet victory it was!!!!!! Thanks be to God, prayer and patience.

MY MARRIAGE

When I met Tom, and we started getting serious about the future, I fervently prayed for God's will. After waiting all this time (I was 34 years old) was this finally the right man for me? Would he be able to withstand all the challenges that he would face with my health conditions? Well, God answered my prayers positively and the test of time has shown that this is the right man for me. I have been truly blessed by his love, devotion and support throughout our marriage.

MY CAREER

I sought out God's wisdom and guidance for the direction in my career path through prayer. I would like to share several of these experiences. I had no idea the obstacles facing me for my first job in Personnel after graduating from college but I learned out later from an acquaintance. He had served as a representative from the Civil Service Commission on the panel that selected me. He said one of the members of the panel did not want to hire me for a job in Personnel because he thought it would "turn off" people from applying if they saw a person with disfigured hands in such a visible position. He was getting the support from the rest of the panel members when this Civil Service Representative told the panel members that a law was just passed but had not had the time to be published to make this kind of reason illegal and that the qualifications of a person had priority for selection. I had prayed if it was God's will that I would be selected and I was.

Later on in my career, I applied for a position at NAS MIRAMAR for a Labor-Management Specialist position. The Personnel Officer was concerned that a woman would be selected for this job, although clearly my qualifications put me at the top of the list for selection, especially after the "hot-seat" interview that I passed. The Personnel Officer told me about a year later that I had proved myself by my performance and he had the courage to apologize for his concerns during my selection. I had really prayed for this position, if it was God's will, as it would serve as a "bridge" which would give me a variety of positions to be promoted into after a year.

My final goal was to become a Training Specialist and I had prayed for God's direction as I had been turned down before. I finally was selected and found it was the right time and right place for my selection. God knows best.

OTHERS BENEFIT FROM THE PRAYER NETWORK

In 2000 we started a Prayer Network from the list of friends who were on our email list since we quite often have friends in need, that Tom and I pray for every day at home. Also in gratitude to God and the many people who had prayed for me when I had the Flesh Eating Bacteria, we had the idea of putting it on the email network. So more people could be prayer partners. As we got acquainted with more people from our travels and activities, they became interested and wanted to be put on the list as well.

We have seen many answers to these prayer requests, and some of them dealing with disease or illness, quite miraculous. One of my friends from High School has heart problems and was in the hospital during the whole summer of 2003, and was Code Blue 5 times. She also had gall bladder complications. We put her on our prayer list and God brought her through with flying colors and today she is doing fine.

Another friend, diagnosed by two neurologists with ALS in May 2003 asked to be placed on our Prayer Network. He also had Laying on of Hands at his church. Three months later his case was reviewed by ALS Specialists and was told he had Myasenia Gravis instead, which is not as serious. Today, over a year later, he is doing fine with only minor neurological challenges and some fatigue Another friend with terminal lung cancer was put on our Prayer Network when she went in to Hospice April 2003. She was told she would not live past October 2003. In October 2003 she was released from Hospice, sent home and was able to celebrate her 48th Anniversary with her husband. She lived until February 2004, when she passed at home in her sleep.

The granddaughter of a friend was born with Down's Syndrome (a preemie) with multiple health problems with her heart, lungs and other organs. The doctor said she had a big hole in her heart. She was put on our Prayer Network for mandatory surgery with many complications. Now, over a year later, she is doing quite well. When she had tests taken just before Christmas, 2004, the doctor reported that the big hole had disappeared, and called it a" Christmas Miracle".

A young 16-year-old high school cheerleader was diagnosed with a brain aneurysm and placed on our Prayer Network. After surgery and a long recovery she is back at high school.
There are so many more who were helped by prayer through eye, joint implant and other kinds of surgery that are too numerous to mention.

There are some who were prayed for that passed on and are now out of their suffering. We never know when God has a better plan but He has shown the way in the Bible for prayer to be used in healing. He uses messengers like us who pray to Him so His will might be done.

THE MEANING OF PRAYER AND MEDITATION FOR ME

Prayer is the channel (or vehicle) that enables me to move, get up and begin each day, live fully and abundantly, love deeply with expression, and spiritually grow to my highest potential that I may be a blessing to others. Meditation is the process that enables me to experience the presence of Christ and attunes my thoughts and actions to a higher path in my journey...one that has the intent of total loving and continually seeks to live a life worthy of His calling.

GOING WITHIN MATTERS

Hymn: Nearer my God to Thee

Scripture: Christ said, "the Kingdom of God is within you" (Luke 17:21) and after I go, a counselor, the Holy

Spirit will come and teach you the truth and all
things...paraphrased   from John 14:26.

MEDITATION

How do we get the motivation to love ourselves and the
energy to love others? The answer is by "going within". Some call it
"inner work" and there are various kinds of meditation. Some say
meditation is really focused thinking. Jon Kabat-Zinn in his book,
Wherever You Go There You Are, talks about "Mindfulness
Meditation, " where one is mindful of one's thoughts and actions and
observes them in an objective way, releasing all judgment.

As I mentioned, prayer for me, is communicating our praise,
thanksgiving and requests, to God. Meditation for me is listening to
God and being still. In the process, I may receive beneficial
information or answers. I never realized what meditation was or the
importance of it until I heard about its positive effect on disease and
illness when I was almost forty years old.

Oftentimes, by just listening, the Holy Spirit will teach us
things we need to know but never thought about before. "Be Still
and Know"...It is really an experience within the inner self where we
"wait on the Lord". We do not ask; we listen for His presence. It
begins by having a regular time every day and is best done in the
same place, a "sacred place" or a place that is quiet and lends itself
to communing with God. Jesus used nature, most often a garden.

Calming oneself by breathing deeply, emptying the mind of
all thoughts except focusing on a single word or concept, such as
Jesus, God or love provides the conditions to become close to our
Creator.

It always helps to read a passage in the Scriptures and say a
short prayer before meditation. ("Breathe on me Breath of God")
Then one needs to totally relax by taking some deep breaths. I do the
following neck exercise to be done slowly, suggested by Edger
Cayce: Allow the head to bend forward and then return to an
upright position (3X), allow the head to bend backwards and return
to an upright position (3X), drop the head to the right, return to an
upright position (3X). Drop the head to the left, return to an upright
position (3X), drop the head forward and rotate in a complete circle

50

to the right (3X), drop the head forward and rotate in a complete circle to the left (3X).

A breathing exercise of inhaling through the nostrils and exhaling through the mouth is also helpful. Practicing the presence of the Creator in our life each day enables us to become more at one with Him. It instills an inner peace that passeth understanding.

I like to mentally picture a garden of prayer, such as one imagines from the hymn, "I Come to the Garden...alone, while the dew is still on the roses..." and mentally say the word, "Jesus", or "God", over and over with each in breath. If my mind wanders, that's okay, I gently bring it back to my breath and continue with the mantra. Soon I am so totally relaxed and at peace that it seems nothing else matters except "being". I always feel this sense of oneness and being connected with everything and everyone. At times I have received information about my health or other guidance about an issue of concern and at other times just absolute refreshment, renewal, love, peace, and contentment from a loving, powerful, overwhelming presence.

After a certain length of time (20-30 minutes), I feel a greater sense of consciousness and awareness of my surroundings and I know it's time to "come back". As I gently bring myself back, I begin to move my limbs, stretch and gradually open my eyes.

FINAL THOUGHT

Prayer and meditation are the basic survival tools for enabling me to not only enjoy my journey, but to keep on the right path. Thanks be to God for these channels of communion, thanksgiving, praise, wisdom, guidance and solace!

CHAPTER 6

SELF-DISCOVERY MATTERS

STRETCHING MY WINGS

Scripture: "Beloved, now we are children of God,.."
(1 John 3:2)
"God created man in His Own Image" (Gen 1:27)
"Be filled with the knowledge of His will" (Col 1:19)

Hymn: Just as I Am
     He Leadeth Me

TAKING ALONG SELF-KNOWLEDGE ON OUR JOURNEY

We all need to learn "who we are" apart from our family and others. First and foremost, we are all God's children and are made in His likeness. Socrates said, "Know thyself". The Bible tells us to love our neighbors as ourselves. How can we do that if we don't know ourselves to begin with? When we know ourselves as best we can, it helps us prayerfully discern who and what we want to become. We all have specific gifts that need to be developed for the purpose that God has for us. We are all in the process of "becoming" and different roads lead us on different journeys in this life. It is only when He is revealed that we become complete.

GROWING SOCIALLY, THROUGH WORK AND TRAVELING

After I recovered from the effects of the cortisone, my parents encouraged me to "stretch my wings" by going to Junior College, joining organizations and socializing. They never intruded on my social life and allowed me the freedom I needed to make my own decisions and the space to be my "own person", even though I still lived at home. My father continued to give me a shot twice a week.

GIRLS SERVICE ORGANIZATION (GSO)

In 1955 my girlfriend, Beverly Piper, invited me to become a member of the GSO (Girls Service Organization), which met at the Armed Services YMCA. It was an organization of young girls, sponsored by the "Y" and led by a woman, almost old enough to be our mother. She was a gem - everyone loved her, including the servicemen. There were monthly group meetings held by elected officers where we planned our schedule for the next month.

Our activities included lots of dances, bingo parties, sing-a-longs (I played the piano), carnivals held for fund raising, beach parties, picnics, etc. which were held for the benefit of the servicemen (similar to the USO). Our sponsor attended all our activities and was always full of fun. Each dance had a theme with appropriate decorations. Servicemen would wander in while we were decorating and always wanted to help. The preparations were often as much fun as the dances themselves. For the time spent helping at the "Y" and for attending each activity, points were given to each girl.

At our meeting the last week of the month the girl with the most points for that month was awarded the title, "Girl of the Month" and was crowned Queen that Friday night. The two runner-ups were her attendants. A professional photographer came in and took her photograph, which was placed on the wall of the "Y" for one year. At the end of the year, the twelve girls were then voted upon by the whole organization and the winner became "Girl of the Year" and the rest of the monthly winners were part of the court. I was the "Girl of the Month" for January 1956 and my girlfriend was "Girl of the Year".

All girls on the court were escorted across the ballroom hall by a serviceman. We were allowed to date the servicemen and because we had so much fun at our group activities, many of our dates were at the "Y". Often a group of us would go out after the dances to have something to eat like "pizza", which was the food rage at that time. When a serviceman would ask me for a date, he always came to my home to pick me up, met my parents and brought me back home. When my dates didn't have a car, we would go on the bus. I never dated with the thought of how much money someone would spend on me or what someone looked like. I always went out with those who treated me nicely and just to have a good time. Of course this was in the day before the sexual revolution. Nothing was expected from either the female or male in those days. Most of the servicemen just wanted female company to talk to and enjoy a fun time as well. Some of the young men I met there I dated steadily and several had serious intentions. The first one had dated me for about eight months, was my escort for "Girl of the Month" in January 1956, was from Arizona and had his parents come over to San Diego to meet my parents. Later on, when we were by ourselves, he pulled out a box with a ring in it. I was quite surprised and cared for this young man but knew I was not ready for any commitment of this sort. I had been sick so much of my life, and felt I was just beginning to live and be somewhat independent. In the most gentle way I could, I turned him down, trying not to hurt him. It was a most difficult time, because I have always been sensitive to the feelings of others. The others let me know their intentions ahead of time before they bought a ring, so it made it easier to handle and I knew more about what I wanted at that time of my life and how to communicate it to them earlier.

CHURCH COLLEGE AGE GROUP (CELTS)

At the same time, I was very active in our church's college age group called the Celts. I always invited the servicemen that I met at the "Y" to our church group meetings and my mother welcomed them for dinner or lunch after morning church services.

We had great Christian fellowship and programs at our Sunday evening meetings. Our sponsors provided us with program material, and we chose how to deliver it. We always had a variety of subjects based on Biblical reference. During that time several of my friends committed themselves to Christ and even a career in the ministry.

Sometimes I played the piano for our hymn sings. After the Sunday evening meetings we would go out as a group to the nearby "eatery", Pizza House, or be invited over to one of the homes for refreshments. My mother provided wonderful home made delicacies for our group quite often. We would continue our fellowship at the homes, raising our voices in song again. We had retreats at the church camp in the mountains with particular themes and some of the ministers would always have an uplifting message. Our "talent nights" at camp were full of fun and comedy.

Once a year we attended a well-known Christian Conference Center (Forest Home) where we were privileged to hear top name Christian speakers like Louis and Coleen Evans and Henrietta Mears. We always had such fun at our activities, whether it was a picnic, an ice cream social at the church, or a desert outing at the vacation home of our sponsors. I will never forget the beach parties and singing "Do Lord" around the campfire. I met some life-long friends at this group (Isabel and Dave Bentley, Gene and Joanne Abshier, Marie Stockon, Vonnie Wolfgram Dahlke, Barbara Winchester Stansfield, Joyce Winchester Stilwell, and many others.)

These groups provided a very meaningful spiritual experience for servicemen, college agers, and especially me during that time when we were choosing the best way to spend our spare time as we "stretched our wings" away from home. It is evidence that good clean fellowship and fun can be found if you look in the right places.

Again, some of these friendships have lasted throughout the years, and these dear people have supported me in prayers many times throughout my life when I have gone through my physical challenges.

MY FIRST JOB AND VACATION TO HAWAII

My first job was a clerk-typist for a Credit Bureau and I scrimped and saved for two years in order to take my first big trip to Hawaii in 1958. My boyfriend, Bill, was transferred to a ship stationed in Oahu and he invited me to come over on my vacation. My parents were concerned that I not neglect my health and asked me how I would take my ACTH shot. I was determined not to let that keep me from going, so I made up my mind I would give it to myself and started practicing on an orange and then gave myself a shot before I left. This was no easy task, as the shot was given intramuscularly in the posterior, and in those days there were no disposable needles, so the needle had to be sterilized by boiling water on a stove. My father got me a sterno burner and I took a little pan to boil water.

Because the ACTH needed to be refrigerated, I had to make arrangements with both the airlines and hotel for this. There were a lot of obstacles to overcome, but I did it. I talked to my girlfriend about going with me so we could share expenses at the "Princess Kaiulani Hotel", which was two blocks from the beach. During the weekdays we took tours and went to the beach. During the weekend and evenings my boyfriend and his buddy took me and my girlfriend out. We went to my first real luau. We were there ten days but it seemed like a dream. However, I was realistic about my boyfriend, knowing he would be stationed in Hawaii for several years.

CIVIL SERVICE EMPLOYMENT

Before I left on my trip, I had taken the Civil Service Examination and when I got back my name had come up for a job offer in China Lake, in the California desert. I thought it would be interesting to work in a different place and my health was pretty good. My family had some friends who lived up there and the woman was a nurse who offered to give me my shot free.

A lot of young people were employed up there and again; I met a whole new group of friends. Verna Rogers, Esther Nemeth, Kay Hautier and I still keep in touch. Mary Jane Bradley Frank and Nola Williams have passed on. We lived in "dorms" similar to those found on college campuses. I learned how to drive and got my first car (a 1955 Chevy) that I paid for myself. I was really becoming quite "independent" and the foundation my parents had given me proved invaluable. On weekends we would take drives to the Sierra foothills or Yosemite, go "rock hounding" in the desert, go to live theater in L.A. or come down to San Diego. The times I stayed on the base, I would attend the community church that had a group for young adults. We had a good time as well.

BACK IN SAN DIEGO

About two years later, I transferred back to a base in San Diego, where I lived at home but paid rent to my folks. My dream was to eventually save money for my own apartment and/or to go back to finish my last two years of college.

VACATION IN MEXICO

However, I loved traveling and when Judy Spondourus Goodman, one of my girlfriends, asked me to go with her on a tour to Mexico, I couldn't resist. I began saving money for the trip and requested vacation time from work. What a terrific time! We joined our tour group in Mexico City where we stayed at the El Presidente Hotel. The history and culture came alive as we saw the Shrine of Guadalupe, the Square and Cathedral in the center of Mexico City, the University of Mexico, the bullfights, and took a side trip to the Pyramids. Our tour guides took us on a nightclub trip in Mexico City and we enjoyed some delicious food and saw some wonderful entertainment, including Flamenco Dancers.

We were surprised to find that, in those days, Mexican blonde women carried an air of mystique about them, which was almost magical. It so happened that Judy, my girlfriend, had blonde hair and looked very much like a famous Mexican actress and singer of the day, so people, particularly men, followed us every where we went. We used to laugh at the excitement she created.

In Acapulco we stayed at both Las Brisas Hilton and El Presidente Hotels and had a wonderful time at the beautiful beach. We visited Cuernavaca, went to the Floating Gardens of Xochimillco, and I was fascinated with the ancient town of Taxco, which still had cobblestone streets and was known as the town of silver, where we all bought beautiful silver jewelry at very low prices. This trip stirred up my interest in learning, so when I got back to San Diego, I obtained my Career status in Civil Service by completing three continuous years of work (enabling me to have employment reinstatement rights), and saved up my money, so I could quit work and go back to college.

FOOT SURGERY

In 1961, my feet were hurting me to the point that something needed to be done and one of my friends, Mary Ann Olson, had recent foot surgery performed by a doctor in Los Angeles that really helped her and she suggested that I get an evaluation from her surgeon. He recommended the same surgery for me, a synovectomy on both feet, which would remove the synovial fluid, causing inflammation. The process also involved removing the crooked joints in all the toes and straightening them. This allowed me to wear shoes without the toes rubbing the tops but as a result my foot was shortened and I must buy children's sized shoes (2-21/2). The downside is that since I have no grip in my toes, I lack balance. However, one learns to trade-off certain things if the bottom line is more function.

CHURCH SINGLE YOUNG ADULT GROUP (SIYADS)

Of course when I came back to San Diego from China Lake, I returned to our church and started attending the Single Young Adult Group, where I became quite active. It was for a group of young people a little older than Celts, the previous group I attended. Most of those I knew from the college age group had either gotten married, moved or were attending this young adult group, so it was just right for me.

Our meetings were more formal and organized. It attracted a cross-section of young people from all faiths, not just from our own church. We had our own church camp by that time and during the summer we attended camp at the Lake Tahoe Presbyterian Conference Grounds. We have had several reunions of the friends I met through this group. Marilyn Rogers Kneeland, Doris Price Scoville, Darlene HedgepethWilson and Joyce Anderson Hanson (dec) were my closest friends in this group.

AMBASSADORETTES AND BRASSHATTERS

At the same time I became a member of the "Ambassadorettes" (a hostess club sponsored by the Marine Corps at

MCRD) and the "Brasshatters" (a hostess club sponsored by the Navy at the Admiral Kidd Club and later at the Naval Station "O" Club). They held dances for the Military Officers and my friends from college as well as all my other single girlfriends attended. I met a lot of my dates and a lot of my friends met their future husbands at the dances, including Barbara Winchester (now Stansfield), Joyce Winchester (now Stilwell), Beverly Piper (now Gonzales), Beverly Beauclair (now Olson), and Darlene Hedgepath (now Wilson). Looking back now, I can say I was there when that first meeting occurred. As a result I was in several weddings and was beginning to feel like I was ready to settle down myself.

I dated a variety of young men, which helped me "sort out" the qualities I would like to have in a mate. Some dates were just for fun and others were more romantically interested.

One time I was out to dinner with a young man and we had tickets for live theater afterwards. I fell over the curb in the parking lot, hurt my leg so it bled and snagged my hose and made a big run in it. My date helped me up and I laughed and said, "Well, now you can say you literally had your date 'fall' for you." He laughed, took me home so I could get cleaned up and we got to the theater in time. Another time I lost my contact lens out on the dance floor and my date had everyone stop dancing and look for my lens until we found it.

One of the helicopter pilots I knew had gone in with several of his buddies to buy a private plane and he wanted to try it out. He suggested that I find one of my girlfriends for his buddy and the four of us fly over to Santa Catalina Island the next weekend. We were good friends and our relationship was more platonic than romantic. I was the adventuresome type and it sounded like fun. However, I made sure he understood certain ground rules about conduct, separate rooms, and then agreed to go only if we paid our own expenses. It was a smooth flight over and the ocean. Cliffs and pretty beach glittered in the sun as we prepared to land. My girlfriend, Marilyn Peterson (now Ackroyd), and I had never been to Catalina and we really enjoyed ourselves, seeing the wild boars and buffalo during the day and the music and beach that evening.

We did have a scare flying back in the plane, though, as the radio went out and we started having engine problems. Thank goodness we were close to land and made it on in with a sputtering engine! Another one of my dates was a pilot and took me up to the base hanger at NAS Miramar where I actually sat in the cockpit of an F-14.

DATING SERIOUSLY

Then I met a Lieutenant that I seriously went with for three years. We liked the same things, and hit it off right away. My folks had recently bought property in the mountains around Julian and had started building a retirement cabin. We had a lot of family gatherings up there as my brother-in-laws helped my parents build their home.

Nolie fit right in with our family. We went to church and did everything together. Even when he had duty on board ship, he invited me to come on board and eat in the Ward Room of the USS Yorktown with him. We went to all the Navy parties and his buddies knew me as his "steady". When the ship went overseas for six months, he left his car with me and wrote me several times a week, sending me packages and gifts from the Orient. I could hardly wait for him to come back but the day finally arrived when I met the ship! He came back loaded with wonderful gifts. We picked up right where we left off. We took drives to the desert, mountains, poppy fields, and went to the beach. Then he got transferred to Long Beach. However, he called all the time and he either came down to San Diego on weekends or I went to visit my sister in Gardena so I was closer to him. We talked about marriage but did not set a date, as we were both saving our money. Everyone, including me, just assumed we would get married sometime in the future.

TRIP BACK EAST

Then Nolie got orders to Philadelphia in July 1965 and that fall he invited me to visit. We went to Germantown, saw the Amish countryside and had delicious food. He took me to see the Liberty Bell and all the historic sights in Philadelphia. I had a wonderful time and we talked about our future. On the trip I also saw my sister, Ruth, and her family in North Carolina and my girlfriend, Pat Barrett, who worked for the government in Washington D.C. While

Pat worked, I toured the White House, Capital, and the rest of the Government Buildings, Monuments and sites.

We took a boat trip on the Potomic and visited Williamsburg, Virginia. Then we traveled to New York by train, where we saw several Broadway shows, including Barbara Streisand in "Funny Girl". We took a carriage ride around Central Park; saw Wall Street and other well-known places. One of the young men I knew from our church group was vacationing in New York at the time and offered to escort my girlfriend and me around at night, so we saw "Top of the Sixes", etc. and went to other evening activities that we would not have gone to otherwise.

HEARTBREAK

Back home once again, I continued to get letters every week from my boyfriend...then they got further and further apart and finally the bad news that he was married to someone else. I was heartbroken! I cried for days and asked God to help me understand. It was hard for me at the time, but God really does know best. Only He knew at that time that in less than four years I would meet my Soulmate.

In the meantime, the mountain retirement home my parents had started building was just about finished and they planned on selling their San Diego home and moving everything up there. This was a good time for me to do something new, so I used my extra money to rent an apartment and started dating again. Since I loved to entertain, I had Open Houses over a one-month period with small groups of friends to celebrate a "new beginning". It was lots of fun and focused my attention on others. However, after the last Open House Party, as I washed and put away my glass lazy susan on the top shelf of my cupboard, the little step stool I was using tipped over and I broke my left pelvis and fractured my left hip. As result I spent two weeks in the hospital (1966). After I recovered, I was ready to go again!

TRIPS

My girlfriend Pat, who worked in Washington D.C. transferred to San Francisco and I visited her on my vacation. She was always lots of fun and knew all kinds of places to visit. We went to the "Purple Onion", frequented coffee houses, participated in the "folk music craze", and saw the "Smothers Brothers". Later on my girlfriend Ellen and I drove to San Francisco in my car, stopping to see one of our mutual friends along the way. We felt so fortunate to be able to see Ella Fitzgerald at the Fairmount.

FIFTIETH ANNIVERSARY FOR MY PARENTS

In August 1967 my parents celebrated their 50th Anniversary. We had a grand celebration and family reunion at the mountain cabin. Everyone was there and we presented my parents with pictures of us and a personal letter telling them how much they meant to us. I was fortunate to be able to get the story of their courtship and wedding on a cassette tape as my brother-in-law Bud asked leading questions. That was a perfect time together. All my sisters fixed their best recipes and we ate my mother's favorites as well. We talked, laughed and my mother played the piano as we all sang along. That was our last good time together as my dad's emphysema got worse and worse.

My girlfriend, Ellen Beyer, and I had planned to take a trip to the Orient but I was concerned over my father's health. He assured me he was going to be all right and encouraged me to continue with my plans. This was so like my parents. They never allowed us to stop or interrupt our plans because of their condition or health and they never put their fears on us.

TRIP TO THE ORIENT (1968)

Ellen and I left in April 1968 and we were gone for six weeks. We met the rest of our tour group in Los Angeles. It was a great fun-loving group of about 20 people (single and married) from all over the United States.

We arrived in Tokyo just in time for the cherry blossoms to open. It was a spectacular sight and one that I will never forget! We stayed at the Tokyo Hilton and toured the city, including the Imperial Palace and countryside. The countryside was so beautiful it took my breath away. We had a Mongolian barbecue luncheon and strolled through the garden with a pond and 500-year-old pagoda.

Everything in a Japanese garden is placed in a special way to create symmetry and harmony. Later in the evening we visited the Ginza. The next day a bus took us to several shrines and the Nikko Highlands National Park were we encountered a sparkling lake and waterfalls amid beautiful mountain scenery.

Kamakura, Japan's 12th century capital with the Daibutsu (immense bronze statue of Buddha) was our destination the next day where we ended up at the mountain resort of Miyanoshita and indulged ourselves with a hot spring bath. We motored through Hakone National Park where Mount Fuji reflects its immaculate beauty. Arriving on a beautiful sunny day, we were lucky enough to see the top of this great mountain.

After a cruise on the lake we stayed at the Hotel Fujia. Then we arrived in Kyoto by the "Tokaido" (world's fastest train going 100 mph-often called "bullet train").

We watched artisans create their beautiful, detailed and time-consuming crafts. I bought a one-of-a-kind 12 place setting of china with a black pine hand painted on all the pieces. We toured more shrines, Nijo Castle, the Gold Pavilion, and enjoyed a delicious Sukiyaki dinner with traditional Japanese seating and chopsticks. Later on we attended a traditional Japanese tea ceremony and listened to Koto and Gagaku music. We enjoyed watching the flower arranging, Kyomai dance and the Geishas. Later on we saw the talented Kabuki dancers perform.

In the morning we motor coached to Nara, which was the capital at one time, and visited a temple with its colossal Buddha image, which is the world's largest bronze statue. Then we went on to Takarazuka where we saw the 400 member All-Girl-Revue Theater.

The next two days were spent on Taiwan (formerly known as Formosa), which is ninety miles off the coast of the China mainland. We stayed at the Grand Hotel in Taipei and went through a hallway where one of the doors had President Eisenhower's name on it since he had stayed there on one of his visits. As we looked out the windows of our room, we could see Chiang-Kai-shek soldiers training at the War College to take over the Chinese mainland again. This dream still existed back in 1968, but the dream never became a reality, of course. We toured the museum where many of China's ancient treasures from the Ming and other dynasties were placed when they were secretly removed from the mainland as Mao took over China. That night we had a delicious 12 course Chinese dinner at the Hotel. It seemed like we ate all night.

The Philippines was the next destination. We saw the Malacanang Palace in Manila. I was lucky enough to have a personal contact (a friend of one of my friends), a Missionary. She escorted us to places not on our tour. The lush countryside and Taal Lake was beautiful, but then there were grim reminders of the war, including the site of the Bataan Death March and the Manila Cemetery, second largest in the world at the time. In the evening we were entertained by bamboo dancers.

Then a flight took us to bustling Hong Kong where we shopped and shopped. This was the place where I got nearly all my gifts for relatives and friends as well as my clothes. I bought a cashmere dress, jacket and matching shoes which were handmade for me, as well as an elegant hand-beaded top and cardigan. I couldn't believe the prices. Now as I look back and am more aware, I can painfully see the discrepancy in how people are paid in other countries and why there is so much poverty in other parts of the world. The people living on sampans were only one example of this.

That evening we had dinner on a floating restaurant and took the tram to Victoria Peak to enjoy a magnificent view of the city at night. We stayed at the Hong Kong Hilton. The next day the trip to Tiger Balm Gardens was fascinating. Later on we went sightseeing to the New Territories, Kowloon and the countryside to a 600-year-old walled village (Kam Tin). We arrived at what was then known as the "Bamboo Curtain" and the barbed wire fence into Red China. (Remember, this was 1968, before President Nixon paved the way for the opening of China.) I was blessed to have the names of a couple living in Kowloon, who knew my friend. He was a doctor and escaped from Red China to Hong Kong on a garbage scow, using only a straw to breathe through with all the garbage piled on top of him. It was an incredible tale of survival.

64

We left the next morning and our flight took us right over Viet Nam. (I even have a picture taken from the airplane window showing the fires from the war below). I was young and adventuresome at the time, but now, sometimes think, what would have happened if we had plane trouble and had to land in Viet Nam. I guess it shows that none of us know-only God does, and He certainly protected us on that trip. We landed for a short time in Kuala Lumpur and then went on to Singapore, our next destination. We saw the Rhesus Monkeys, which are sacred over there as well as Fakirs with snakes. Sightseeing tours took us to Hindu Temples, Moslem Mosques and the Palace of the Sultan. We stayed at the Raffles Hotel in Singapore.

Our next stop was Bangkok, Thailand. where we went to Wat Po, the most extensive temple in Bangkok, and saw the reclining Buddha. The next day we toured more temples, the canals, the floating market, and saw the Royal Barges-a sleek fleet of beautifully carved and decorated wooden boats. We went shopping and I bought a Thai Star Sapphire (my birthstone) and Thai silk material. That evening we had a wonderful Thai dinner and were entertained by an unforgettable performance of classical Thai dancing. The next day we saw the Grand Palace and other sites.

The next day, Ellen and I left the tour group and ventured out on our own. We wanted to go back to Japan to experience the stay at a traditional Japanese Resort. Our tour guide recommended Beppu. We flew to Kobe and took the Kansai Line boat cruise up the Inland Sea between Japan and Korea. Our accommodations were totally Oriental. A futon for us to sleep on was placed on the floor of a Japanese style room. Japanese robes were laid out for us and there was a small table with hot tea and cookies awaiting us when we returned from our Japanese hot spring bath, The Japanese gardens there were spectacular and very few employees spoke English.

It was truly a delightful memory to have of our last visit to an enchanting country with such mystic beauty. We flew to Tokyo where our plane was waiting for us to board, since our departure from Beppu had been delayed. We were personally taken through the gates by the JAL officials and escorted to the plane by limousine. We stopped in Hawaii for a couple of days to relax and get our reality bearings before coming back home.

THOUGHTS ON KNOWING ONESELF

1. Pray and meditate.

2. Take Psychology Courses, such as Transactional Analysis.

3 Take an inventory profile that includes physical, mental, emotional and spiritual attributes to find out how a more balanced lifestyle would be of benefit,

4. Analyze your interests, abilities, skills and knowledge. Find out your strengths and weaknesses through tests and self-examination.

5. Love yourself as you are, but also love yourself enough so that you are motivated to improve and grow in your weak areas.

CHAPTER 7

CONTRIBUTING TO SOCIETY MATTERS

DEVELOPING MY TALENTS AND ABILITIES THROUGH WORK

Scripture: "As each one has received a gift, minister it to one another, as good stewards and of the manifold grace of God." (1 Peter 4:10)

Hymn: I'll Go Where You Want Me To Go
Here I am Lord

TAKING ALONG AND USING OUR GIFTS ON OUR JOURNEY

God makes us in His image but makes each one of us special and unique as well. He has given each one of us gifts and talents to be developed in our DNA. Our genes combine with our family's encouragement and nurturing so that these talents and gifts are developed. In the parable of the talents (Matt 25:15-29) Christ gives us talents to use according to our ability and warned us to use these talents wisely. We use our talents or gifts wisely by contributing to society. There are many ways to do this, i.e., working in a profession, career, job, raising a family, volunteering, etc.

Tom and I agreed not to have children because of my health. However, I did have the education to work professionally for the Federal Government for twenty-five years and I have volunteered in many ways. Tom worked as a Quality Engineer and volunteered with me as well.

GETTING STARTED

As I said in the last chapter, after Junior College, I worked as a Clerk-Typist two years for a Credit Bureau and three years for Civil Service before going back to college to obtain my Bachelor's Degree.

It was very helpful for me to be out in the work force because it helped me decide what kind of work I really wanted to do, where and for whom I wanted to work, as well as what major to take. Before I applied for the Civil Service Test, my mother and I had already talked over the benefits it would provide me, however, as always, she wanted the final decision to be mine. I have my mother to thank for my choice of government employment as she pointed out some important considerations. We both agreed that I could have problems over organizations/people not wanting to hire me with my history of Arthritis.

Since one of my sisters had experience in Civil Service, my mother thought the Government would be fairer in their hiring practices than private industry in selecting qualified people with disabilities. She had said, if I was hired for the Government, the opportunity to get good health insurance would probably be more important than the salary. She was right! As it turned out I was able to have good health insurance as well as a good salary with promotional opportunities.

While I was working I also had a chance to talk to people in various kinds of jobs and departments, and find out what was required to qualify for those positions. My sister was in Personnel and I had a chance to talk with her and others in the Personnel Department.

DETERMINING QUALIFICATIONS FOR A JOB

I learned that people qualify for specific jobs or positions by meeting the requirements, which are written down in terms of skills, abilities, and knowledge. A skill is usually a hands-on type of craft, trade or training requiring manual dexterity (typing, painting, woodworking). Abilities are usually defined as experience demonstrating "the ability to supervise a group of people", or "the ability to speak and write clearly" It is the natural or acquired capacity to do things or to carry them out, i.e. talent. Knowledge is usually determined by education or training courses, degrees or certificates. It is to be well acquainted with certain facts or information about a specific subject or issue. Interests determine how well one likes what one does and how long one stays with that job.

The key to getting a job that you like and are qualified for is to have a perfect match (or as perfect as possible) of your interests with the skills, abilities and knowledge required for that position. It is also important to remember that if you want promotions up a career ladder, that initiative, responsibility, and accountability are a necessary part of career development.

One must exercise initiative and take responsibility at a level commensurate with the position title and be prepared to take the consequences or be accountable for the things that happen (failures as well as successes) at that level.

One of the strengths given to me from my parents was to take responsibility and face the consequences of my actions, so I was prepared for that. I enjoyed working with people (interest) and I understood there was promotional opportunity with a career in personnel but that I lacked the knowledge and experience to qualify for a professional position.

Therefore, that made me determined to go back to college and get my Degree in Business with a Psychology Minor. I was able to complete the requirements in a year and a half. As a result, I applied and was selected for a Personnel Clerk GS-5 in the Personnel Department. Eight years later, I happened to meet up with a man who had worked for the Civil Service Commission, at the time I was selected for that job. He had coordinated my selection with the Civilian Personnel Officer at the base that had the Personnel Clerk vacancy. He told me that the Personnel Officer had been reluctant to hire me because my fingers were somewhat deformed due to the Arthritis and thought that people might either be repulsed or would find it awkward to deal with me since the Personnel Office was in such public view. This man had been quite firm with the Personnel Officer, letting him know that such an attitude was discriminatory and that since I was qualified that I should be hired. I'm glad I didn't know about it at the time, but eight years later, I could laugh about it, since after a year in that job I had received a commendation from the Commanding Officer on a project I had worked on.

The next year a similar situation arose which challenged my courage and integrity. According to the regulations, if the first three candidates on a job certificate (ranked according to their qualifying score) are available, the selecting officer cannot hire anyone with a lower score on the same certificate. One of the Department Heads wanted to hire the daughter of a friend who ranked below the top three candidates and asked the Personnel Officer to help him. The Personnel Officer then came to me and requested that I mark one of the top three candidates as not available so that the Department Head would be able to select his friend's daughter. I asked him if he was serious, because I couldn't believe he was asking me to do something that was not right. He tried to make it sound like it wasn't that bad, that it would be just like a typing error.

It was very intimidating as my immediate supervisor was not there at the time. It took a lot of courage for me, as a GS-5, to politely tell a GS-12, that I could not do that, but if he wanted to sign the certificate with his signature I would turn it over to him. He very abruptly declined and said he was just testing me. My supervisor never had any knowledge of what happened. She was fair, followed procedures and I liked her very much. However, in government work, the head boss supersedes a lower level supervisor.

DEVELOPING MY POTENTIAL

I applied for a Personnel Intern Program, because I wanted to move ahead in my career. A young man was selected over me, but I was determined to move ahead, and applied through the promotion bulletin for a Personnel Staffing Specialist GS-7 at another base and was selected for that. I had learned an important lesson in my career development. If things don't go the way you plan them, think of alternate strategies to accomplish the same purpose! God always provides a better way.

The Personnel Officer at the next base had a lot of integrity and my immediate supervisor, Virginia, was a gem. I learned many things from her, not only about my job, but also about life in general. She was a great mentor, teacher and absolutely the best supervisor I ever had. We keep in touch to this very day. I loved my job but had a thirst for learning new abilities and knowledge.

BRANCHING OUT TO GAIN MORE EXPERIENCE

After three years, I decided to branch out into a new field of personnel; Labor-Management Relations at NAS Miramar. Again, I applied through the Promotional Bulletin. The position required being on Management's Team and serving as liaison with the Base Union as well. It also required serving as employee-relations counselor for employees who had grievances and heading up the Equal Opportunity Program. I would also be responsible for writing up Command Directives and Instructions explaining how each of my programs was to be carried out. It would require walking a fine line and using a clear head for making decisions. A panel of five men, one of whom was the Personnel Officer, interviewed me for about an hour. It was termed a "hot seat" interview.

They presented me with several cases and asked how I would handle them, and then when it seemed that I might have contradicted myself, they asked me to explain. Thank God I didn't get rattled and was able to clarify the difference. I was in the process of working on my Master's Degree and some of the courses that I had just completed really helped me.

Arriving a little ahead of time, I sat in my car reading my Bible and praying, so I was calm when I went in. Several days later, I was notified of my selection and after a year was promoted to the next level. At that time, the Personnel Officer told me that I had proven him wrong. Among the panel of five men, he was the lone holdout who felt a female would not be strong enough to deal with the hard core Union Officers and walk the fine line that this job required, but he told me that watching me perform in an exemplary fashion had changed his mind and that I more than deserved the promotion. I also received an award from the Commanding Officer for my performance.

The next Commanding Officer was quite different, outspoken and was known for his penchant of embarrassing others and/or placing them in a most unusual predicament. I was giving a training session for supervisors when the Commanding Officer (C.O.) happened to walk in. As I was finishing a particular segment, I asked if there were any questions and the C.O. (Commanding Officer) said, "Nancy, is that a wig you're wearing?" Well, I was taken aback to say the least, but was able to come back with an appropriate reply of "Only my husband and hairdresser know for sure." Everyone laughed and it showed I could handle unexpected remarks with humor (which helps not only in work organizations, but just about any circumstance).

It was during this time that I met and married my husband, which is related in the next chapter. However, I will say that the Commanding Officer had his secretary call me and ask for a personal invitation to my wedding and he really did attend!

HELPING TO ELIMINATE RACISM

The next position I held was a Race Relations Facilitator for the Navy's program in working towards eliminating prejudice and racial discrimination. I had three weeks intensive training at a Naval Base in Florida to prepare me for this job. When I returned I was part of a team of three (two military men) which conducted three week intensive training seminars in Race Relations for about thirty-two military personnel assigned in teams of two from different ships or commands. Each team would include one Caucasian and one person of another race who would be trained by us to give a two and one half day seminar, called "Understanding Personal Worth and Racial Dignity" (UPWARD) to their command or ship when they returned.

The three-week training we provided was very intensive (very much like an encounter group) and often went from 8:00 A.M. to 9:00 P.M. with short breaks to eat. Issues were brought up which were at the core of one's emotions, because it involved our parenting and what myths we were taught about other races. We would not stop until we brought emotional closure to the whole group. Then the other two members of our team and I would "process" what went on during the day and discuss how to proceed with the next day's training.

A part of this program was to become aware of logos or advertisements, which stereotyped certain races, and I was partly responsible for the removal of the "lazy Mexican under the cactus" from the Frito-Lay chip packages. It was one of the most challenging and rewarding positions I ever held with the government and was presented a Superior Achievement Award. I can truly say I was part of a very widespread nation-wide movement to eliminate some of the hatred and behavior that pits one group or person against another and that I contributed towards making this world a better place.

After about two years, the program was completed and I faced a Reduction-in-Force but due to my variety of experience, education and training, I had no break in employment. I went to work the next Monday at another base but worked there only a short time until I found another job that I really wanted.

HELPING TO ELIMINATE SEXISM IN JOBS

My next job as a Federal Women's Program Coordinator was an extension of the Navy's Equal Employment Opportunity Program to eliminate prejudice among civilian personnel as well. The purpose was to help women develop their skills, abilities and knowledge so they could qualify for jobs that they wanted. It was 1975 and women were beginning to go into types of jobs that they hadn't held since World War II. Through the Career Counseling Program I developed, women applied for training to become welders, carpenters and hold other blue collar jobs, as well as qualifying for and moving up the ladder to professional positions. It also required holding training classes for hard-core blue-collar foremen who did not want women in their shops. I can remember giving a workshop preparing macho male supervisors for this change when one of the supervisors slammed his fist on the table in front of him exclaiming he would never have a woman working under him. I challenged him, saying "Good supervisors can train anyone and if you are as half as good a supervisor as I've heard you are, you will demonstrate to me and your peers that you can train a woman to do just as good a job as a man".

Of course his peers wouldn't let him get out of that one so he backed down. This same supervisor came to me later and told me that after two years of training, the young lady in his shop was just as good or better than most of his male employees! The Transactional Analysis training and background I had proved very beneficial in changing their attitudes. In fact, I was asked to give a course on base, sponsored by Community College and held after working hours. It was called, "TA for Supervisors", and helped present and prospective supervisors gain insight and application in positive communication skills.

RECOGNITION AND AN AWARD

The program was such a success that I received a Superior Performance Award and my supervisor nominated me for a national award. In the meantime, in July 1976, I had my first artificial knee implant but was back to work after six weeks. Later on that year, I was notified that the government would fly my husband and me to Washington D.C. to receive the national award from Chief of Naval Material for developing the career counseling program. It was quite an honor to be presented the award at a banquet in Washington, D. C. in December 1976. However, we had an embarrassing moment that we laugh about now. Upon arriving at the awards banquet, Tom was winding his way around the crowd so he could check my coat. After excusing himself many times, he still was finding it hard to get through and accidentally stepped on the shoes of one of the Admirals. He apologized but when he got to our assigned table later, found the same Admiral seated at our table.

DISCRIMINATION AND HELPING TO MAKE CHANGE

Again, as part of my contribution to change the stereotype of women not being responsible, I challenged a New York Nursery doing business in California. A credit application I filled out from them required the signature of my husband in order for me to obtain credit. As a result of my challenge, they had to change their credit application. In 1970, I felt the sting of discrimination and intrusion into my personal life when we filled out the loan application on our home, which required me to sign a statement that I would not get pregnant in order for my salary to be used to qualify for the house. I decided at that time that I would become involved in women's rights and issues and I was fortunate enough to be in the right place at the right time with the appropriate education and experience to obtain a position that would allow me to do this. However, sometimes if you stay in the same field of work too long, you can get "labeled" and others may feel that you do not have a broad enough experience or are not flexible enough to adopt to other position titles with career potential or which may fit your interests at that time.

It became increasingly clear to me that my greatest sense of job satisfaction came from sharing knowledge or information I had with others in order to help them grow or develop and I knew the position of Training Specialist would give me a broad field in which to do just this. However, the timing must be just right and I decided to build up more experience in a "bridge"" position.

BRIDGE POSITION

So, the next step in my career path led me to the Civil Service Commission, as a Personnel Staffing Specialist. This position had wide visibility and variety. It included Personnel Staffing work as well as some training and I was assigned to give training to other agencies in San Diego and Los Angeles. I was exposed to all the career opportunities at all the agencies and bases. As a result, after a year and a half, I became aware of an open Training Specialist position at one of the bases. I applied and was selected at last! If at first you don't succeed, try, try again!

FULFILLMENT OF MY POTENTIAL

I finally was selected as a Training Specialist, a career goal I had wanted and prepared for, for some time. The job was located at NAS North Island. This is a lesson in patience, perseverance and waiting for just the right time for things to break. This job enabled me to combine all my interests, including giving workshops, seminars, counseling, and assisting people to fulfill their potential. I developed another career counseling program as well as being responsible for the Engineering Development Program (a combined college and work program to train employees to become engineers). I saw young women complete this program with high honors and go on to become very competent in their field.

I was rewarded with several Superior Performance Awards for this work. During this time and until 1984, Tom and I were both active in the American Society for Training Directors (ASTD) and attended meetings regularly. When I left my North Island position in 1981, my supervisor hosted a beautiful going away party for me at the Hotel Del Coronado.

NAVAL SUPPLY CENTER

A call came in asking me to apply for another Training Specialist, GS-11, at a base closer to my home. I thought about it, and although I loved what I was doing, not having to drive so far, seemed too tempting to turn down, so I applied and was selected. I was responsible for an intern program at this base as well, but the content in general did not give me the broad variety that I had before. However, the trade-off in reducing my commute time paid off. Sometimes you have to give up some things you like in order to get other things that compensate you in a different way.

TIME TO RETIRE

Several years later my left knee started going out on me and my shoulders and elbows were giving me so much pain, it was difficult to work. I had wanted to work thirty years with the government to qualify for regular retirement. However, faced with more implant surgeries, I had to accept Disability Retirement with twenty-five years service. When I stop to think of it now, that really is pretty good considering nearly all my doctors have been totally amazed that I kept working that long. One of them stated that most people would have accepted Social Security Disability years ago rather than to put up with the pain and persevere in the presence of the kind of challenge I had with my body. However, I can hold my head up high and say, "God and I did it our way"! The government provided a wonderful career opportunity for me that gave me the ability to create programs to help others and rewarded me with great satisfaction and achievement. One of the interns that I had mentored was responsible for planning a wonderful surprise retirement party for me that I will never forget.

THOUGHTS ON CONTRIBUTING TO SOCIETY

1. It is important to know oneself and follow the guidelines under "THOUGHTS" at the end of the last chapter before working, if at all possible; or certainly before moving ahead in a career.

2. Everyone can learn a great deal by working outside of the home, sometime, even if it is only temporary. It teaches one responsibility, discipline, how to keep deadlines, and how to interrelate and work with other adults in a team effort.

3. Volunteering is always needed by church, school, charities and other organizations and provides many intangible rewards for oneself as well as benefits for others.

CHAPTER 8

LOVE MATTERS

Hymn: Love Divine

Scripture: "...if I have a faith that can move mountains, but have not love, I am nothing." (1 Cor: 13:2)

> "Love is patient, love is kind. It does not envy, it does not boast, it is not proud. It is not rude, it is not self-seeking, it is not easily angered, it keeps no record of wrongs. Love does not delight in evil but rejoices with the truth. It always protects, always trusts, always hopes, always perseveres. Love never fails.........." (1 Cor 13:4-8)

> "And now these three remain: faith, hope and love. But the greatest of these is love (1 Cor 13:13)

> "Thou shalt love the Lord Thy God with All thy Heart, and with All thy Soul, and with All thy Mind. This is the First and Great Commandment. The second is like unto it: Thou shalt love thy neighbor as thy self..." (Matt: 22: 37-39);

TAKING ALONG LOVE ON OUR JOURNEY

Loving God and loving others as ourselves, I believe is the most important lesson we can ever learn. Because, if we do this, everything else falls into place.

KINDS OF LOVE

AGAPE love is total unconditional love that neither requests nor requires anything in return. It is a never-ending love. It involves loving people regardless of their behavior. This kind of love transcends human understanding. This is the kind of love that comes from God. "God so loved the world, that He gave His only begotten Son, that whosoever believeth on Him should not perish but have everlasting life." (John 3:16)

LOVING OUR ENEMIES

We are called on by Christ to even love our enemies as an extension of the love given to us by God. This is quite a challenge and requires letting go of anger, judging others and forgiving ourselves and others. "Love your enemies; bless them that curse you; do good to them that hate you; pray for them who despitely use you." (Matt 5:44)

FAMILY

Family love is a result of being born into a situation where one is nurtured and loved by parents and siblings. Regardless of different ways of thinking, beliefs or lifestyles, there is an unconditional love that cements relationships together, even though some specific behavior of one or more of the family members is disapproved. I was born into such a family and I credit my parents for providing the faith, hope and love I needed to give me the foundation for living a victorious life under challenging circumstances. Unfortunately, some are born unto parents who do not want them or where the family is totally dysfunctional. My heart aches for these people and I have no answer, except to say we can pray for strangers in this situation and if we know of anyone like this, we need to show them the love they never received in their families as well as share with them how God loves them and can help them.

CHURCH FAMILY

Our church family is another form of family, although not genetically related, we are one body or family through Christ. We are blessed to be members of a church such as this where we love, care for and pray for each other.

WORLD FAMILY

Even though we may not recognize it, we are members of the human family all over the world. We are all reflections of one another and are intertwined in our thoughts, words and deeds as well as through God. We need to love, care for and pray more for our brothers and sisters all over the world.

FRIENDS

This kind of love occurs as we get to know someone deeply as a friend and have a lot of things in common as well as really caring about the person's welfare. I have been blessed beyond belief with such friends all my life and hope I have been as good a friend to them.

ROMANTIC

Romantic love can be just infatuation when a person first meets someone and there is a "click" of chemistry, usually sexual, but it can be spiritual, as in the case of "soulmates". If it is sexual, it can lead one to "fall in love with love" which leads to the idyllic story of Miss American Beauty marrying her Handsome Prince Charming. Sometimes the test of time and life's experiences can take its toll and divorce ensues, or if it is real the test of time will prevail.

INTIMATE COMMITTED LOVE

Both parties are attracted to each other but it will only last if "what really matters" is on the inside. This kind of love will pass the test of time as two people grow and pray with each other "through joys and sorrows, sickness and health, etc." It is important to learn that men and women communicate differently and work at understanding your partner's ways and both parties appropriately adjust. As you will see, again I have been blessed with this kind of unconditional love from Tom that involves total acceptance and commitment.

MEETING AND MARRYING MY SOULMATE

My supervisor, Virginia Anderson, during the period 1966-1969 turned out to be my best mentor, spiritual advisor and one of my best friends. I asked her one-day when do people really know they are in love. She responded, "you don't have to ask, you just know inside." Well, I thought I knew I was in love when I was seriously involved with my Lieutenant for three years, but now that was over.

The summer of 1968 was sort of slow, although my work kept me busy during the day. After my big trip to the Orient, my dad passed away and it was a low period in my life. My close girlfriend, Ellen that went to the Orient with me was getting married soon, another one was engaged (I was with both of them the nights they met their fiancées) and it seemed like life was passing me by. Now, it was September 1968, I had just turned 33 years old, and my girlfriend, Marilyn Rogers, and I were out observing the single scene.

There seemed to be no good marriage prospects in store for either of our futures, although both of us were dating off and on. Agreeing that we both needed a new focus, we decided to forget about men and concentrate on our education to improve our careers. So, we made a commitment to enroll in the Master's Degree Program for our respective majors. We did so but little did we know that the next year I would meet Tom and she would meet Bill, our life partners. Well, I found plenty to keep me busy, working hard and attending night classes for my Master's. Anyway, I had given up on any thoughts of eligible men, hadn't I? My friend, Virginia, was a Spiritualist Minister and had predicted that 1970 would be my year and when the flowers were blooming I would walk down the aisle with my True Love. Well, I appreciated her optimism, but things looked pretty dismal to me. My engaged girlfriend, Darlene, was getting married in Missouri and wanted me to be in the wedding. Since all my savings were going towards paying for my education, I didn't have any spare money for the flight to Missouri. It was July 27, 1969, the day of her wedding and I was feeling pretty low.

However, that day would be one of the most eventful and biggest life-changing days of my life. Some of my other single friends had invited me to a Singles Dance that evening, but I wasn't too interested so I decided to go to a church program. It ended earlier than I had thought, so when it was over, I dropped in at the Singles Dance to see my friends, since it was close by. One of my friends was across the room dancing with a young man and my friend, Joyce Anderson, was sitting at a big booth with another young man. I was talking to her and had just about decided to leave when this other tall handsome young man came back from the dance floor to this same booth. Joyce introduced us and Tom asked me to join them, so I did, as I needed cheering up. Well, we talked and talked and talked and danced and talked. We had so much in common that time just flew and before I knew it, the place was closing. He asked if he could take me to get something to eat, so I agreed and we talked some more. His last words were, "I wish this night would never end".

I wondered if it was all just a dream but when Tom called the next evening as he said he would, I knew it was for real. We arranged for a symphony date for that next weekend. We both loved music and would often go to several lounges to hear our favorite pianists.

We went to church, group and family activities, concerts, Starlight Opera, out to eat, and double dated with close friends. Sometimes I would invite Tom over to dinner to test my culinary skills. We were both money conscious so were careful not to overspend. I had a book of restaurant and entertainment 2 for 1 offers so we utilized these quite often. The Naval Air Station where I worked had discount coupons to Disneyland, so one weekend we spent a day up there.

I will never forget this picture that sticks in my mind to this very day-Tom had on an iridescent green shirt and as we were going up the ramp to the G.E. Display Building, he held out his hand to me and as he looked back, his eyes were sort of twinkling with an invitation of fun. It was like he was sending me a telepathic message inviting me to share a lifetime of adventure with him. I knew at that moment that I loved him and wanted to marry him. However, it would be three months later before I knew whether it was just my imagination or if Tom really felt the same way. I prayed a lot about our relationship, because I didn't want a broken heart but if I was going to get married, I wanted it to be God's will so that it would last.

A lot of our dates were picnics out in nature, a walk on the beach or we would go for drives to visit my mother at the cabin in the mountains. Since I had a lot of homework with my Master's Degree, Tom would often come over to the apartment and read while I worked on class assignments, or we would discuss some of my class subjects. I found I often gained a new perspective from his point of view.

Marilyn, who made the commitment with me to start our Master's Program together, was engaged to Bill and they had set the wedding date for several days after Christmas. At their wedding, I caught the bride's bouquet and Tom caught the garter. Tom had talked about getting married and I "sort of knew" he would pop the question while they were on their honeymoon, so we told them the news then. On New Year's Eve we had plans to double date at the Officer's Club Party with our friends, Darlene and Bob, who got married in Missouri the night I met Tom. We were all out on the dance floor when midnight arrived, and as Tom kissed me, he asked me to marry him. It was one of the happiest moments of my life.

I am a dreamer, but I am also a realist. The questions started coming to my mind - would Tom still love me if my health got worse? How would we manage finances? We both had good jobs, but had not saved anything. I realized we needed to talk seriously about a lot of things before we set a date. I asked Tom to make an appointment with my doctor and get a worse case scenario about my health.

I loved this man dearly, and it took a lot of courage, but I wanted him to marry me, without sympathy or a sense of obligation, knowing all the details from a doctor's viewpoint. He did and when he came back he said, "When you love someone enough to get married, the love is unconditional, so whatever the medical condition is, doesn't matter - it is love that matters."

It affirmed my faith that with God's help, He would give us the strength to get through anything. One of my friends used money as a criteria for a mate. She had said, "you can fall in love with a rich man as well as a poor man and I'm going to make sure I marry a rich man". Well, that was all right for her, but my criteria was love and I knew God would help us with the rest. Another one of my friends even said I shouldn't marry Tom because he did not have a college degree and I was working on my Master's. I told her the same thing that I was marrying for love and that one of the things that attracted me about Tom was his innate intelligence and his own program of self-education.

By the way, the latter friend never did marry. Now, thirty-five years later, Tom and I are quite financially well off and are still reading and holding college level intelligent discussions. We started with love and God did provide all the rest!

While we were dating, Tom had already shared many things he had to overcome in his life. Rejection and lack of self-worth took its toll in his life as a result of some of the things that happened in his early years. As a child he developed Dyslexia. Since his eyes were affected, learning has not been easy and he was thrown out of school, church and some groups because they did not understand. Later on, one of his friends threw a firecracker in his face and since then he has had Tinnitus in his ears. Lower back problems surfaced when he worked for a bowling alley as a teenager. He was already familiar with medical problems since his mother and sister had had polio, but with a great deal of treatment, both were able to recover without any visible affects.

As Tom and I have discussed many times, even though there is no visible evidence, it does not mean a person is free of a disease or an ailment (cancer, heart problems and a host of other health problems are not visible). Emotional and mental scars can be just as debilitating. The issue is how a person overcomes and goes on to lead a victorious life. As Dr. Robert Schuller says, "turn your scars into stars". It is also a life lesson to understand the problems of others. The phrases "until you have walked in someone else's shoes" and "there for but the grace of God go I" come to mind. We all are in the process of overcoming something and it is up to those of us who have been blessed by the grace of God in being victorious to share our message with others to help them overcome.

MAKING PLANS

From that point on, Tom and I settled down to making plans. We made up a budget for our first year of marriage and talked about real issues of living. We decided not to have any children because of my health and the medications I had had all my life.

OUR WEDDING

We set the date of May 2, 1970 for our wedding. My mother made my wedding dress and it was beautiful. The hem was the only thing left undone when she had a bad heart attack close to our wedding date. We consulted with the family about postponing the wedding and were told that is not what mom would want us to do. When she was well enough, I asked her personally and she was adamant about us going ahead. That was my mom-she never asked us to nor would she want us to deny ourselves any change in plans because of her. In fact she was so unselfish, that it would probably have affected her adversely had we done so. A neighborhood dressmaker finished the hem on my wedding dress.

Tom and I had the standard pre-marriage counseling session at our church and arrangements were made for the reception in the church lounge. With some help from our families and friends, Tom and I pretty much took care of the plans for our wedding. We ordered the invitations and sent them out ourselves, ordered the cake and made arrangements for a photographer and flowers. My Horizon Club leader, Jean Kenneally, who was President of the Rose Society, provided roses for the church pews.

The colors were white and yellow. I had one attendant - a Matron of Honor (Darlene). Her husband, Bob, had duty orders for the East Coast and so couldn't be there. One of our dear friends, Hal Smith, was Best Man. My oldest sister, Charlotte, stood in for my mom, who was still hospitalized, and her husband, Bud, walked me down the aisle in place of my dad. It was a small wedding (about 200 attended) in our church chapel. The wedding ceremony went off without a hitch except I almost forgot to kiss Tom and I signed my maiden name on the Marriage Certificate, which is ironic after practicing writing my married name millions of times while we were courting.

After the reception in the church lounge, Tom and I went to the hospital to visit my mom and take her some flowers. My sister, Edith, had stayed with my mom while the ceremony was going on. That night we stayed at our apartment and the next day headed off for our honeymoon (Santa Barbara, Big Sur, Monterey, Carmel). We used 2 for 1 coupons from our Let's Dine Out Book for hotels to economize. We took a picture of the phrase we wrote in the sand on the beach at Santa Barbara, which is "I Love You". We had car trouble on the way back, and Tom investigated and found out that the linkage on the carburetor broke. Tom, with his ingenuity, was able to bend a coat hanger correctly so that it replaced the linkage until we returned to San Diego We were gone a week and as soon as we got back, went to see my mom again in the hospital.

FIRST FIVE YEARS-1970-1975

SIGNS THAT WE ARE SOULMATES

As Tom was helping me unpack my belongings from my single life, he came across a colored portrait of me and asked, "Was this picture ever hung on the walls of the Armed Services YMCA?" and I said, "Yes, when I was Girl of the Month for January 1956". That was when we pieced together the story of the time when we almost met 13 years earlier.

Tom had been in the Marine Corps, stationed at Camp Pendleton and had come into the "Y" while we were having a fund-raiser. He remembered seeing me play the piano (it was getting close to Christmas) while servicemen were gathered around singing Christmas Carols and thinking he would like to meet me. At that point, I stopped playing and went into our "Dime a Dance" room. He wanted to go in but found he didn't have a dime and couldn't find me after that, but remembered seeing my picture hung on the "Y" wall. So I guess we were supposed to meet. His first girlfriend and ex-wife were both named Nancy and he jokes that he just didn't get the right one first.

As Tom was unpacking his things, he found an old postcard collection. There was a postcard from the Sunset Auto and Trailer Park that he and his folks stayed in, when they came out from Wisconsin. I uttered a strange sound and said, "My goodness, that is the first place we stayed in when we came to California, since it was owned by my Uncle, who had asked my Dad to come down from Idaho and help him manage the place." And then, there was the prediction from my friend and mentor, Virginia, that I would get married to my True Love in 1970.

MY MOTHER

My mother had moved from the hospital to a convalescent home and I visited her often, alternating with my two sisters who lived in town. I would sometimes visit after work since it was close by or Tom would go with me later in the evening. Later on, when she was discharged, she lived at my sisters' homes in San Diego. She realized she could no longer live by herself in the mountain cabin she and my dad built and that we all loved so much, so it was sold. She gave me and each sister the choice of money or a part of the remaining mountain acreage surrounding the cabin. Of course I took the land, which was on top of the mountain, which was accessible only by hiking and 4 wheel drive. However, we took many hikes up there and enjoyed the scenery anew each time. We finally sold it in 1980, after we had property in Oregon.

SHARING RESPONSIBILITIES

Early on Tom and I talked about responsibilities and the necessary things that have to be accomplished in running a household together. We were honest about our likes, dislikes, preferences, strengths and weaknesses. We made endless lists and compromised often. Since both of us had been on our own for some time (working and living by ourselves) we were familiar with what needed to be done. It was a matter of dividing up the chores. Since math had been one of my weaker points and paying the bills on time was a stronger point, we agreed to divide the checkbook duties. I would pay the bills, log the check inventory and Tom would balance the checkbook with our statements, so we would both be aware of money coming in and going out. My paycheck was to be automatically deposited in the bank, and Tom's paycheck was to be cashed for living expenses.

Since we wanted to save some money, we agreed to talk everything over before we bought anything over $20.00. If we couldn't afford it, we wouldn't buy it. There were so many things we wanted, but we decided to wait. We were fortunate to have the furniture, dishes and cooking utensils that I had bought for my apartment when I was single, and the beautiful bedroom set was given to us by our families as a wedding gift. We had one credit card and agreed that we would never carry any finance charges on it, and would pay off the amount due in full each month. We went grocery shopping together and itemized the costs as we went along. I had a book of 101 ways to fix hamburger and that first year we ate a lot of hamburger (that was before I learned my lessons about cholesterol and saturated fat).

Since we were both working outside of home, Tom said that it was only right that he help me around the house when I needed it and not hesitate to ask him to help. Before marriage we had talked about the importance of sexual equality in the workplace as well as at home. I realize how fortunate I was to have married a "liberated" man since some of my friends had not fared so well (this was 1970). Because I wanted to show how much I appreciated him, I did most of the cooking and cleaning for the first fifteen years.

LITTLE THINGS MEAN A LOT

Since we were both working, we realized the importance of having a balanced life. We went to church almost every Sunday and prayed every day. I was finishing my Thesis for my Master's Degree, so that kept me busy and Tom had lots of reading. However, we have always made time for fun. Every day as I made his lunch, I would stick little love notes with cute pictures of animal cutouts inside. He would stick some in my lunch as well when I wasn't looking. We would squeeze in private time for ourselves, go for walks on the beach or in a park, watch a sunset or listen to music.

HAVING FUN IN THE OUTDOORS

We saved up enough money to rent a cabin on Lake Arrowhead with friends, Hal and Ellen, for the July 4th weekend and had fun boating on the lake. Tom and I had talked often about our love for nature and since I grew up with the love of camping with my parents, we decided to try it out for ourselves. My sister loaned us their tent and so the week after Labor Day we camped in the Sequoia National Park. We had a grand time, hiking to Mist Falls, where Tom boosted me up over rocks, so I could get there, going for a splash in the cold river water and just plain having fun. We decided camping was for us and wanted it to be a part of our lives. It seemed to be the least expensive way to enjoy vacation time so we vowed to get our own equipment as soon as we could afford it.

FIRST SURGERY

Around November, I started having tremendous pains in my right side. It was so bad I thought I was going to die. I would get up at night and go in the living room, doubling over with pain on the couch, so I wouldn't wake Tom. After some tests, the doctor said my gallbladder needed to come out, and surgery was scheduled. This was Tom's first exposure to the hospital with me. Little did he know he would spend a lot more time with me in hospitals during the course of our marriage. The surgery went well, but I got an infection and had to have my stay extended for an extra week.

COMPROMISES

One of the stark realities of marriage is to recognize that two individuals are united in love but were brought up differently, with each other's family having specific traditions and ways of doing things. This is especially true around the Holiday Season. Many compromises need to be made.

Since both families lived in the same town, we could spend Thanksgiving with both families and we decided to alternate spending Christmas Eve one year with Tom's family and the next year with mine. My family had always celebrated Christmas Eve with a big dinner, opening of gifts, my mother playing the piano with the rest of the family singing carols, and then going to midnight church service.

Tom's family had always celebrated Christmas Eve with a big dinner, opening of gifts and spending the evening with family at home. So we compromised and enjoyed both alternately.

INVESTMENTS

Tom had come from a family that put money in stocks rather than land. I came from a family that believed in buying land. We educated each other, bought both, and now thirty-five years later, have the best of both worlds.

My father had always said renting was like putting equity in someone else's pockets and it was just as easy to buy a home and be putting the monthly payments towards your own equity. So, the first opportunity we had, Tom and I went to look at houses. I had said, "maybe in 2,3, or 4 years we would buy a house." Well, we had looked at used homes, property and new developments, but then one day in February 1971, we looked at the model homes in Tierrasanta. Before we left we had signed papers and put a $100.00 down payment. It was the last money we had in our checkbook, and had been designated to pay the doctor's balance on my gallbladder surgery (we paid the doctor the next month).

In those days, I had to sign a paper guaranteeing that I would not get pregnant so my salary could be used in order for the loan to be approved. Even though we were not planning to have children, I didn't think it was anyone's business. This practice is illegal now. An interesting note is that we were paying $180 a month rent for our apartment and our house payments were $179.84 a month which meant that we saved sixteen cents each month for twenty-nine years, so my father was right!

Another investment we made about the same time, was a van camper. The Plan of the Day at the Base where I worked listed a for sale item. One of the Squadron Officers had to sell his van camper since he had immediate orders to Vietnam. It was first come, first serve. I called immediately, and that evening Tom and I went to his house and took it out for a test drive. We were able to arrange financing through the Navy Credit Union and so now we had our camping plans resolved. Tom sold his old car and drove the van to work, so it served two purposes.

ANOTHER FRIEND MARRIED

My good friend, Joyce Anderson, who was with me the night that I met Tom, became engaged. She asked me to be her Matron of Honor at the wedding in April, where she became Mrs. Ken Hanson. The wedding was very beautiful and I was so happy for her. Except for a few single friends remaining, most of us who went to single activities together were now married.

FIRST ANNIVERSARY-May 2, 1971

When Tom and I celebrated our first anniversary in May, we really had something to celebrate - the dream of having a home of our own would be a reality within the first year and one-half of our marriage, we had our van camper and I had completed my Master's Thesis! Each anniversary we have a tradition that we started on our first anniversary and have followed it every year since then, without fail.

We always go out to dinner, light our Lilly of the Valley Wedding Candle that was given to us for our wedding (it is one of those real tall beautiful candles that lasts a lifetime as long as you only light them once a year), get out our wedding album to look at the pictures and listen to the recording of our wedding ceremony while we exchange vows again. It helps you remember why you got married and rekindles those embers of love and commitment. If more couples practiced this tradition, I believe there would be less divorce.

I graduated with my Master's Degree in June 1971 and celebrated with Tom. (I had remembered that I had started my Master's Program with the intent of focusing solely on my education and career to forget about the dismal prospects of marriage). Now God had blessed me with both my Master's Degree and the most wonderful husband anyone could have!

HAVING FUN CAMPING

That summer, we tried out our van camper with a two-week camping trip to Oregon. We fell in love with the beautiful forests and campgrounds and talked about buying retirement property up there one day. One of the State Campgrounds we went to was called Silver Falls. The camping sites were in a separate area, so we took our van and parked it in a nearby parking lot close to the falls. We started walking down stairs that led to a plateau with falls, and then we went down some more stairs that led to another set of falls. As we walked down further, we found ourselves in a wonderland of lush vegetation. The area was long and narrow with a total of about 200 steps. There was a total of seven falls and each one was unique and different from all the rest but had its own special beauty. One fall splashed over a large overhanging cliff so we were able to walk underneath it. We were so enthralled with the beauty that the day just flew by and before we knew it, dusk was upon us and they closed the falls area with gates for the night.

We weren't quite sure how to get back to the parking lot where our van was located and I was so tired that I could hardly move. Well, we talked about it and just had faith that God would show us the way. Going back the way we came was full of stairs, so we didn't want to do that, but we took the next trail up out of the falls valley and I just kept putting one foot in front of the other as Tom kept encouraging me. We finally reached the top and lo and behold came out right where our van was located so we had made the entire circle of the falls valley, about a mile and a half.

Over Labor Day weekend, we went camping with our friends, Hal and Ellen at a place called Wilderness Lakes. We had lots of fun during the day and during the night; I heard a sound like a moan around the location of their tent. I woke up Tom, because as I lifted the curtains and looked out the window, I could see Hal with a lantern talking to a man with his back to our van. Tom went out to see if he could help Hal and the man had blood all over him. He was in shock and wasn't making any sense, so Tom and Hal were going to take him into town to the ER. Just as the light shone on his face, Tom recognized him as the man camped on the other side of us. They woke up his wife and the following is what happened as the story was pieced together.

92

This man was fishing and drinking too much, so his wife made him sleep in the truck, instead of the cab over camper. He opened the door of the truck to go to the restroom, and in his stupor, had walked the wrong way and fallen into the ice-cold lake. After climbing out of the lake in shock. He stumbled into trees, causing the bleeding, until he found Hal's tent. It was the first experience camping for Hal and Ellen and turned out to be quite an adventure story for all of us to retell in our later years.

BUYING OUR HOME

When we bought our home, the developers had not even started construction at the time, so we have a picture of me holding some rocks and dirt and pointing to the ground indicating our home would be built on that property. It was fun watching the house being built and Tom went out every day after work to check the progress. He caught several errors (crooked door frames, etc.) and talked to the supervisor until things were redone. Tom took pictures as the house progressed, so we knew where all the outlets were being placed. Around the end of September, Tom received notice that his company would be moving to Anaheim and he was offered a large salary increase to move with the company. He turned down the offer, knowing that my job was secure and since we were in the process of buying a house in San Diego, had faith that God would provide him with other employment in the area.

God didn't let us down. The Monday after his last day at the old company, he started a new job at the Myron L. Company in Encinitas. The developers for our home had given us many completion dates that had been changed, and every time we notified our landlords we would be moving. As a result our landlords got tired of the changes and rented our apartment, so we had to move. The house was nearly finished when we moved in November 1971. Our loan papers were misplaced which caused a delay on the processing of our mortgage, so for the first two months, we had to rent our own home until the papers were approved. Finally, January 1972 we were homeowners - what a wonderful feeling and we thanked God and still thank God. I have always been aware that so many people are less fortunate than us and do not have shelters of their own.

Now that we had a new home, we needed new furniture to match, but we were cognizant of the commitment we made earlier not to buy things until we could afford them, so we did with what we had, used lots of big pillows and crates and had large areas which were void of furnishings until much later. As we could afford things, we bought them, including a beautiful hand made oak entertainment center, telephone table with cabinet, and bar that Tom had designed. It was five years before we had the money saved to buy these pieces. The entertainment center was seven feet tall to cover our big living room wall and had to be moved in the house in two pieces and finished inside. After waiting for five years, we really appreciated the beauty of this piece and how nicely it fit in with the rest of our furniture.

NEIGHBORS

Our home was located on a cul-de-sac and I wanted to get to know the neighbors, but since Tom and I both worked, we were tired when we got home and had only gotten acquainted with the people who lived behind us.

We knew the names of the other neighbors, but that was all. About three months had passed when the man who lived directly across from us was notified that the location of his job was being changed. The family had to move and they put their house up for sale.

Marie, who lived diagonally across the cul-de-sac, came up to our house and wanted me to sign a petition stating that we did not want "colored people" in our neighborhood since she said she saw some looking at the house up for sale. Marie did not know my values or she never would have asked me to do something like that. Part of my job with Civil Service at N.A.S. Miramar included being Equal Employment Coordinator and I had strong beliefs about equal opportunity for all races in employment, housing and all other areas. I was very upset and told her in no uncertain terms never to come to our door again if she was going to peddle such trash. I also told her Tom and I did not appreciate living by people like her, who were so prejudiced and that we would welcome an African-American family into our cul-de-sac. As a result, when the Hayes moved in, Marie and her husband moved out and a Hispanic family, the Richardson's bought their home. Carol and Tony moved in behind us about a year later and we have all lived happily here ever since.

We count ourselves to be so blessed because now we have the best neighbors anyone could ever have. Frances Tamayo (our "Angel") lives to the right of our house in the next cul-de-sac. She is a retired nurse and volunteered for services refusing to take any payment, helping me many times, with baths, massages, etc. after my coming home from the hospital or being injured in a fall, as when I broke my pelvis in 2002.

We look after each other and at the same time respect each other's privacy. An example of that is when Kim Hayes was about five years old (she is the youngest daughter of the Hayes family) used to meet me at the driveway when I would come home from work. She would help me carry my things into the house but always would go home then, even though I invited her to stay, saying "My momma told me to help you whenever I could but not to stay because you work hard and need to rest after work."

One day, she saw me outside and brought her stuffed turtle over to me. She said, "I love my turtle and since I love you too I want you to have my turtle." I was astounded and said, "Oh honey, I can't take your favorite plaything." She said, "Yes, I want you to have it, cause I love you so much."

Well, needless to say, I was overwhelmed at the love this sweet little girl had. I told her I would take good care of it and would put it on top of our pillows after I made the bed each day. We have glass doors from our bedroom that open up to the patio and told her she could come in the back yard anytime and look through the glass doors at her turtle sitting on our bed to make sure it was okay. Also if she ever wanted it back or wanted to visit it at our house she was welcome to. I kept it in good condition and when Kim got married, I had wrapped her turtle up with her wedding gift and gave it to her so she could give to her children.

Since Tom and I did not have any children, we have delighted in watching the Hayes children grow up. Fred is the oldest and then Michelle, Regina and Kim. They used to put on plays in the garage and send us invitations. We always went and enjoyed their sense of creativity so much. Now they are all married and have kids of their own that we enjoy just as much when they come over to see Pappy and Daisy (Grandma and Grandpa). We always take time to

95

"Ohhh and Ahhhh" when we see them out in the cul-de-sac jumping rope, skating, playing ball, etc. and always tell them how good they are doing. I think it's important for kids to get compliments from people other than parents as well as us taking time to just talk to them and find out what they are doing in school, etc. They are all very smart and really nice young folks.

When we go on motor home trips, Carol and Tony, living behind us, always pick up any papers around our home from solicitors and have our email address to let us know if anything goes wrong. It is very comforting to know we can be gone for months at a time and feel secure about our home with our wonderful neighbors looking after it. We stop our daily newspaper and have a slot in the garage door for the mail. Scott, our nephew, has a key to the garage, and comes over to check our mail flow in the box we have below the slot. When the box is full, he places the mail in a big hefty plastic bag, so the box is emptied for more mail.

HAVING FUN CAMPING AGAIN

We always took advantage of the three day holiday weekends to start our vacations and so we used the Memorial Day Weekend of 1972 to take our first long trip through California, Nevada, Utah, to Yellowstone National Park and the Grand Tetons in Wyoming, then back through Idaho, Oregon to California. Tom captured a beautiful 3-D picture of Tower Falls in Yellowstone and when we got home we were so happy with it that we took the negative to a company that was able to put it on canvas for us that still hangs on our living room wall. The rain had just stopped, and a large pine tree in the foreground had a drop of water just about to fall from the tree branch as Tom snapped the camera with the sun glistening on the raindrop. In the background falling from the mountainside is Tower Falls, surrounded by smaller pine trees in the lush valley below with a blue violet mist covering the sky. He also took a picture of me with a rainbow ending at the top of my head.

GROWING TOGETHER IN KNOWLEDGE

Tom and I have always been interested in Psychology and the way people behave and communicate. In my Master's Program, I had training in Transactional Analysis (T.A.) and Tom had done some studying in it as well. Both Tom and I were interested in improving ourselves and I wanted to learn more about ways that I could use my mind to overcome the pain of Arthritis. I also thought I might obtain my Psychology License and go into private practice, now that I had my Master's Degree, but that would require specialized training and supervision. It seemed that joining the ITAA (International Association of Transactional Analysis) would meet all of our above needs.

We had group meetings in La Jolla, studied, and went to classes and seminars, and teaching sessions. The La Jolla home of the Psychologist who founded the San Diego Group was big enough to hold weekend marathons, where we took our sleeping bags (males had one room and females had another for sleeping), but the objective was to stretch our minds (no drugs or alcohol allowed, even if this was the 1970's), learn why we do the things we do, how we are programmed by overt and covert messages from parents, and how we relate and communicate with others, with the end purpose of changing for the better.

Tom and I both went to all the functions and attended out of town conferences in San Francisco. We were taught by pioneers in the field who knew and worked personally with Eric Berne (the founder of T.A.), before he passed in 1970. It was one of the most life-changing times of our lives and both Tom and I received a tremendous amount of benefit from our ten-year association with the organization. No, I did not go into private practice as a result, but did hold T.A. therapy groups in our home and later taught the subject through San Diego Community College. Tom and I still find practical use for the T.A. concepts to this day. I would recommend the book. *Born to Win*, by Muriel James and Dorothy Jongeward to anyone wanting to improve their life.

WORK CHALLENGES

The next job I had (1973) was a Human Resource Specialist for the Navy's Racial Awareness Facilitator Training Program. Right away, I had to leave for a three-week training program in Florida and was the first time I was away from Tom. We spent a lot of money on telephone calls and I flew back home one weekend to attend my High School's 20th Reunion. It was worth it just to be able to see Tom again after two weeks away from him.

Back in San Diego again, after the training, I was kept quite busy serving as part of a three person teaching team which facilitated three week training sessions for a group of about 30 Military Personnel.

Since we educated attendees on the origins of prejudice and facilitated awareness discussions about the negative results caused by prejudice, with the hope of eliminating all forms of racial, sexual, ethnic and religious bigotry and hatred from the Navy, it required continuing the class until the subject at hand was brought to closure without any issues or feelings left unresolved.

There were many times I did not get home from work until quite late, and I was very appreciative of the fact that Tom understood my commitment and purpose to such an important work. My part of that work was completed in a year and a half, but it was one of the most rewarding experiences I have ever had. During that time, the heel of my shoe caught in the space on the steps as I leaving work late and I broke my ankle. Since it was late, I just ignored it, thinking it was just a sprain. I went to work and stood on it the next day but that night it was quite inflamed and after having it x-rayed found out it was broken. (I have always had a high tolerance for pain). The doctor gave me a walking cast and after a day off work, I went back. My ankle healed nicely.

ANOTHER SURGERY

Also during that time, after continuous problems with my menses, my Gynecologist had informed me that I needed a hysterectomy (I had already had three D&C's before marriage with pap smears ranging to Class 4). Tom and I talked to my doctor together and since we had not planned on having children anyway, surgery was scheduled as soon as possible. It took about six weeks recovery before I could drive to work again and I had early Menopause as a result, but the ordeal was very minimal compared to the rest of the surgeries and health challenges I have faced in this life.

BUYING OUR FIRST CLASS C MINI MOTOR HOME

During 1974 we had a gas shortage, but Tom and I have always been optimists while everyone else is living in a fear state, so we found it worked to our advantage and bought a new Jamboree, 18 foot Class C Mini Motor home at an extreme savings. I thanked God for our blessings - it was all so wonderful! We now had a real bathroom with shower, toilet and sink, a refrigerator and stove. We folded down the dinette for our bed like we did with our van. However, our van camper just had an ice chest and we cooked outside using a propane stove. We either used a campground shower or rigged a hose up with a shower curtain when we were out in the wilds and carried a porta potty with us.

We took our first trip in our Jamboree over Memorial Day Weekend in 1974 and stayed on my sister's land in Harrison Park (the Julian Mountain property that my folks had, since our property was inaccessible by motor home). During the day we hiked up to our property on top of the mountain and came down in the evening to sleep in our motor home. However, when we awoke the next morning we were met with a surprise! That night some cold weather settled in and it snowed! Our Jamboree was parked on a plateau on top of a hill and Tom had to back down the hill in snow without chains - what a challenge with a new motor home but he did an outstanding job!

Our next trip with the Jamboree was over the July 4th holiday and we went to the Sequoias. Well, going up the steep incline entrance to the Park, our distributor gave out and we coasted downhill into our campsite. We were able to call a maintenance shop in the valley having a RV tow truck that came up to the top of the Sequoias. The repair man pounded a piece of redwood bark to hold the metal plate in the distributor until we could get back to San Diego and have it fixed right. He fixed it in a short amount of time with very little expense to us. I said a prayer of thanks to God. This is an example of how all during our marriage, when both small and big things go wrong, we turn it over to God in prayer and we never take it for granted but always thank God for all things. "In everything give thanks." (1 Thes: 5:18)

SHARING COMMON INTERESTS

We got married because we loved each other and wanted to share our common interests. We did that by buying summer season tickets to Starlight Opera, to the summer Symphony Pops Concerts and to other concerts that we attended. We loved nature and enjoyed camping by ourselves or with friends. Idyllwild was a favorite camping spot for us and our friends. We bought a Camping Membership into Silent Valley, a camping resort between Banning and Idyllwild that we still enjoy to this day.

FACING THE LOSS OF MY MOTHER

In January 1975, my mother had a stroke that left her in a semicomitose state in a nursing home. My two sisters in San Diego and I alternated our visits. We always talked to her just like we always did, even though she couldn't answer. From what I know now of the subconscious state, I know she heard us even if there was no acknowledgement. We always told her how much we loved her. When you love someone deeply, it is very hard to see them suffer, and I prayed that God, in His mercy would not allow her to suffer long. So when she passed in June, we felt it was a blessing even though we missed her physical presence.

Prior to that time. the doctor told us she could be in a semicomitose state for ten days or ten years and that we needed to go on with our lives. Tom and I were the first to have scheduled vacations, and my sisters agreed that we should go ahead with it. We told my sisters we would continuously call and check on my mother's condition. We left on our three-week vacation just before Memorial Day, to meet friends in the mountains above Taos, New Mexico. We took the wrong fork in the road and ended up in the backyard of some mountain people and before we knew it, five men with bib overalls and shotguns came running out of this shack towards our motor home. Well, Tom turned around so fast my head spun and we headed out of there and found the right turn to the campground where our friends were.

We were heading on our way back, and stopped in Grand Junction, Colorado to call my sister about my Mom, when we found she had just passed. We took the fastest route home. As I said, since she had been suffering so much, it was a blessing to know that this wonderful woman who had given her family so much, was finally released to a life without pain. When you believe, there is no fear of the hereafter and we have always felt we could talk to her Spirit.

NEXT TEN YEARS 1976-1986

MY FIRST ARTIFICIAL JOINT IMPLANT

In May 1976 I started having severe pains in my right knee and gradually my leg became weaker, until it started collapsing on me. I was referred to an Orthopedic Surgeon who said I needed an artificial knee joint. European doctors had been performing this surgery for a year or so, but it was a fairly new procedure in this country. Well, it appeared that there was no alternative, so we prayed and it was one of many implant surgeries Tom would go through with me. I was able to talk to the anesthesiologist, Dr. Karl Eckhardt, prior to surgery and somehow God spiritually guided the discussion as I shared my faith with him and mentioned that besides going to my church, I watched Dr. Schuller on TV. Then, I found out he went to the Crystal Cathedral in Garden Grove, and he said he would say a prayer in my ear just before I went under the anesthetic.

Well, everything went well, and on July 4th, 1976, when everyone else was celebrating the centennial, I was in the hospital recovering from knee surgery. In those days, physical therapy was pretty much up to the patient, and those that did not do the required exercises on their own, just did not recover properly. The artificial joint is medicinally glued in place, which makes the leg completely straight, and it will only become flexible through continuous exercise.

101

My Surgeon, Dr. Richard Braun, had given me a set of exercises to do at home throughout the day, every day, until my next appointment. I remember Tom, at my request, forcing my knee back further and further each day until I screamed, but gradually my knee loosened up and I learned how to walk with an artificial joint. I was back to work in six weeks.

OUR VACATION LAND

We had always wanted river front property for our retirement and since we loved Oregon, kept looking at the Sunday paper classifieds. In April we saw an ad from people who lived in Carlsbad, but who wanted to sell some acreage from an estate in a place called Murphy, Oregon. We visited them in Carlsbad and since we had planned our camping vacation in Oregon over Memorial Day, they gave us a map of the property and permission to camp on it and look it over. I had told my sister Charlotte about it and she and her husband met us at the property with their motor home. We all had a great time and fell in love with the property immediately as it was located right on the Applegate River. The land was full of Douglas Fir, Sugar Pines, Madrone, and Oak trees, besides undergrowth, wildflowers and blackberry bushes. When we came back from our vacation we signed the papers to buy ten acres.

Since we already had our vacation we thought we would camp by the Colorado River over July 4th that some friends had told us about. When we got there, we found out it was too hot (110 degrees) and turned around and headed for San Jacinto State Park in Idyllwild. When we got there, we found it was full, but the ranger pointed us in the direction of a new campground just being opened up by Ramada Inns. It was beautiful and we enjoyed our stay. This eventually became a Thousand Trails Campground, which we enjoy to this day.

APPOINTED TO THE ARTHRITIS FOUNDATION BOARD OF GOVERNORS

We had been attending the Arthritis Foundation meetings and I was asked to be on the Telethon in May of 1977. I was also appointed on the Board of Governors and was the only layperson to serve on the Medical and Scientific Committee. I served on this committee and the Board of Governors for four years. My suggestion about the Arthritis Foundation sponsoring water therapy exercise classes has since been put into place.

About that time we bought our first Jacuzzi and placed it in our back yard. The hot water therapy really helped me when I came home from work full of pain in my joints.

FACING ANOTHER CHALLENGE

In December 1977, we got a phone call from a foreman of a logging firm in Oregon. They had been hired to cut some trees on the adjacent property to our vacationland; somehow had crossed over to our property and cut down twenty-two of our trees. The man wanted to come down and talk to us about rectifying the situation. At first we were quite devastated; needed time to think and asked him to call back the next day. He was visiting some relatives in California about 50 miles away and when he called back the next day, we invited him down.

After prayerful consideration, we decided that we needed to see for ourselves what our property looked like after the cutting, since we had bought the property for the beauty of the trees and natural scenery. The foreman, who was very nice, said he was authorized by the company to make a settlement and asked us what we wanted. Of course they were afraid we would sue, but that is not what our life is about. Honest mistakes are often made and we believe God wanted us to work out a peaceful accommodating solution.

They agreed to fly us up to Oregon in January, meet us at the airport and take us to our hotel where they would pay for our lodging for three days. They took us to our property and showed us the number of trees cut. Well, when we saw it, it wasn't nearly as bad as we had thought, since the land is full of trees. They agreed to put in a road, a locked gate, clean up the brush, take the trees they cut to the mill and pay us for them. When we bought the property, we agreed to keep it under a forestry management program, which called for cutting of some larger trees so the seedlings and smaller trees could get sun and putting in a fire road. Because the land is being taken care of according to good forestry principles, we get a cut on our taxes.

The logging company agreed to meet all the requirements under our forestry management program and so they actually did us a favor that we would have paid someone else to do. We also got a nice check for $2,500 for the trees that were taken to the mill. This is what is called turning your negative situations into blessings. It was a win-win situation for both parties.

SEARCHING FOR WAYS TO MANAGE MY R.A.

Because I wanted to find other ways besides prescription drugs to manage the Rheumatoid Arthritis, Tom and I joined the Mandala Holistic Health Association in San Diego, which sponsored classes and workshops on natural health and healing. In the summer of 1978, they sponsored a two-week course at U.C.S.D. in holistic health, which I attended, and I met Dr. Norman Shealy, the first president of the American Holistic Medical Association. This was a life-changing event for me. He was the first M.D. who gave me hope of living a successful life without the use of steroids for my Rheumatoid Arthritis.

At the time he had written a book called "*90 Days to Self-Health*", which advocated mind-body management of diseases. He also suggested a list of other books and magazines to assist me in a new direction for my well being. After the seminar, I went out and bought every book I could find on holistic health/medicine or mind-body connection, started subscribing to the magazines recommended and read voraciously. The message of "the healer/physician is within" seemed to resonate inside of me. The Bible tells us that our body is the Temple of the Holy Spirit and the practice of "going within" fit in with my spiritual faith. I took more workshops and learned about Edgar Cayce, the father of holistic medicine.

He left a legacy called the Association for Research and Enlightenment (A.R.E.) which I joined, and attend chapter meetings in San Diego. I have since given several presentations to this group and other groups, including San Diego Homeopathic Society concerning the help that natural remedies (herbs, homeopathies, etc.) and alternative methods of healing and have given me.

I was excited - a whole new way of looking at dis-ease was being presented to me and every chance I got I shared it with others, taking magazines and books with me on our camping trips. Over the years I have used both conventional and alternative forms of treatment for illness with success and believe that God guides a person as to what will help him/her the most at that particular time.

NEW VENTURES

Over the Labor Day Holiday, we decided to go back to the campground in Idyllwild that we went to the year before and found out it had been bought by Thousand Trails, a campground organization that had campgrounds spread out over the United States. We listened to a sales presentation and because we love camping so much, felt it was a good proposition for us to buy into the organization. Each year we enjoy our stay at several of the campgrounds plus we meet some of the nicest people.
We also invested in a Time Share Condominium and although we have not "banked" (used) it to go to other places, we have rented it out each year. We have since sold this venture.

TOM'S WORK ASSIGNMENT OVERSEAS AND OUR VACATION IN HAWAII

In October 1978, Tom was assigned to start up a new plant in Hong Kong for DSI (Duluth Scientific Inc.), and was there for four weeks training employees. He called me nearly 5 times a week. When He finished, as a reward, his company gave him a week's paid vacation in Hawaii on the way back. He called and asked if I could get vacation time from work so I could join him. God heard my prayers and my supervisor at the Civil Service Commission approved my leave, which was on the books. As soon as I could make the arrangements for our hotels and condos, I was on the plane. We stayed on each Island (Oahu, Kauaii, and Hawaii) for 2 and 1/2 days. We saw Waimea Canyon and Bay, Sunset Beach and many other famous places. Our condo in Kauii was close to the beach where the female lead sang, "I'm Going to Wash That Man Right Out of My Hair" from "South Pacific" as it was being filmed.

Tom even got a picture taken of me "pretending"" to wash my hair and singing that song on the same beach. We took a boat cruise to "The Grotto" and did so many other fun things. On the big Island of Hawaii, we saw all the Volcano fields and walked through several of them. We had a great time spending Thanksgiving in Hawaii and it was like a second honeymoon.

BACK HOME AGAIN

When we got back we received a phone call from the people we bought the Murphy, Oregon property from and they offered us a good price on an additional six plus acres right next to our other ten acres, so we bought that and now have incorporated it all under one deed.

SUMMER TRIP TO OREGON 1979

During the trip to our Oregon property the next year, we decided we wanted to have our road extended, have other work done and as we drove into town asked a gas station owner if they knew of anyone. Within a short time, this man called "Dutch" came up and rode with us to our property. He ran a dozer service and we showed him what we wanted done. We then took off and went to some of our favorite campgrounds, while he did the work.

When we got back, everything was just as we wanted it. We also talked to him about cleaning out some of the fallen trees and he said his church had a program where they used fallen trees for fire wood to take to the elderly and sick for the winter and asked permission if they could use our fallen trees for that purpose. Of course we said yes. They sent us an accounting of the wood collected at the end of each year from the church and we were able to deduct it for income taxes, so it was a win-win situation again.

Every year for about ten years this took place and when Dutch told us he was moving, we asked him for the name of someone who could put in gravel on the road for us. We didn't hear anything from him, but the next year when we went up the work was all done. We called and asked Dutch how much we owed him, since it was just what we wanted. He refused to take any money and said it was what the church wanted to do for us because of all the wood they had collected. He and his family left the next morning. We have really been blessed by the people we have met in Oregon.

1980-1985

TOM'S CAREER PROMOTION

Tom completed his work with DSI and started a new job with Scientific Atlanta around 1980 as a Quality Engineer, which opened new doors for his career. During 1982 Tom was hired by MA/Com Linkabit, the first company started by Irwin Jacobs and Andrew Viturbi, that put him on a career path leading to Sr Quality Engineer, which was destined to bring us financial security for the rest of our lives. As a part of this work experience, Tom traveled to Minnesota and Puerto Rico.

SECOND NEAR DEATH EXPERIENCE

My allergies started flaring up again and I was having a lot of muscle, nerve and joint pain. By that time I had trouble keeping most food down and when I could, had severe cramps afterwards. We had been praying for some kind of an answer when a friend referred me to a holistic M.D. who specialized in allergies and Acupuncture. I was tested for allergies and found out that I was allergic to mold, other environmental contaminants, and many foods, including wheat, milk, corn, yeast, soy, eggs and chicken.

The doctor started me off on a long allergy treatment program. For three months I had to avoid all wheat, milk, yeast and corn and I rotated the rest of my food, so if I had a certain food on Tuesday, I couldn't have it again for another four days. We had to educate ourselves to a new way of shopping (reading all labels) and eating, including making our own bread.

We found out that soup and nearly all canned goods contain either some form of wheat or corn. We shopped at a Health Food Market started eating new grains, such as kasha, quinoa, amaranth and whole rye (without wheat). I ate a lot of fish, yogurt (without corn sweetener) and brown rice. We got new recipe books and even

107

hired a cook to make things for us while we were at work. After three months I was able to gradually add in my most common allergens (wheat, milk, yeast and corn) and then I had to rotate them as well.

After two years, my allergies were finally under control. The doctor also said the ACTH that I had been on for 30 year for my arthritis was causing adverse reactions severe enough to cause my death and recommended that I be taken off this steroid gradually using acupuncture supported with natural remedies.

He advised me that there was a chance I could die even then and I signed a waiver releasing him from any responsibility. This was a great step in my life for the better to take responsibility for my own health instead of relying solely on a doctor.

Being taken off a steroid after thirty years is an extreme jolt to the immune system even when doing it gradually and even with the support of Acupuncture and natural remedies, I had delirium tremens and felt the shock to my body. I started in with three acupuncture appointments a week and then graduated to weekly appointments. This used up a great deal of my sick leave and at times, it felt like I was dying. It took a total of nine months of acupuncture treatments before I finally got off steroids and months later before we found out that my immune system was again functioning on its own after being suppressed for thirty years! What a miracle! I survived my second Near Death Experience.

ARTHRITIS TAKES ITS TOLL

However, the Arthritis had taken its toll and after a visit to my Orthopedic Surgeon in the summer of 1984, he said my left knee was going out on me and that I would need to have it replaced with an artificial joint before the end of the year.

TIME TO RETIRE

By that time three of my doctors were recommending that I retire from my Civil Service Career in order to take care of my health. It was with real regret and sadness that I submitted my application for retirement, but after listening to my body and praying, I knew it was for the best. I have always enjoyed the creative aspect of work, the sense of achievement it gave me, the rewards that I received from being in a helping profession, seeing others benefit from my knowledge and training, and contributing to many groundbreaking changes in society that were taking place at that time. My last day of work was in November 1984, but my official date of retirement was May 1985, since I still had enough sick leave on the books to carry me to that date. My leg was bad enough that by the first of November I had to walk with a crutch in order to get around. However, one of the interns in my program area planned a most wonderful surprise retirement party with invitations to relatives, co-workers, long time friends and people that I had worked with over the years. It was a wonderful sendoff.

OUR SECOND FIFTEEN YEARS

1985-2000

MORE SURGERIES

A week later I had my second artificial knee joint implanted. I knew what to expect, and technology had improved in 8 years so it was a little easier. However, no joint implant is ever easy! My right wrist had been extremely painful for some time and in February 1985 I had surgery to have my right wrist fused, since my orthopedic surgeon had said that wrist implants had not been perfected enough. This was something else and the recovery time took much longer since the fusion has to set. A vise with visible screws on both ends was surgically inserted into my wrist until the fusion was complete and then the vise was pulled out. A rod was also inserted in my right forearm above the wrist to stabilize the fusion. However, that bothered me so much that it was surgically removed a year and one half later.

MORE TIME TO HEAL

Since retirement, I noticed a considerable release from stress and I was able to get more rest. It allowed me time to take care of myself and heal, so I could enjoy life more.

TRAVELING

Tom and I had always wanted to travel abroad more, but never had time with our work and our love for camping vacations. However, since I was retired and Tom was able to get some extra time off, we made plans to go on a group tour to both the North and South Islands of New Zealand, plus a short stay in Sydney, Australia. Our wonderful trip is documented in Chapter 16.

PART TIME WORK AFTER RETIREMENT

I was doing well the first part of 1986 and decided that I would like to get a part time job. I was hired by Nutri-System, a weight loss firm as a Behavior Modification Specialist. I enjoyed my work and since it was part-time, I was able to keep up my own health care program. It gave my mind the mental stimulation I needed and I met many friends that I still keep in touch with today.

ANOTHER HEALTH CHALLENGE

In December 1986, I developed blisters on my right ankle and additional blisters that popped out on nerve pathways on other parts of my body. I was diagnosed with Shingles, (Herpes Zoster), a terrible disease related to the Chicken Pox Virus that causes extreme nerve pain even after the blisters heal.

MORE IMPLANT SURGERIES

This evidently set my immune system off, because my Arthritis flared up uncontrollably and during 1987 and 1988 I had a total of six surgeries. A rod was put in my left thumb to help me write, since I am left-handed. Also, because the rod that was placed in my right forearm for the wrist fusion was causing problems, it was surgically removed. Both my left and right shoulders and my left and right elbows were removed and artificial joints were surgically implanted. About the time I would recover from one surgery, the next one was being scheduled. My right elbow, which was the last joint replaced was the worst since I had to be treated for infection, because the wound had rubbed against the cast. Since I worked part-time, I was lucky to be able to come back to my job as Behavior Modification Specialist as others filled in for me while I was out.

NEW JAMBOREE

During this time, as optimistic as we are, we traded in our 18-foot Jamboree for a new 24-foot Jamboree motor home.

VACATION TRIP TO EAST COAST -1987

Despite all my surgeries, we did find time to take a camping vacation in our new motor home back to North Carolina to see my sister Ruth and her family. We got our first video cam for the trip. I even had a cast on my left elbow during our trip, which wasn't due to come off until I got back. I stayed in the motor home while Tom took the strenuous hikes to the waterfalls and video-came the scenery, so at least I was able to see pictures of what I had missed after we got home. We visited Cade's Cove in the Smoky Mountains and Tom got out to look at all the old pioneer cabins. He was looking at this one cabin when a voice said, "Do you know what you are looking at?" Tom turned around and a living descendant of the pioneer who owned that particular cabin introduced himself.

He had pictures of the original cabin and his pioneer relatives that lived there. He showed Tom how the chimney had been replaced and provided him with the original story of this pioneer family. It was quite a blessing to hear first-hand how this pioneer family survived the rough challenges of those days.

TOM'S WORK

In 1987, Tom's work with MA/Com split up into different branches and Tom's Branch was sold to Hughes Network Systems, but was still located in San Diego.

SURPRISING TOM

It was June 1988, when, with the help of friends I surprised Tom with a big party celebrating his 50th birthday (even though he was 51). Our friend Joyce Stilwell always had a summer party and a Christmas party, and about eight months before, I was talking to her about her caterer for the party I wanted to give Tom. She volunteered to help me by offering her home for Tom's party and I used her caterer as well. She sent out an invitation to us that looked like her annual summer party, so Tom was not suspicious. Then I sent off invitations to all our friends and relatives, his co-workers and other friends letting them know it was a "surprise party" and providing a map with directions to Joyce's home. They were to arrive a half-hour earlier than we were so when we came in, they all jumped up and yelled, "surprise".

Tom was truly surprised, as everyone had kept the secret. It was one of the greatest joys of my life to be able to do something for Tom, as he has always done so much for me. It was a sit down dinner out by the pool with delicious food and a big cake provided by the caterer. Friends, Barbara (Joyce's sister) and Orlin Stansfield helped me with the food and drinks. We had music and everyone told their favorite story about Tom, so it was sort of a "roast" as well. What fun we had that night!

LOSING ONE OF MY BEST FRIENDS

Hal and Ellen had not come to the party, as Ellen wasn't feeling well. Besides Lupus, she had Angina and passed in her sleep the next night. This was very hard for me as Ellen and I were very close and had taken trips to San Francisco, the Orient and had chummed around so much together when we were single and in our marriage, Tom and I had enjoyed camping so many times with Hal and Ellen.

TOM'S CHANGE OF EMPLOYMENT

In December1988 Tom was hired as a temporary Sr. Quality Engineer for QUALCOMM, and a year later, in December 1989, Tom was offered a permanent Sr. Quality Engineering position with QUALCOMM. As a part of the benefits for his position, he was offered stock options, which have provided for us to be financially secure for the rest of our lives.

STUDYING MIND-BODY-SPIRIT CONNECTION

I was laid off from Nutri-System, which gave me more time to explore natural health and healing. By this time, more doctors were writing books about the importance of the mind-body-spirit connection. In 1989 I read the book, *Vibrational Medicine*, by Dr. Richard Gerber, and learned about the healing power of flower essences as well as other methods of esoteric healing I had studied, including Laying On of Hands and Faith Healing. I studied meditation and meditated regularly. For some time, friends had referred other people to me who had Rheumatoid Arthritis or other diseases because they had seen how I was able to take responsibility for my health and live a victorious life. I had been counseling these people and sharing with them the things that had helped me. Many people had said I needed to start my own business to help others.

OUR OWN BUSINESS

As I meditated about this one day, it became clear that I should start a business called

WELLNESS
INFORMATION
NETWORK or WIN

113

So in December 1989, after taking a class on "How to Start Your Own Business", we applied for a trademark under that name and had it registered. The goal was to provide information through workshops and consultations on wellness, using alternate methods, techniques and natural remedies. As I gathered new knowledge, techniques, or became certified in particular areas, such as Flower Essence Practitioner, or licensed as a Hypnotherapist, these arts were added to the consultations as well.

LOSING MY FIRST SISTER

In January 1991, my sister, Mary, passed on. It was quite a shock because of her age (66) and because she went to the hospital for a simple gallbladder surgery and died from a heart attack.

STUDYING FOR MY DOCTORATE

In 1990 I applied to the University of Metaphysics in Los Angeles to start working on my Doctorate in Metaphysical Sciences. It included obtaining a Bachelor's and Master's Degree in Metaphysical Sciences as a precursor for the Doctorate. I had to do another Master's Thesis dealing with using guided imagery prior to surgery for a successful outcome, as well as my Doctoral Dissertation on the "Metaphysical Meaning and Healing of Rheumatoid Arthritis". I completed my degree in 1992. During this time, I obtained my California Lifetime Teaching Credential and taught classes, part time, through San Diego Community College to seniors on Healthy Lifestyles, Nutrition and Mind-Body Connection. In September 1992, Tom and I attended the Second Annual Flower Essence Convention in Australia and had a wonderful vacation along with it, which is documented in Chapter 16.

YOGA CLASS

When I got back, I started attending a class called BLISSWORK (Body Lengthening, and Integrated Structural Strengthening Klasses) I learned a lot of Yoga positions beneficial to my health that I still practice and met some wonderful new friends.

The summer of 1993 I took intensive training with the Flower Essence Services in the High Sierras to become a Flower Essence Practitioner, and incorporated this service into our business.

CHANGES IN OUR LIFE

In 1994, on our camping vacation to Oregon, we contracted for two concrete pads to be constructed on our property. It has made the arrival and setting up of our RV on our property much easier.

PASSING OF MY OLDEST BROTHER-IN-LAW

In 1994, Bud Wennstrom, husband of my oldest sister, Charlotte, passed on.

This was my first brother-in-law to pass on. He had filled in at our wedding for my father as he walked me down the aisle, so there was a special attachment for us. It was a very difficult time for Charlotte, as they had been married for over fifty years.

CHURCH

We had been members of the same church, ever since we had been married, but when our long-time minister retired, the selection committee brought in a new minister who had a much narrower system of beliefs and seemed to exclude certain groups of people. After hearing quite a few of his sermons, Tom and I decided to leave in 1994, along with quite a large group of other parishioners for a church which was more inclusive and loving. We are very happy we did, as it provided an opportunity for much more lay participation and a closer feeling of being a part of Christ's ministry.

At First United Methodist Church in San Diego, Tom and I have served in the Care Ministries Program, the Lay Hospital Visiting Team, the Home Bound Visiting Program, the Covenant Circle and the Prayer Partner Program. I have also participated as a Scripture Lay Reader. Their Motto is, "Open Minds, Open Hearts, Open Doors," and the mission is "to worship God in spirit and in truth, to grow in the image of Christ, to care for one another in Christian love, to share the good news of what God has done in Christ and to follow His example of humble service to all people." There is a strong emphasis on living what we believe, with active involvement in the community and the world, for those in need-the hungry, the ill, for people with AIDS, disaster relief.

We attend a Monday Neighborhood Bible Study a well as a Sunday School Class which meets after church on Sundays and occasionally attend Vespers on Wednesday evenings and the Active Adult Program Meetings, which meet monthly on Wednesdays. The Church is always sponsoring stimulating workshops and classes, through the San Diego School of Christian Studies, on Saturdays or in the evenings. Tom and I go to as many of these as we can. All these programs act to deepen our faith and help us live a more vital and active Christian life. Our pastor, Dr. Jim Standiford, is a down-to-earth person who remembers everyone's name, is very outgoing, friendly and his sermons always provide insight on strengthening our spiritual connection. We love attending the monthly concerts and take great joy in listening to our church choir during the worship service.

BECOMING A HYPNOTHERAPIST

Tom and I have always been interested in the power of the mind to help people change for the better so we went to an introductory workshop on Hypnotherapy. I had also been studying it in my studies in Metaphysical Science as well. It provided a better way of understanding how negative behaviors can be released more easily by seeing the past in a new way, which opens the door for growth into a brighter and better future.

Hypnotherapy Training

I took my training sponsored by the American Board of Hypnotherapy to become a Clinical Hypnotherapist in 1994. Tom took the same training in 1995, which enabled both of us to practice Hypnotherapy in our business. We leased an office nearby and were able to help many people lose weight, stop smoking and release many negative behaviors, thoughts and emotions. I specialized in helping people release pain. My certification in November 1996 as a Hypno-Anesthesia Therapist added to my abilities to help people. My Rheumatologist and Orthopedic Surgeon were so impressed by what I had accomplished in my own life with Hypnotherapy that they sent me patients and it was very rewarding to see people responding to a non-invasive method. I made tapes for patients having joint implant surgeries which enabled them to go through the surgery with less medication, recuperate and be released from the hospital faster.

TOM'S RETIREMENT

Qualcomm gave Tom a wonderful retirement party in 1995 with a gold watch and a wonderful fishing pole, which he put right to use on our three-month vacation to Canada, which is documented in Chapter 16.

HIP IMPLANT SURGERY

My left hip began giving me trouble and in July 1996 I had surgery for a left hip implant. Because I made my own Hypnotherapy tape, I did not require any pre or post pain medications, and I recuperated and was released from the hospital in record time. Tom made a videotape of my speedy recovery showing how the use of hypnotherapy can help expedite healing. Five weeks later, we left for our motor home vacation to Oregon and continued the videotape showing how I was able to hike and enjoy myself after such a short recovery period. Videotape copies were made for the doctor's offices and one copy was provided to our church. As a result I was able to help Carol Blum, a woman from our church who was scheduled to undergo a hip implant soon by making a tape which she used to make her surgery go easier. Since Carol and her husband Ed live in Tierrasanta, we have become very good friends.

REDOING HOME

Since our home was getting to the point that several things needed redoing, we asked a contractor working on our neighbor's home if he could do ours next. We replaced our roof, carpet, had inside and outside painting done while we went camping in a nearby Thousand Trails Camp.

HAWAII TRIP

Since Tom and I had visited all the Hawaiian Islands, except Maui, we decided to take a trip there in April 1997. We landed in Oahu and stayed a couple of nights there, meeting some friends of ours, Dawn and Scott Seaver. Then we flew to Maui, rented a condo and a car, so we could tour the Island. We really enjoyed the drive up to the Volcano Haleakala and going through Iao Valley. The lush beauty of the drive to Hana with waterfalls, flowers and ferns around every corner provided many backgrounds for taking pictures. We really took our time and just relaxed, taking in all the beauty of this grand Island. We had a wonderful time but on the way back my right knee was injured on the chair lifting me into the airplane.

MORE HYPNOTHERAPY TRAINING

Time Line Therapy was developed as a faster method of therapy than the method used in Clinical Hypnotherapy where a longer amount of time is taken to relax clients and place them in a trance. Clients view their time line of the past, present and future by going above their time line to act as an observer. In this way past traumas are released without experiencing the original pain and ongoing present state challenges or issues can be dealt with productively as well as creating a positive future. It is good to be trained in both the slower method as well as Time Line Hypnotherapy. Some people do better with one or the other depending on their need to use deeper relaxation methods. Therefore Tom and I added this training to our skills in a weeklong training session in Seattle in May 1997.

REVISION OF RIGHT KNEE IMPLANT

As I said, my right knee was injured on the way back from Hawaii and the old knee implant was twenty-one years old and needed revision anyway. As a result, I had my right knee implant revision surgery in August 1997. During the interim, new technology was developed, so the one I have now is much stronger. Of course I made my Hypnotherapy Tape again which allowed me to recuperate faster and expedite my release from the hospital. Since I incorporated a statement about minimal bleeding on the tape, my surgeon said I bled the least amount of any patient in his thirty-four year career as an Orthopedic Surgeon and he was truly amazed at the fast and optimum results of my recovery.

LIVING TRUST

Tom and I have always planned for the future so before the end of 1997, we had a Living Trust prepared.

NEW MOTOR HOME

In March 1998 we bought our first Class A motor home, a Rexhall, 25'6" Vision with a full dinette as well as a Queen sized bed that was as comfortable as the one we have in our bedroom. We were thrilled with it and used it for a short getaway at a campground nearby.

1998 VACATION TO OREGON AND IDAHO

That summer of 1998, we took our annual camping trip in our new motor home to Oregon, and Idaho. We stayed on our Oregon property for a while before heading off to Idaho. We were at a campground in Idaho Falls, when a man came up with a flyer, letting us know about the Rexhall International RV Club for owners of Rexhall Motor Homes and the Rallies they have every year. It sounded like fun so we signed up to become a member of the Rexhall Chapter as well as a member of the Family Motor Coach Association (FMCA). After camping along the Salmon River, we went to Sun Valley and saw Joe Fos at the Lodge and the Ice Show with Surya Bonalei (sp?) and a lot of other ice Stars.

The most memorable time was at Bonner's Ferry, where we got the last campsite available as they had a re-enactment of pioneers crossing the Snake River in covered wagons. Everyone was dressed in 1890's clothing, Native American guides led the group and the crossing was as historically correct as it could be. One wagon was even caught by the swift river currents and tipped over, but the occupants, including an Idaho Senator were soon rescued.

On the way back to our property, we stopped at an Oregon campground where we met some terrific people, Carol and Terry Richards, who were camped right across from us. On the back of their motor home was a sign, "Heart transplant in '89, spending my extra time". We got acquainted and they joined us later for a campfire songfest of hymns. Terry played the harmonica and Carol had an electronic keyboard, as she played the piano for the church they belonged to.

We had a wonderful time and the next morning we took down names, addresses and phone numbers and departed on our separate ways. They were going East to La Grande to see Carol's mother and we were heading west with the next planned stop at Paradise Campground, McKenzie Bridge (one of our favorite campgrounds). As it turned out McKenzie Bridge is where they lived. We arrived at Paradise campground, got our site and I was sitting in a chair outside when this minivan drove up and this young lady with two kids got out. She came up to me and said, "Are you Nancy Burk?"

Well, I was stunned to say the least, because I didn't recognize her. It turned out she was Carol's daughter, Denise and Carol had called her from La Grande, telling her what kind of a motor home we had and to go to the campground and find us. Carol wanted us to use their other car, while we were camped there, so we could go sightseeing and not have to use our motor home and move it.

Here we were, being offered the use of a car and the owners didn't even know that much about us .We were honored to think that Carol and Terry trusted us that much. We followed Denise back to their property and picked up the car, which we used with great care. We went to their church on Sunday before we returned the car and left on our way. That was the start of a beautiful friendship that continues to this day. We enjoyed camping with Carol and Terry on several camping trips after that. Terry passed away in 2000 and Carol remarried Jim Lauman in September 2002. We met Jim the next year and enjoy our times with both Carol and Jim each year when we go to Oregon. We came back from our 1998 vacation with a lot of fun memories, which helped to tide me over some very rough health challenges that followed.

FLESH-EATING BACTERIA

Out of the blue in September 1998 I was diagnosed with the Flesh-Eating Bacteria, which is a story in itself and is detailed in Chapter 11-Amazing Grace. Interestingly, during this time, when I almost lost my life, our QUALCOMM stock took off and hit an all time high that will provide us with financial security the rest of our lives and were able to designate a greater gift in our trust to our church.

LOSING MY SISTER EDITH

My sister, Edith, had been sick for some time with Pancreatitis and respiratory problems, and in October 1998 almost passed on. However, she came back and had seven more months before she finally passed in June 1999. I just had my chest catheter removed and so Tom and I flew up to Grass Valley, California for her service. When I was small, Edith was like a second mother to me and I have always been close to her.

Her husband, Carl, passed in January 2001, just two weeks away from my other brother-in-law, Cal Pollard, who had been ill with Parkinson's for some time.

TRIP TO NORTHERN CALIFORNIA, OREGON AND WASHINGTON 1999

In June 1999, we left for a three-month motor home camping trip to Northern California, Washington and Oregon, which really helped me on the road to healing from the Flesh-Eating Bacteria.

We traveled around Northern California, mostly the Big Sur area where we honeymooned in 1970, and then headed for Oregon and Washington. We were camped at the Thousand Trails Campground in Leavenworth, Washington and were just coming back from a walk when we saw this couple trying to get in our motor home. It turned out they had just bought a Rexhall Vision, just like ours and mistook our motor home for theirs. Well we got acquainted with Trudy and Bob Roswald and have enjoyed meeting them at different campgrounds and the Rexhall rallies every since. In fact we ended up camping next to them at the La Conner Thousand Trails Campground after we left Leavenworth. After we returned to Grants Pass in August, we saw an advertisement for a litter of four Shih Tzu's that were for sale. We had wanted one for some time as we had read about what good traveling dogs they are, and are so creative, intelligent and loyal. We fell in love with this eight week old puppy that we named Tao, because of his black and white markings and because sometimes he seemed to be more passive and calm (yin) and sometimes more active and energetic (yang). He is really a great therapy aid!

REXHALL MOTOR HOME RALLY

In Oct 1999, we attended the Rexhall Homecoming Rally at Lancaster, California, along with Trudy and Bob Roswald and had a wonderful time. We were quite surprised when Tom's name was called out in a drawing and he won a $50.00 Rexhall camping jacket. Then he ordered one for me so we would have matching jackets.

RECOVERING FROM PNEUMONIA TO CELEBRATION IN THE NEW YEAR

We spent Christmas Eve with Tom's family in Ramona at his nephew Steven's home. Tom's mother had the flu and wasn't feeling well the whole evening. Later on she was taken to the hospital where she was diagnosed with Pneumonia and treated for a week During that week, Tom and I came down with the flu, and since mine wouldn't go away, went to the doctor. After taking chest X-rays and tests, he diagnosed me with Pneumonia and I was placed on Antibiotics again. I was sick the whole month of January 2000, but recovered just in time to attend the Retirement Party of Orlin Stansfield at the Bel Aggio in Las Vegas, from February 28 to March 3, given by his wife Barbara. We stayed at the Monte Carlo, along with a lot of the other guests and friends we had in common, and we had a wonderful time.

OUR LIFE FROM 2000 TO THE PRESENT

We did the groundwork for our Income Taxes, had them officially prepared and then April 15, 2000, and took off for a 26 state, six-month trip in our motor home, which will be documented in Chapter 16.

We had been gone not quite a month and were in Houston, Texas, when we were notified of the passing of Tom's mother. We were staying at a Thousand Trails Camp and they allowed us to leave our motor home there while we rented a car, took our doggie, Tao and came back for the service and so Tom could settle the estate, since he was the Executor. This vacation would also be the last time we would see my two brother-in-laws, Cal Pollard and Carl Daffin, as they both passed the next January. My brother-law, Paul Casad (Mary's husband) passed away with cancer in December 2000. In December, I also fell at home and hurt my shoulder but after X-rays were taken, found no broken bones so was quite thankful.

HOME PAID OFF

Since the 30-year loan on our home was just about up, we decided to pay the balance, so we are completely free of large debt now. What a great feeling!

2001

In February, I lost my balance, fell and twisted my body (lumbar sprain). I had a lot of pain but no broken bones, and healed after three months.

123

The first part of 2001 we started planning a revision of our backyard that we had long talked about. We had a new spa with decking all round and a four foot artificial waterfall put in before we took off on our summer camping motor home vacation May 31st and went to B.C. again, but just stayed on Vancouver Island, came down through Washington and to Oregon. This trip is also documented in Chapter 16. Our backyard revision was completed with a Japanese style sun house that we use as our "Sacred Spot" to mediate and pray. It also provides us with an opportunity to be close to nature as it has a beautiful view of and opens up into our Japanese style garden filled with beautiful flowers.

2002

In March 2002, I volunteered to serve on the Reunion Committee for our 50th Point Loma High School Reunion to be held the weekend of September 19-20, 2003. I was web site coordinator for Classmates.com, where a number of classmates were registered and located, who had previously moved and there were no forwarding address. With Tom's help, we also searched on the Internet and located many classmates whose addresses had been missing, as they had never attended a reunion. This kept me busy but had many rewards since I have "connected" with a lot of old friends. We also had a lot of laughs over the comments from classmates who thought I had passed on. Evidently they had heard something about me having the Flesh-Eating Bacteria. As it turned out, I have outlasted half the football team and many others who were a lot stronger and healthier than I was in High School. Everyone always thought I would be the first to go.

ANOTHER HEALTH CHALLENGE

Our summer trip to Oregon in 2002 was short-lived. We left on June 16 and met friends Tom and Kathie King who were in Oregon for a car show. After visiting with them on our property and going to lunch, we left for Fish Lake. Tom was out fishing when I attempted to get in our motor home and the magnetic latch of our screen door stuck and then came open with such a force that I did a backward flip into the air and landed seven feet away on a gravel pad. Tao was in his playpen and saw the whole thing. The next thing I knew, a man was standing over me.... he said he had heard our doggie crying and he thought Tao was hurt. Instead he saw me lying in a pool of blood. He beeped Tom and he called E.R. I was taken to Medford Hospital 40 miles away. They determined it was a broken pelvis and a mild concussion. I was extremely blessed as I could have been killed, broken my back or been paralyzed for life. I believe Angels were around me when I fell, as I remember saying, when I felt I was losing my balance, "O God please help me."

I was even protected in the hospital when they gave me an overdose of Demerol and I went into convulsions, and they had to correct it. To make a long story short, we came back to San Diego, where my pelvis could heal and I would be under the care of a doctor who knew my case history.

Tom packed lots of pillows around me on the bed, as I couldn't sit up. It took a painful three months for therapy and to learn to walk again. I used a walker to walk on the sidewalk around the house, and started in with one round in the morning, then the next day two rounds, and the next three rounds and so on until I reached ten trips. Then I did two rounds a day, until I could walk on my own. Every step I took, I said, "I take this step through the strength Christ gives me."

2003

CAMPING TRIP TO ARIZONA - FEBRUARY

In February 2003, after our annual Hypnotherapy Training in Irvine, we visited with one of my classmates in Irvine and with our motor home took a three week trip to Arizona where we saw some of my classmates living over there. Reconnecting with old friends is a lot of fun. On the way back, we stopped at Colorado River Adventures, and became campground members there, so now we have a place to camp in the winters.

LOSS OF ANOTHER GOOD FRIEND

In March 2003, Joyce (Anderson) Hanson, who had been with me the night I met Tom passed with heart complications. She was taken to the hospital on Friday, we visited her on Saturday and on Monday morning she was gone.

ANOTHER BROKEN BONE

I was rushing around at home, turned fast and caught my toe under the leg of a chair the last of April. I felt myself going down and after an X-ray found out I broke my left arm in-between the two inches of bone between my elbow and shoulder joint implants. I was advised to go to the Orthopedic Surgeon who did my arm implants for an evaluation. I entered his office and said, "Hello Dr. Braun, I'm still walking around." He said," Nancy, long after your obituary appears in the paper, you'll still be walking around." We both laughed. A splint was made for my arm and he advised me to be careful. My Rheumatologist, Dr. Nguyen, started me on a new injection medication called Forteo, which helps to rebuild bones. Since I was doing well otherwise, she said it was safe for us to go ahead on our planned vacation in May.

TRIP TO LAS VEGAS AND OREGON

We left in May, as scheduled for Las Vegas to see the Celine Dione show at Ceasar's Palace. She truly is a great talent. I had just begun having problems with my stomach, so after calling my doctor in San Diego, she advised me to see a doctor in Las Vegas for a Colonoscopy. After viewing the results of the Colonoscopy, that doctor diagnosed me with Colitis, but gave me medication so we could continue our trip to Oregon which is documented in Chapter 16.

When we got back I had another X-ray of my arm and it had totally healed.

50th POINT LOMA HIGH SCHOOL REUNION

The time for our long awaited 50th High School Reunion finally arrived-September 19-20, 2003. Friday afternoon a bus tour took our classmates to all the old hangouts as well as the new developments in San Diego. A lot of changes occur within fifty years. That night we had our "Mixer" at the Bali Hai Restaurant in Point Loma, where appetizers were served and we got re-acquainted.

The next night the U. S. Grant Hotel was the site of our dressy dinner and dance. Appetizers were served before dinner while classmates mingled around conversing with each other. We were then escorted to the Ballroom where we took our seats at tables beautifully decorated with monogrammed wine glasses and a bottle of wine. Dinner started out with salad followed by a combined entree of filet mignon and salmon with potato, vegetables and bread with tiramisu for desert.

The surprise of the evening was the entrance of the 2003 Point Loma High Cheer Team from two back doors in a "V" formation to the front where they performed 3-tier acrobatics and cheers. A 1950's lounge singer also entertained us with our favorite songs. A drawing for prizes and a band playing 1950's rock and roll music as well as slow dance ballads topped off the evening. The next day, those that selected an optional seven-day cruise to the Mexican Riviera left for their adventure.

Tom and I stayed in town where a special gathering was held at Dedi Ridenouer's home for the Rosettes Horizon Club members. Tom and I picked up "Miss Jean", our leader.... it was so good to have her there. We all shared with her how much she meant to each of us About sixteen of us plus spouses attended. We had a delicious buffet, shared memories of old times, laughed, and had lots of fun. We celebrated the life of Mary KleinWade, who had passed on two years before, with a candle ceremony arranged by Dedi.

FIRESTORM OCTOBER 2003-EVACUATED HOUSE

It was Sunday, October 26, 2003 and we were preparing the motor home to attend the Rexhall Annual Homecoming Rally. The

127

day before fires had started in the rural areas of San Diego, as they often do during the hot Santa Ana winds of the season but they are soon extinguished. A neighbor who had been serving as a volunteer fire security guard had come back from Ramona, near the fire site and shouted to us as he ran into his home, "Get ready to evacuate, the fire is roaring towards Scripps Ranch and Tierrasanta." We looked up just in time to see for ourselves that the encroaching flames were coming up over a distant hill. We finished last minute packing and left with our Tao.

As we moved into the congested traffic leaving the neighborhood, the flames were within 1/2 mile of our home and we were in a bumper-to-bumper traffic situation. The flames were moving faster than we were as I looked out the rearview mirror. I audibly said, "Lord, please deliver us" and just a moment later there was a security guard at the intersection that directed our lane into a faster route so we could get down to Highway 8 and we headed west straight for the beach.

We spent the night in our motor home in Mission Bay Park. The air quality was better there than anyplace in the City and with my breathing problems felt that was best. There were about thirty motor homes and about forty cars with us. People even spent the night in their cars...but we were SAFE.

When we were allowed back in our neighborhood the next day, we found our home had no damage!!!!! We said a prayer of thanks for our home being saved and also prayed for those not so fortunate, realizing that it could have been ours..."There but for the grace of God go I".
We went on to the Rexhall Rally after checking our property.

ENDING A BUSY YEAR

We took a cruise to the Mexican Riviera in November for eleven days this is detailed in Chapter 16.

The Holidays were rather subdued after the fires, but we enjoyed spending them with Tom's sister Lynn and her husband Ed; Scott, Kim and daughter Rachel; Steven, Sandi and son, Tommie; and Kathy, Ray...son, James and daughter, Sierra. Tom and I treated everyone to the usual pizza dinner and then we headed to Lynn and

Ed's home for opening of gifts. We again enjoyed our annual New Year's Eve dinner celebration with Marilyn and Bill Kneeland.

2004

CLEANING PROJECT LEADS TO HOME REPAIR

We had already started a cleaning project around the house and as we cleared away some items that had not been moved in quite awhile in the back bedroom that we were making into a computer room, we noticed some water damage to the back wall. We called in a contractor to check the damage. After finding a broken water pipe in the backyard that had been the source of the water damage, he said repairs were definitely needed, so we decided to go ahead with a lot of work that had to be done. (New back wall, new windows and window doors from the kitchen and major bedroom out to the patio, as well as a new patio cover.) At the same time, our clothes dryer went out, so we had another purchase.

PREPARATION FOR TRIP TO ALASKA

We have always wanted to take a trip to Alaska and drive the Alcan Highway, so since I was doing well health-wise on my current medications of Forteo, (Osteoporosis) Enbrel (Arthritis), Colazal (Colitis) and Nexium (Acid Reflex), we decided this would be the year and we started making preparations by doing maintenance and repair work on our motor home. Tom saw an advertisement through Camping World President's Club for a Motor home Caravan tour to Alaska. We got the itinerary and it seemed to have just what we were looking for and the price was right, so we signed up.

We left the 12th of May to take a slow trip through Oregon, seeing both Carol and Don, who were camping up there and my sister Charlotte and her family. We enjoyed our trip through British Columbia and joined our Alaskan Tour Group June 20th at Dawson Creek. There were twenty-eight motor homes; Four people were in one motor home, two others had single drivers, and in the rest of the motor homes, there were two people. They were very special and we bonded right away. Someone was always there to help Tom as some of the side trips were quite a challenge for me, but with God's help and our wonderful tour friends, we did it!

ALASKA

Our Alaskan trip was a dream of a lifetime and our tour guides, Mary and Gene Springer, led us through thirty-seven days of awesome beauty up the Alcan Highway to Fort Nelson, Muncho Lake, Watson Lake in B.C., Whitehorse and Kluane in the Yukon, and Tok, Valdez, Palmer, Anchorage, Seward, Homer Spit, Kenai Fjords, Fairbanks, Denali, Skagway and Juneau, in Alaska. And is detailed in Chapter 16. The tour ended July 27, and we spent the rest of August in Oregon, visiting Carol and Jim Lauman in Summerville and staying on our property in Murphy.

ANOTHER FALL

We were back from our Alaskan trip only two weeks, when I attended a workshop and fell again. Tom took me to E.R. with a bloody face and open wound on my left hand. I had five stitches above my upper lip and the doctor took tweezers and placed the skin back on my left hand where it was peeled back sealing it up with medicinal glue. I had a Cat Scan and an MRI, which indicated my neck, was broken, but since I was having no pain in my neck, it didn't sound logical. I was referred to a Neurosurgeon who made a detailed study of the MRI. His final diagnosis was Cervical Myelopathy, which means, that the base of my skull is very close to my spine and another fall or destruction of spine due to aging process, Rheumatoid Arthritis and Osteoporosis could cause paralysis if skull presses on nerve. I am being very careful when I walk and have faith that God will take care the rest.

DIAGNOSED WITH SLEEP APNEA

For some time I have had problems with breathing in my sleep. One of the doctors noticed it when I was sick with the bacteria six years ago. It seems after a trauma, especially a fall, it gets worse.

130

Because it flared up after falling on my face, my doctor recommended that I be tested by a Sleep Diagnostic Technician. This was set up through New Millennium Diagnostics, who sent out a technician to our home for an all night study.

I was tested with a Polysomnogram, which measures physiologic responses during sleep. A multitude of electrodes was attached to various parts of my body. During the first 3-4 hours my normal sleep patterns were recorded showing the number of disturbances during sleep, which indicate the severity. Enough disturbances were recorded, so I was placed on a CPAP (continuous positive airway pressure) device, which has a mask that fits over the nose and straps around the head.

This device provides a flow of positive pressure air through the mask to keep the airway open during sleep. Results of the sleep study showed I had Severe Obstructive Sleep Apnea, which means I stop breathing for at least ten seconds during sleep because my airway collapses and prevents air from getting into my lungs. Sixty-three disturbances per hour were recorded. As a result, my doctor prescribed the CPAP equipment, which I used for two months with unsatisfactory results, since none of the three different sized masks provided fit right because of my small face and bone structure.

After talking to my Homeopathic M.D., he said success had been achieved in many cases using a homeopathic remedy. I am being treated with this remedy and it appears to be working for me. This is the advantage of understanding that there are both complimentary and alternate forms of treatments for a variety of health conditions. Many cases of illness or disease are unable to be treated by conventional medicine or equipment either because there is none available or the treatment available is not suited for every individual due to allergies or adverse reactions to medication or equipment.

CELEBRATION OF LIFE

Sally Bonham Clark Mozingo, one of our Rosette Horizon Club members, was diagnosed with Lung Cancer in 2002. The doctor indicated she would not live beyond December. She not only attended our 50th High School Reunion in September 2003, but a small group of us helped her celebrate her 69th Birthday earlier this year. Sally passed on in September and Dedi again invited us to her home the first week of October to celebrate Sally's life with a candle lighting ceremony and a delicious buffet. Those living out of state were unable to attend but Sally's husband, Jimmy and her sister Betsy, along with a small group living here in San Diego attended. Tom and I were delighted when Miss Jean said she could come along with her caretaker, Melissa, so we took them with us.

MOTOR HOME ENGINE GOES OUT ON WAY TO REXHALL RALLY

We were on our way to the Rexhall Annual Homecoming Rally the middle of October when we were a little North of Escondido and the engine started smoking. We had to be towed to the Ford Dealers in Escondido. They told us the engine had to be replaced, and that it would take a week to order it and have it installed, so we had to miss the Rally.

DECISION TO HAVE MOTOR HOME BUILT FOR US TO SUIT OUR NEEDS

Since we wanted to travel to the East Coast in 2005, we decided to have a new motor home built with all the modifications needed for my physical challenges already in the motor home from the beginning rather than to have it modified afterwards. We contracted with Rexhall to start the construction and in December we decided to donate our1998 Rexhall motor home to the Children's Hospital.

DECEMBER 2004

We enjoyed the Balboa Park Holiday Christmas program and our church's annual Christmas concert. We again spent Christmas Eve with Tom's sister, Lynn and her family. Christmas Day we had turkey dinner at our home, inviting Sue Casad, my niece (daughter of my deceased Mary and husband Paul) and her fiancé, Malcolm. Our New Year's Eve annual dinner celebration with Marilyn and Bill Kneeland was delicious and fun.

2005

I am concluding this chapter with our plans for 2005. With our new motor home, we are taking two long trips, in celebration of our 35th Wedding Anniversary in May. We leave in February to go to Louisiana and Florida (two states we missed on our trip to the East Coast in 2000) and on the way will see friends and relatives in most of the states in between and on the way back see friends and relatives in states below the Mason-Dixon Line. We return to San Diego the end of May or the beginning of June. We leave again the beginning of July for Oregon, up through Washington, following the outline of the United States to the East Coast. We will take in North Dakota, Michigan and see the New England States in the Fall, as well as seeing friends and relatives in States above the Mason-Dixon Line. We plan to return to San Diego in October and by that time will have visited every state in the United States.

Our lives are an adventure and we enjoy each day to the fullest. Part of our enjoyment is asking God for opportunities to be a blessing to others. We never know what He has in store for us but we know He holds the future and will bring us blessings as He leads us through our journey of love, as messengers for Him, taking along what matters.

MY THOUGHTS ON LOVE AND MARRIAGE

Marriage starts out as a wondrous adventure. "Stuff" happens as time goes by. There are disappointments, health challenges, relationship problems within families, financial changes, job stresses, loss of family and friends, both parties grow and change in unexpected ways. It is up to both parties to continually remember, renew, and celebrate the love that is at the core of the relationship, to grow with one another (instead of apart from one another), to support and console each other as "stuff" happens, to go to church regularly, to have daily prayers together asking for guidance, having the faith that things will work out with the help of God, forgiving one another constantly, and having fun together.

133

It is important to understand, accept, respect and trust the other party and to continually acknowledge your love verbally and in all actions. Showing appreciation, thanking the other party, making little notes and surprises for each other are thoughtful ways of expressing, "I'm happy I married you". Throughout this book, I have shared some of the things we have done, but Tom has been such a love and support when I have been in pain, that one Thanksgiving when the San Diego Union was asking for people to write in letters about what they were thankful for. I couldn't resist sending the following in that I wrote about Tom:

ONE WHO'S ALWAYS THERE

Darling Tom:

Thanks for: Being you;
The courage to marry me with my arthritis pain;
Massaging my joints day or night;
Supporting me with love, prayers and humor through surgeries and recovery;
Helping me when I can't do it alone;
Encouraging me when I can;
Faith that our faith and minds will overcome all adversities;
Respecting my career achievements;
Being my best friend;
The joy of having you by my side awake or asleep.
Love Forever,
Nancy Burk, San Diego

We have always had some little saying that we repeat to each other to make the other one smile. One is, "I wish this night would never end", which is what Tom told me the first night I met him. On our first anniversary, Tom gave me a little statue with a couple hugging and the below verse inscribed on it. This motto has stayed with us every since:
Me and You,
You and Me
That's the Way It'll Always Be.

134

Another time we were looking at TV one night when an interviewer of a couple who were celebrating their 70th wedding anniversary asked the question, "What is the most important ingredient that has kept you together all these years?" As they held hands, and looked at each other, he answered, "I love her and she loves me and that's the way it is." That sums up our relationship, exactly.

CHAPTER 9

MIND MATTERS

Hymn: Be Thou My Vision

Scripture: "Let this mind be in you which was also in Christ Jesus." (Phil 2:5)

"For God has not given us a spirit of fear, but of power and of love, and of a sound mind." (2 Tim 1:7)

"And do not be conformed to this world, but be transformed by the renewing of your mind, that you may prove what is that good and acceptable and perfect will of God." (Rom12: 2)

TAKING AND USING OUR MIND PROPERLY IN OUR JOURNEY

What we think about and focus on most of the time, becomes who we are. Where our mind goes, the energy follows. Thoughts are forms of energy. We cannot focus on two opposites at the same time, so, if we think negative thoughts, that's where we will stay, unless we make a conscious effort to change the way we think to positive. We can make ourselves sick by thinking about it a great deal. That's why a POSITIVE ATTITUDE is so important for life's journey and healing.

ARE YOU CARRYING AROUND EXTRA MENTAL BAGGAGE?

No matter how much we love our parents, most of them pass on faulty or some negative mind programming to children, simply because it was passed down to them due to ethnic heritage, fear or some unknown reason. They may have accumulated additional faulty programming in their life experiences as well. However, each of us is responsible for becoming aware of our faulty or negative programmed messages, either passed on to us, or accumulated in our life experiences. Transactional Analysis (TA) is a good therapy method to help you eliminate these programmed messages. The book, *Born to Win,* by Muriel James and Dorothy Jongeward is excellent and has exercises at the end of each chapter. Eliminate that negative excess baggage on your spiritual journey!

"The Mind is the Builder, The Spirit is the Life Force and the Physical is the Result."

Edger Cayce, Prophet

"The curious paradox is that when I accept myself just as I am, then I can change."

Carl Rogers, Psychologist

MAKING UP OUR MIND AND TAKING RESPONSIBILITY

Taking responsibility for the choices we make in life is one of the most important things we can do. This eliminates blaming anything else or anyone else. It also involves admitting when we are wrong and being big enough to take accountability for it. Taking proper responsibility means we look at options and the consequences of our proposed decisions before we act. We need to create WIN-WIN solutions, which will be in the best interests of everyone instead of the "us" versus "them" mentality that leads to dissension. In today's world, this might be called "thinking outside the box". Using our minds creatively for positive solutions is what God wants us to do.

"Enter into the mind of Jesus and think from there."

Norman Vincent Peale, Minister/Author

MIND TECHNIQUES TO HELP US CHANGE OR MINDING OUR BODY

AFFIRMATIONS AND IMAGINATION

Einstein said that imagination was more important than knowledge. Knowledge comes from the past, but imagination is an aid to envision the future.

Affirmations are POSITIVE statements of being, placed in the present tense that states what one wants to happen or what one wants to become. As one makes the affirmative statement, it is also important to imagine the results already taking place. As we said, our thoughts are followed by energy that makes changes, so by repeating these positive statements and imagining the results over and over and over, the affirmation becomes a reality and we become the change that we have affirmed.

These are some examples of affirmations that have helped me:

THE LIGHT OF GOD SURROUNDS ME,
THE LOVE OF GOD ENFOLDS ME,
THE POWER OF GOD PROTECTS ME,
THE PRESENCE OF GOD IS IN ME AND WITH ME
ALWAYS AND FOREVER.

I AM WHOLE, HEALED AND FREE
AS GOD INTENDED ME TO BE.
THANK YOU GOD.

A person sits in a chair or lies down in a comfortable position (legs and arms need to be uncrossed) while saying the following either internally or out loud (one is actually talking to his/her body and asking it to do what he/she asks...and the body will actually do this over time, but it takes practice.) This is called Biofeedback or Mind/Body/Spirit Healing.

When I use (3X) it means the phrase needs to be repeated three times, one right after the other.

MY ARMS AND LEGS ARE HEAVY AND WARM (3X)
MY HEARTBEAT IS CALM AND REGULAR (3X)
MY BODY BREATHES ITSELF FREELY AND
COMFORTABLY (3X)
MY ABDOMEN IS WARM (3X)
MY FOREHEAD IS COOL   (3X)
MY MIND IS QUIET AND STILL (3X)
I AM AT PEACE
I AM TOTALLY, COMPLETELY RELAXED AND
COMFORTABLE

The above is taken from a book I recommend called, *90 Days to Self-Health,* by C. Norman Shealy, M.D. He is a Holistic M.D. and I have had classes and seminars from him. He practices in Springfield, Mo. The book is published by Bantam Paperback Books. There are other Affirmations and Guided Imagery Exercises, which follow the above that are helpful and are all included in the book.

VISUALIZATION

Visualization is another technique to help us change. We close our eyes in a relaxed state and visualize or "internally see" (at the location of the nose bridge between the eyes or what is known as the "third eye") the change we wish to become. One can practice this by closing the eyes and visualizing a favorite piece of clothing, car or place they enjoy. Mentally, "see" the color, "hear" the sounds, "smell" any odors, (like the smell of flowers or the seashore), "feel" any textures, (like velvet, or the sand at the seashore), etc. Then, if you are practicing how to better a relationship, mentally, "see" yourself and this person having a conversation, and your positive words coming out just right so that the other person is responding with positive behavior to what you say, and your corresponding behavior also comes out in a positive manner.

GUIDED IMAGERY

A trained person gently leads the client through a process of relaxation by placing them in a garden, the mountains, the seashore, or a vacation spot that they enjoy and that is pleasurable. Then the client is given affirmations for the change they wish to become and at the same time visualizes the change taking place.

DREAMS

Dreams are messages from our subconscious that give us clues about understanding our daily life and how to live it better. It is best if one has been to a workshop on dreams, consulted a dream therapist or read books to understand what certain images or symbols in dreams convey. I have used all of the above aids and have benefited from each one. I would like to share a dream of mine that has had a profound effect on my life. I call it Step by Step:

STEP BY STEP-A DREAM

I was standing in front of a big thicket with thorns and big thistles all over. Across from the thicket was a beautiful meadow and behind it was a forest and mountains. I knew I had to get across the thicket but I was paralyzed with fear and couldn't move. I didn't know how I was going to make it across. I decided to put out my left foot and see how far it would go. Suddenly a path opened up in front of my left foot. I was amazed! Then I put out my right foot and a path appeared in front of it. Each time I took a step the path opened up in front of me but it extended only about two feet in front of me. As I walked faster and faster, the path spread faster. About half way through, I stopped to look around and the path stopped. Then I started again step-by-step, and again the path opened up. I was able to gain confidence and move faster and faster. I reached the other side and It was beautiful. There was a stream in the meadow and I could see animals in front of the trees ahead. The birds were singing and I gave thanks to God. I had reached my destination. It was like the promised land.

WHAT MAKES IT POSSIBLE TO CHANGE

God has designed the brain and mind with the structure and DNA to make it possible to change.

THE BRAIN

The brain is the physical part of our thinking ability; it is the mass of nerve tissue located in the cranium. The left-brain contains our logical or linear thinking and the right brain is where our imagination (visualization) and spatial ability is located. The mind is not centered in the brain, it is in every cell of our organs and body, including the brain, and has three parts:

CONSCIOUS MIND

The conscious mind is that part of the mind that is known as the rational state, uses the analytical process, has temporary memory and uses the will power to make decisions and choices. Awareness is not always a part of the conscious mind. AWARENESS comes with an effort to understand the real reason or truth underlying a concept or issue and carries with it an "a-ha" or sense that now "I have seen the light". It is a cognizant state that resonates with an inner sense of knowing.

SUBCONSCIOUS MIND

The subconscious mind (sometimes called the unconscious mind), is that part of the mind, which regulates our breathing, heartbeat, coordination, etc. It also often controls our actions without us ever realizing it, because it carries permanent memory, emotions, past traumas, imagination and a protective process. If you do something and afterwards wonder, "Why did I do that?" it is because the subconscious takes over and protects us from something in the past that may have hurt or caused us harm.

141

SUPER CONSCIOUS MIND

The super conscious mind is that part of the mind which contains our spiritual experiences and connects us to God through the Holy Spirit. This is where we get our intuition or sense of "inner knowing".

HYPNOTHERAPY HELPS PEOPLE CHANGE

Hypnotherapy helps people to stop smoking, lose weight, have successful relationships, manage/release pain, release past trauma, deal with and release any issue or problem facing them. It then replaces that problem or issue by creating success in that area. A trained hypnotherapist places a person in a relaxed (altered) state which bypasses the conscious state.

There are various methods to do this and I will illustrate by the method I have used. This is done by asking the person to breath deeply while focusing on a particular spot. The person counts backwards while the therapist suggests to the client that he/she allow the eyelids to gently flutter until they are tired and then just allow them to close. Once a person is in this relaxed state, the subconscious mind, can be more easily accessed, the reason for the habit or trauma is understood and released. What the client once perceived as harmful to survival is altered and change can be implemented through positive suggestion.

Hypnotherapy has been used for centuries to help people make changes in order to have a better life. The AMA approved the use of Hypnotherapy as a valid therapeutic tool in 1958. Since I am trained and licensed hypnotherapist, my Rheumatologist and Orthopedic Surgeon both referred their patients to me for Hypnotherapy after they saw the results of using it in my own life.

I have used it to understand and manage my pain as well as help me control my bleeding and help my body/mind to be relaxed during the surgery process so I could recover faster and easier. I have made my own audio hypnotherapy tapes, which I listen to while undergoing surgery. The tape plays over and over until the surgery is finished (for joint implants, it is a five hour surgery). The result is that I do not use pre or post surgery pain medication; I have more strength and am able to leave the hospital in half the time as the usual patient. As my doctors referred their patients to me, I helped them in the same way.

THE PAIN CYCLE

Focusing on how bad the pain is only causes more tension, anxiety and more pain. Once one has experienced pain, it creates fear that the pain will return. This leads to anxiety, more tension and thus more pain. It is a viscous cycle. Of course one needs to be diagnosed by a doctor to first determine the cause of pain, but once this is done, using these methods can reduce the amount of medication needed.

TECHNIQUES TO MANAGE PAIN:

Dis-association:

Mentally see the pain get smaller and smaller until it disappears, or mentally picture it being removed by God and put into a wastebasket or a helium balloon to be carried away by the wind. You can also mentally picture all your fears or troubles being carried away in a helium balloon as well.

Distraction:

Distraction helps one to refocus on things that are enjoyable or to focus on something new. Remember you cannot hold two conflicting images in your mind at the same time.

Perception:

Remember, if we perceive pain (or anything else, for that matter), it can remain, until we alter the perception. To do this, we change the pain into something else, such as an object (ball, for instance) with a particular size, color, shape, sound, texture, scent, etc. Then we can change the size, and find we have the ability to increase or decrease our pain by changing the perception! With practice, we can reduce the intensity of our pain with our mind. I have done this for so long that I have the ability to totally "transcend" pain.

However, in times of undue stress, I need to be in an environment where I can pray, meditate and place myself in a trance. Other times when I am more "balanced", it comes more naturally. When I had the Flesh-Eating Bacteria, in 1998, the doctors automatically gave me morphine for pain and when Tom found out, he had them take me off of it (knowing how I felt about being "overmedicated"). The doctors didn't want to do it, but finally gave in. They were amazed to see that I was not yelling with excruciating pain. I was in a "state" of transcendence that I believe was spiritual as well as from practicing that kind of "state" for so long.

Once in a while when the pain is quite severe, I may temporarily be depressed or despair but I ask God to help me change my state of mind; or I may shed tears and this does help me to cleanse...it serves as a wonderful catharsis and helps me to relax. Then I can use other methods to transcend the pain.

USE OF SPIRITUAL HYPNOTHERAPY

Since I am a spiritual person, in 1995, I began developing and using my form of spiritual hypnotherapy on myself and on clients desiring this emphasis. To help clients relax, I suggest that they envision the light of God filling them with light and love. Then when they are n a relaxed state I describe a beautiful garden where Jesus appears, (I use the words from "I Come to the Garden Alone") and they "talk with Him and walk with Him" and in the process, receive a healing.

I also use the words from "Breathe on me breath of God, fill me with life anew...that I may live as Thou dost live and do what Thou woulds't do."

144

OTHER TECHNIQUES USED IN HYPNOTHERAPY

Reframing Technique

Instead of using the word "stress", as it conjures up negative feelings, use a substitute word or phrase like "life's little surprises" to describe situations that are uncomfortable. One can "reframe" any situation or issue this way into a more positive, tolerable one.

Creating Techniques:

There are as many ways to do Hypnotherapy, as there are people. The wonderful thing is that, with the mind, one never seems to run out of options. It is the last final frontier. Einstein believed that we only used about 10% of our potential, so we have a long ways to go in discovering what WE CAN DO. So take along this magnificent potential with you as your journey continues. Norman Vincent Peale said, "Change your thoughts and you change the world."

MY THOUGHTS ON THE MIND

The mind is a great frontier of knowledge and help for healing as we see in the next Chapter. There is so much to learn about how the mind can help us to better relate and communicate with each other and how the Superconscious Mind can help us commune and relate with God by being "at One" with Him. The future has much to teach us in this area.

"Let this mind be in you which was also in Christ Jesus." (Phil 2:5)

The application of this Scripture is the way to peace, the answer to al our challenges and everything that matters on our journey.

CHAPTER 10

HEALTH AND HEALING MATTER

TAKING RESPONSIBILITY FOR ONE'S OWN HEALTH

Hymns: Open My Eyes That I May See
Breathe on me Breath of God

Scripture: Be healed and go and sin no more, (John 8: 11)
Phys heal thyself (Luke 4:23)
Who sinned this man or his father? Neither so the Glory of God may be made manifold (John 9: 23)

THINGS TO LEAVE BEHIND OR THROW AWAY

Before we can talk about what to take along on our journey for health and healing, we need to look at what dirt and trash we have picked up in the process of traveling that we need to "wash off", leave behind or throw away. Christ talked about sin and evil, Carl Jung talked about the "Shadow Self," and some call it the dark side. Whatever it is called, it is all the same. We look at war, violence, crime, and the lack of moral standards in society as something "other than us". However, because we are all interconnected and because people make up society's ills, each person must look deep within himself/herself, as all these vices are an extension or an exaggeration of the sins that beset each one of us.

Maxie Dunham and Kimberly Dunham Reisman, in their book, *The Workbook on the 7 Deadly Sins*, remind us that if we look closely at ourselves, we discover "how often we give in to low passions which debase our humanity, and fall short of God's intention for us." (P1), Upper Room Books, Nashville, TN, 1997.

I urge each person to get this workbook and go through it slowly and painstakingly, with prayer and meditation. It is very revealing and cleansing. The 7 deadly sins are listed below:

PRIDE

I think of this in terms of ego out of control and forgetting to search for God's will in our lives through prayer. Following God's will means being able to release our willful self. As Christ said, "...Yet not as I will, but as you will." (Matt: 26:39)

ENVY

We often look at the material goods or even the happiness of others and wish we had it, not realizing that true happiness and contentment lies within us. "Seek ye first the kingdom of heaven and all these things shall be added unto you." (Matt 6:33)

ANGER

Anger is the first step towards rage and violence. If we look at what is happening today on our highways, we find ourselves becoming impatient, irritated or frustrated which can lead to "road rage". Stories of domestic violence and other crime, and now, even at schools are on the news constantly. We all need to take a serious look at our part in this sin and work on dealing with it. Some hold anger in and others explode, neither one of which is healthy or a solution. "If we are not a part of the solution, we are part of the problem". Being able to express ourselves in a calm but assertive way, respecting the rights of others takes practice, but it is something we all need to do until we can appropriately express ourselves.
"Be slow to anger, abounding in love." (Ex: 34:6)

SLOTH

The Dictionary defines this word as disinclination to work or exert oneself, laziness. Christ calls us to a service of love...loving

147

God, ourselves, others and all creation. It is a living and action based faith.

AVARICE

Greedy is a good substitute word...hoarding or wanting everything for oneself and not sharing. The moral decay of some corporate executives falls into this category. However, power, money and the so-called "good life" are all traps waiting to catch any of us. "...walk by the Spirit, and do not gratify the desires of the flesh." (Gal 5:16) Praying every day and asking God to provide opportunities to bless others is a good antidote.

LUST

The Dictionary defines this as "an intense or extreme desire, especially sexual desire." "But put on the Lord Jesus Christ, and make no provision for the flesh, to gratify its desires." (Rom: 13:14) By keeping our eyes upon Jesus, we can stay out of this trap.

GLUTTONY

Gluttony is the habit of excessive eating. We fall into this trap because food and advertisements for food are so prevalent in our society...they are all around us. We need to look at the real reason of why we eat so much. So often we use food to comfort us rather than looking at the lack in our lives which can be filled by using spiritual means. Christ reminded us our bodies are to be used as a "temple to the Holy Spirit". (1 Cor: 6:19)

AFFECT OF EMOTIONS AND BEHAVIOR ON HEALTH

All of the "7 Deadly Sins" have to do with emotions/behavior but many studies have been done showing the affect they have on one's physical health. Because of the mind-body-spirit connection, anything that affects one's physical health, also affects one's mental, emotional and spiritual health.

Pride can lead to prejudice and being mentally off balanced. Envy can lead to stomach sickness, and possibly to cancer as jealousy can literally "eat up" one's insides. Anger can lead to High Blood Pressure, Strokes and Heart Attacks. Exercise is important to one's health and if one is slothful or lazy, there is not much motivation in keeping physically fit. Avarice, being greedy or hoarding can lead one to be overly suspicious that someone is going to get what you have and cause one to be mentally unbalanced. If lusting is the focus of one's life, it not only violates God's commandments, but also violates one's own mental health and/or body. Gluttony or excessive eating leads to obesity, Diabetes, Heart problems and many other diseases. Addictions can result from any one of these "sins".

TAKING ALONG RESPONSIBILITY FOR HEALTH ON OUR JOURNEY

HEALTH IS A QUESTION OF BALANCE

Overcoming the physical and emotional challenges of life starts with taking responsibility for one's own health. This means we do everything possible to take care of our health in order to prevent disease. Preventing disease begins with living a balanced life, i.e., physically, mentally, emotionally and spiritually. Research has shown that almost every illness can be changed for the better and some can even be prevented or reversed by a change in lifestyle, including exercise, nutrition and balancing self physically, mentally, emotionally, and spiritually. According to a report in the *Journal of the American Medical Association*, almost two-thirds of adult Americans are overweight or obese. There has been a lot of publicity about the Atkins Diet or South Beach Diet. Before starting in on any of these, please check with your doctor and know enough about your current physical condition or illness to know if these diets are appropriate for you.

Each of us is an individual and what may help one, may harm someone else's health. More than 18 million Americans have Diabetes, a disease that is greatly influenced by weight and in most cases can be entirely controlled by change in lifestyle and healthy behaviors. The *New England Journal of Medicine* reported a study in which subjects taking a placebo as well as following a healthy diet and moderate exercise for a three year period, reduced by 58 percent, the incidence of full blown diabetes, while patients taking a prescribed diabetes medication only reduced the incidence of the disease by 33 percent. Reducing food portion sizes and total calories, increasing whole grains and total fiber as well as paying attention to the Glycemic Index, lowering fat intake while eliminating meat and maintaining complex carbohydrates, getting a good exercise workout every day and having a "can do" attitude are all important.

Even arthritis is affected by the excess weight on bones and joints. The recovery time and success of joint implant surgeries is influenced by a patient's weight The incidence of heart attacks, strokes, and high blood pressure are all increased by being overweight as well as by lack of anger management. Smoking takes its toll in heart problems, strokes, lung cancer and other lung diseases. Handling emotions appropriately, healthy eating, a healthy lifestyle, including exercises are important factors in reducing cancer or any other disease.

I will briefly mention techniques that I use to balance myself in all the four areas mentioned above.

SPIRITUALLY:

I feel that living a balanced spiritual life is most important, so I will share with you what works for me.

When I first wake up in the morning, before anything else, I ask God for spiritual strength for the coming day and I breathe deeply, inhaling through the nose and exhaling through the mouth, while I visualize God's white healing light going to the center of my heart and spreading out in all directions to every part of my body. After listening to my body to determine what I need, I get up and take a flower or healing essence. Then on my bed, I listen to a tape while I do about 40-45 minutes of range of motion exercises, weight bearing exercises and exercises prescribed for my joint implants. Then I get cleaned up and dressed and Tom and I have prayer together. The prayer begins by thanking God for the beautiful day (regardless of the weather), asking God to protect us and guide us; that His will be our will; that the words of our mouths and meditations of our hearts be acceptable to God and that God will bless us. We end by asking God to present us with opportunities to share hope, faith and love with others that we may be a blessing to them.

Then before we have breakfast, I take time to look at our little doggie, Tao. massage his ears (which he loves), and sing him a little song called "Tao we love you". The look on his face is so captivating; one can't help but smile or laugh. It is a good way to balance the emotions. After breakfast is a good time for reading the Scriptures and meditating. I meditate on how God wants me to apply His teachings or just take time to listen to God.

PHYSICALLY:

"Or do you not know that your body is the temple of the Holy Spirit, who is in you, whom you have from God, and you are not your own?" (1 Cor 6:19)

EXERCISE:

The old adage, "use it or lose it" is really important from my perspective, so I do exercises every day (range of motion which I just described, weight bearing (with one-pound weights on each ankle and on each wrist) and thirty minutes of aerobic walking a day to get my heart rate going. It is important for everyone to listen to his/her body, analyze and determine which exercises are best for him/her. I also do a lot of stretching and simple yoga positions when I can. I took a Yoga Class for three years when I was younger. Studies have shown that strength-training and range-of-motion exercises help Rheumatoid Arthritis (R.A.), walking wards off weight gain as well as helps R.A., exercise eases back pain and moderate-intensity physical activity helps high blood pressure and heart disease as well as reduce incidence of diabetes.

RELAXATION:

Relaxation Techniques are important with the rapid pace of living, which we seem to get caught up in nowadays. The following technique is one I use called Progressive Relaxation developed by Edmund Jacobson, a physician. Lie flat on your back. Do whatever you need to get comfortable (pillows for head, knees). Tense and hold for three seconds and then gradually release each major muscle group in your body and repeat three times before going on. Start with your feet, go to your calves, thighs, buttocks, stomach, chest, back, hand, arms, shoulders, neck, and face (scrunch and frown to tense). After you are finished, relax five minutes before getting up.

NUTRITION:

Everyone needs to determine what is appropriate for his/her body condition and eat healthy foods accordingly. Some bodies need more protein than others, diabetics have to watch sweets, etc. However, it is important to read and understand labels, watch fat, sugar, salt and calorie intake. I recommend either a book by Andrew Weil, M.D., titled, *Eight Weeks to Optimum Health,* or a book by Mark Hyman, M.D. and Mark Liponis, M. D., called *Ultraprevention: The 6-week Plan That Will Make you Healthy for Life (Scribner),* to help one understand nutrition.

LIFESTYLE:

It is important to eliminate smoking, excess alcohol, excess food and anything else that causes one's body to become unhealthy. We need to keep in mind that the body is the Temple of the Holy Spirit and anything unhealthy that we put into our body dishonors the Holy Spirit. Also, any unkind word that come out of the mouth or anything we say that is not loving stifles our spirit and dishonors God.

MENTALLY:

One keeps balanced mentally by releasing negative states of mind and keeping a positive attitude. Sometimes therapy is needed as well. Transactional Analysis (T.A.) Therapy and training helped me tremendously in being able to understand the pain of Rheumatoid Arthritis as well as my communication patterns and

152

thereby benefited me in improving my relationships with people. I share my techniques in Chapter 9.

EMOTIONALLY:

One keeps balanced emotionally by releasing negative emotions such as anger, by the use of hypnotherapy, or other forms of therapy (T.A.) and applying the guidelines in the Bible, i.e., releasing judgments, forgiving, loving and receiving love, being joyful, etc.

Loving God, loving ourselves and loving others as well as forgiving ourselves and others are the main keys to a healthy life. Forgiveness results from releasing the hold that anger and resentment have over one, which can cause high blood pressure, pulse rate and even heart attack. Since 9/11, there seems to be a mindset of revenge and aggression in this country. We use misinterpretation of facts to justify the means. We don't realize we are setting up the conditions for a self-fulfilling prophecy of more terror and aggression by doing this. We become more effective negotiators and peacemakers by seeing things from the opposite point of view, having empathy and forgiving. We don't have to condone the actions of the other side or agree with them, but the exercise in itself provides new options that lead to a better solution.

In our daily lives, as well, we say things without thinking that are hurtful to others. It is important to catch ourselves as soon as possible to say, "cancel" to the universe and "I'm sorry", to the person we hurt. Hearing an apology from the perpetrator of a wrong lowers the blood pressure of the wronged person and aids the perpetrator in releasing feelings of guilt, which fosters an emotional healing and leads the wronged person to reach a state of forgiveness. According to research in the book, *The Power of Apology,* (John Wiley & Sons), by family therapist Beverly Engle, one study showed that an apology by the perpetrator allows the victim to experience empathy for the perpetrator, which is crucial to the victim's ability to forgive and move on. What keeps us from apologizing so often is the old willful self or ego in a state of denial keeping us from taking responsibility for our actions.

DEALING WITH ILLNESS

TAKING ALONG THE UNDERSTANDING OF HEALING IN OUR JOURNEY

When something unforeseen happens and we are diagnosed with a disease, we do not blame God, the doctors, ourselves, or anyone else. We may feel that we are letting others down...that if our faith were just strong enough, we would be healed. However, there are those of us who have weak genes or a weak immune system, or at a certain point in our lives, our body just gives out - it just happens. However, we CAN make a difference by having a positive attitude and being responsible for how we heal. It is my belief that there is a purpose to everything and that things happen fo a reason.

When we are sick, it gives us time to reflect on the most important things of life, such as faith and love. We have time to look at our unfinished business (relationships as well as the direction in which our lives are going), so that when we get well, we can do something about it. Sometimes we do not always get well, and we live our lives with a chronic disease, or it is our time to pass on. As one who has lived with a chronic disease since age 10, along with several other diseases diagnosed along the way, I can say that, although it is not an easy life, it can be a happy and victorious life if one relies on faith in God and the strength in Christ. God often uses these people as an example to others who do not have as strong a spirit to show that with God, nothing is impossible.

If the diagnosis is terminal, we or our loved ones cannot blame God, the doctors or anyone else. Grieving and going through the stages named by Elizabeth Kubler Ross is important but releasing blame is one of the most important parts of the process. The lesson is to depend on God's love and comfort to see us through He will never let us down and in the ensuing days He will show us how to live our lives anew.

DOCTORS ASSIST US IN OUR HEALING. THEY DO NOT HEAL US. GOD IS THE SOURCE OF ALL HEALING.

For instance, when I had the Flesh-Eating Bacteria, it was my Infectious Disease Doctor who started the antibiotic treatment, checked my status continuously and my Plastic Surgeon, who did my excellent skin grafts, that assisted my healing, but because of all my health complications, living without amputation and recovering was through prayers of others and the grace of God, as well as the strength He gave me to do the things I needed to do to regain the ability to walk and function again. In my case, it took almost two years to recover and I still have some residual limitations. However, the test is to keep the faith throughout it all.

When I talk about healing, I am referring to the whole person, including physical, mental, emotional and spiritual healing. Since our body is the temple of the Holy Spirit, healing is an internal or inner process.

Some people may wait for God to heal them externally and this can happen, but in my experience, God gives us the strength to take responsibility for the choices we make and the things we need to do to allow our own inner healing process to take place (mentally, emotionally, spiritually and physically) and then the healing proceeds to the outside. This may mean changing our lifestyle (eating habits, exercise, etc.), listening to what our body is telling us, analyzing our thinking process (thoughts are things and have energy which affects what happens to our body), looking at our relationships and paying attention to our spiritual practices, including being still and listening to God).

This also means educating ourselves on how the body functions and learning as much about our disease or health challenge as we can. It might mean getting another opinion or prayerfully considering alternate or holistic forms of treatment. If we have lived a full life and feel God is calling us home, it might also mean prayerful consideration to refuse invasive medication, treatment or hospitalization. Loved ones need to be respectful and honor our prayerful wishes. Whatever we do, it is important to pray and really listen for God's will and answer.

HEALING POWER

SPIRITUAL

I firmly believe that the source of all healing power comes from God and some churches have healing services with laying on of hands and/or anointing with oil. The church Tom and I go to (First United Methodist Church of San Diego) that has healing services with anointing of the oil, once every month.

The Scriptures chronicle multitudes of healing that took place by Jesus. Besides the healing, Jesus would add an admonition, such as, "Your faith has made you whole" or "Go and sin no more". This means that healing involves more than just the physical, and we need to become aware of and change our thoughts, words, behavior and lifestyle to a life that is forgiving, loving, and cares for all people and all the creatures of the Creator.

There are sins of omission as well as sins of commission. Sometimes we think only self-evident things we do wrong are important for forgiveness. However, we forget the sins of omission. We allow so many lost opportunities to go by...times when we could have helped someone else, times when we could have made a difference for equality, for peace, for the world and times when we needed to stand up for our beliefs. Even sins and behaviors that are self-evident, we try to ignore or say they are part of human nature. We need to become aware of our fear, anger and emotion that hurt. The phrase "Be not afraid" or "Do not be afraid" is listed more than any other in the Bible. We need to eliminate prejudices and hatreds, (racial, ethnic, national, religious). We need to release all judgments and think peace and act peacefully. In other words, we need to pray every day the words of this hymn, "Breathe on me breath of God, fill me with life anew, that I may live as Thou dost live, and do what Thou Dost do." The words of another hymn are appropriate as well "Open my eyes that I may see glimpses of truth Thou hast for me"

Studies have shown that belief in a Higher Power and going to church is healing in itself. It is true, some churches and cults have abused their power to the extent that injuries and even death have occurred to other people, such as the old southern churches supporting the Ku Klux Klan, but that is not the focus of this book. Again, searching by attending various churches and discernment through prayer and meditation is the key to which church is best for each person. However, there is no "perfect church" as the church is really the people that attend that church and people are not perfect. Tom and I have had a very loving and healing experience at First United Methodist Church. There is a committee to serve every need and lay participation is encouraged. It is not only a Christ centered church but also truly puts into practice the teachings of Christ. When I had the Flesh-Eating Bacteria, the Parish Nurse of our church was at the hospital every day for two weeks, while I was in and out of life and death. I describe the involvement of our church in meeting the needs of the community and the world in Chapter 8.

HEALING PROFESSIONALS

Becoming a doctor or healing professional is a high calling and God works through these people. I have had many competent and caring doctors, but unfortunately, I have also had the other kind. However, doctors are people too, and after going to doctors since age 10, I have learned to make choices after prayerful consideration concerning the doctors I return to for treatment. I have had great success in my joint implant surgeries but have found out the negative side of medicine by experiencing many adverse reactions from drugs. Because of this, I have found that sometimes conventional medicine is appropriate and sometimes it is not.

COMPLIMENTARY OR ALTERNATE FORMS OF HEALING

I have used complimentary or alternative forms of healing very effectively for Rheumatoid Arthritis. There are so many things one can do to help himself/herself. I take Epsom Salts Baths, use cold pressed castor oil, other lotions or creams on my joints and muscles On camping trips, we always take along elastic bandages (to use if my joints swell), a massage wand, heating pads, gel packs that can be heated in the microwave or frozen. There are so many books that describe these techniques now that I would suggest one trying out each method and see what works best. One first needs to do a lot of searching, reading, training, praying and meditating before using or practicing any of these methods. I started my search in Holistic Healing twenty-five years ago by joining the American Holistic Association, attending seminars, workshops and training by doctors practicing alternative methods and reading multitudes of books. After intensive training I was certified as a Flower Essence Practitioner in 1993 and again after intensive training I became licensed as a Certified Clinical Hypnotherapist.

ENERGY HEALING

There are many methods and techniques involved in Energy Healing, and Dr. Richard Gerber, M.D., has a chapter on each one in his book, *Vibrational Medicine.* In the book, *Hands of Light,* by Barbara Brennan, a one-time NASA scientist turned spiritual healer, it describes how she uses energy healing for boosting physical and emotional health.

MY USE OF ALTERNATE AND COMPLIMENTARY HEALING

I will briefly mention the alternate or complimentary healing remedies and techniques that I have used the most and where I have described them in this book.

PRAYER AND MEDITATION-see Chapter 5

NATURE AND A GREEN ENVIRONMENT

I have long known the health benefits for me of nature through camping. When I was working, Tom and I made a conscious decision to get away "in the green" at least one weekend a month. The spiritual meaning of this is described in Chapter 13, under our responsibility to take care of the environment and again, when our fun times are recorded in Chapter 16. Recent studies reported in *American Journal of Public Health,* and the magazine, *Environment and Behavior*, (University of Illinois at Urbana-

Champaign-Frances Kuo, Researcher; Cornell University-Nancy Wells and Gary Evans-Researchers; Ohio State-Nasar and Jean Marie Cackowski, Researchers) have proven that natural settings help both children and adults release stress, reduce levels of aggression and violence, lower mental fatigue and help kids with ADD reduce the severity of their problems. It was found that even road rage and levels of frustration were contained when the traffic was routed through a scenic area rather than having traffic go through an area with almost nothing but concrete and man-made structures.

LAYING ON OF HANDS

This is a form of Spiritual and Energy Healing that I have experienced through various churches and organizations. Usually the "Healer" (this person acknowledges that he/she is being used as a channel for God's healing energy) stands behind a chair in which a person is sitting and places their hands over a person's head and then follows the outline of the body or aura. Usually a sense of heightened energy, tingling and warmth is felt throughout the body

HYPNOTHERAPY-see Chapter 9

AFFIRMATIONS-see Chapter 9

VISUALIZATIONS-see Chapter 9

GUIDED IMAGERY-see Chapter 9

TRANSACTIONAL ANALYSIS (T.A.)-see Chapter 9

VITAMINS, MINERALS, HERBS, ENZYMES, NUTRIENTS

I use a standardized multivitamin and mineral pill daily, along with Calcium, extra B Complex, and Vitamin C when I need it. The herbs I use, on an "as needed basis", are Yucca, which contains Sapponins, a pain reliever, Butcher's Broom, (helps to sweep out impurities and toxins from the circulatory system), Eyebright, Bilberry, (both for eyes), Hawthorne Berry, (for Heart Support), Maca (for energy), Valerian (for better sleep), St. John's Wort, (for sadness). Since I take RX Nexium and Colazal, the only enzyme I now use is Papaya (for absorption, digestion and abdominal discomfort). Nutrients I take on an "as needed basis", are Bioastin, Pycnogenol and NAC (anti-oxidants for eyes), Cranberry, Jarridopholous (an excellent form of acidophilous), fish oil (for Omega 3 and 6-reduces inflammation), as well as Colostrum, and sometimes SAMe which give me a sense of well being. I use liquid Iodine for eliminating toxins and take before meals. Before starting Forteo, I used to take Glucosamine and Chondroitin for the Arthritis

OTHER PRODUCTS USED TOPICALLY

I have had allergies to certain foods and medication since the 1980's and sometimes I get red bumps or hives that have been as large as quarters. Aloe Vera Gel (99 cents for a small tube that lasts a long time) takes them down right away. When I was in the hospital, after having hip-implant surgery, they gave me blood plasma, which caused giant hives. I tried unsuccessfully to tell the nurse that the Aloe Vera gel in my suitcase would take them down, and my doctor had written in my chart that it was all right to use it as well as my other alternative remedies to assist me. After several hours of the hives spreading almost to my bandage with the incision, a doctor finally came in and used the Aloe Vera Gel and the hives were gone within 15 minutes. Epsom Salts baths are good for eliminating toxins, Caster Oil packs are good for digestion and the roll on Caster Oil is good topically for pain. Palm Christi lotion is wonderful for moisturizing the skin and helping it keep its elasticity.

HOMEOPATHY AND HOMEOPATHIC REMEDIES:

Homeopathy, used throughout the world for over 200 years, is a safe, effective treatment for a variety of illnesses. Dr. Samuel Hanemann, a German Physician, discovered how Homeopathy works and benefits patients. The underlying principle is "like cures

160

like", i.e., a substance causing symptoms in a healthy person, can also be used to stimulate the healing of a sick person with similar symptoms. When a person takes the proper homeopathic remedy, it simulates that person's own physical, mental, emotional and spiritual ability to heal itself. The homeopathic remedy is made from natural sources in extremely small amounts. A trained homeopathic practitioner takes an extensive case study of the whole person to determine the proper remedy and dose. There are thousands of remedies, but there is one best remedy that is specific for each individual's case. Remedies come in liquid, pill or tablet form There are remedies for "Acute" or short-term cases and there are remedies for "Chronic" or long-term cases. Some of the remedies that I have used successfully are:

Rhus Tox, (for Arthritis and Sciatica that is better for movement),

Apis (for bee stings), Hypericum for helping nerves recover, especially after surgery.

Arnica helps sore muscles recover and is also good for surgeries

There are also homeopathic creams, lotions and gels for topical use as well.

Califlora, a gel or calendula oil is used for wounds or sores, and Arnica oil or Arniflora is used for muscle soreness Any person interested in his/her own healing is encouraged to become involved in a Homeopathic Study Group to learn more about this particular method of healing. See Appendix for the address of the NCH and referral to a study group in your locale

FLOWER ESSENCES:

Flower Essences are a vibrational liquid made from flower blossoms immersed in spring or distilled water. The essence of the blossom is diffused into the water by the power and heat of the sun over a period of about 3-4 hours. The blossoms are then removed and the resulting liquid becomes the stock bottle. A small portion of the liquid from that bottle is then placed in another dropper bottle with a preservative and is ready for distribution/sale. A person buys a specific flower essence to assist in healing or to heal a specific emotional, mental. physical or spiritual issue. Each flower essence has a particular purpose, related to the name of the flower, which aids in this healing. Flower essences are usually taken underneath the tongue from the dropper bottle using 3-4 drops at a time, or in some cases up to 7 drops. Some can be used topically and others can be used in bath water.

FLOWER ESSENCE PRODUCERS/ESSENCES I USE MOST

The flower essences I use most often are Rescue Remedy (Bach Flowers) or Five Flower Remedy (FES) for stress, Yerba Santa (FES) for sadness, Yarrow Environmental (FES) for allergies or negative environmental pollution, Harvest Brodaeia (FES) for eye discomfort, Balance and Stability (Stars), Candystick (Pacific), for allignment of the pelvis, Authenticity (Himalayan), for Throat discomfort, Turtle head (3 Flowers Healing) for managing emotions and Round Leaf Bluebell (3 Flowers Healing) for Pulse Breathing.

GEM ELIXIRS, COMBINATIONS AND SEA ESSENCES

The gem elixirs use gems, such as Silver, Diamond and the sea essences use sea creatures or products in place of flowers, but the process is the same. Combination essences are made up of a combination of flowers and other essences to provide a synergistic and a stronger effect for a specific challenge. Examples of gem elixirs I use are Silver (Pegasus), for stress, easing tension, Gold (Pegasus), for greater love, opening up heart, Sugalite (Stars) for any difficult or challenging healing. Examples of sea essences I use are Sea Horse (Pacific), for taming the nervous system, Rainbow Kelp (Pacific), for alignment of head, brain, and Sea Lettuce (Pacific), for release of toxins.

Combinations I use are Super Immune (Stars), Super Vitality (Pacific) and Heart Spirit (Pacific).

AROMA THERAPY

The essential oils of flowers are used in healing by applying a few drops topically on the skin, in bath water or through spraying the area or smelling the oils. The important thing is to know the purpose of each oil and use it for the purpose intended. Lavender is a very calming flower oil and is wonderful to use in bath water when one is stressed out. I have had Sinusitis, my nose gets clogged up, and I have trouble breathing. On those days, which are particularly troublesome, I carry around a bottle of Eucalyptus oil and when my nose is clogged up from sinus problems, I take the cap off the bottle and pass it in front of my nose several times until my nose becomes clear. Lavender is good to use for calming down or putting in the bath water to relax.

ANGELIC ESSENCES tm

As Ruth Joy, founder of Angelic Essences, states in her brochure, "Angelic Essences are co-created with the guidance and assistance of the Angelic and Spirit realms. These essences are offered as direct resources to energies to awaken our consciousness, shift our vibration and put us into contact with our Source and possibilities."
They act to "heal and awaken the body, mind, emotions and spirit." Essences I use most frequently are: Angelic Healing, Balance and Integration, Wholeness, Freedom from Fear, Rejuvenation, Solid Center, Peaceful Heart, and essences to balance the energy centers: root center, solar plexus, heart, throat and third eye centers.

EDGAR CAYCE REMEDIES:

Edgar Cayce, is known as the "Father of Holistic Medicine". He recommended the use of Castor Oil, Epsom Salt Baths and many other remedies. I have used cold pressed Castor Oil with great success to relieve inflammation on particular parts of my body (there is a roll on container to relieve pain) and when used with warm flannel and a heating pad over the abdomen it releases gastrointestinal problems. Epsom Salts baths release toxins and

163

provide a wonderful relaxation. I always shower after I take the baths.

MASSAGE

Massage by a therapist is best and is a wonderful treatment for sore joints and muscles and a boon for release of stress and obtaining relaxation. There are various kinds of massage and it is best for one to read up on each kind and determine which is best for the needs of each individual. (Use the Internet-Google or call offices having different types of massage and ask if they have brochures explaining procedure).

Lymph massage is one I used for recovery from the Flesh Eating Bacteria and was beneficial in the draining and releasing of toxins from the lymph nodes of my body.

Massage Wands, pillows, and aids are available from a variety of stores and catalogues. I have used many of these to stimulate circulation and release pain. My massage wand is electric and Tom helps me by moving it around the sore spots on my body. Battery operated massage aids I use are: Eye goggles that relieve eye irritation and nose congestion (use once a day for five minutes at a time), plastic foot slippers I usually use at night for thirty minutes while reading or watching TV, neck pillows (for neck pain) and seat or back pillows (relief of sciatic pain and sitting so much at a time).

These are all wonderful aids that can be used at night, while traveling or at a moment's notice to relieve pain. The point is, that if one does research and obtains the aids that help, pain can be diminished, reduced or eliminated completely. We are so used to calling a doctor, depending on other people and not using our minds to help ourselves that we suffer needlessly. For deep pain, I have used a TENS (transcutaneous nerve stimulator, needing a doctor's prescription and which my insurance company paid for). It is a battery-operated device that hooks on to waistband and contains four wires with small round pads at the end, which are attached to pain spots on the body. There are dials on the device, which allow the user to control the amount of electricity being conducted through the wires to the nerves as well as a dial that the user can control whether the electricity is delivered in a continuous mode or interrupted pulse mode. In a way it serves as a modified portable acupressure pain reliever. Most doctors never inform the patient of the existence of such a device. My doctor allowed me to test one out for a trial period before I even ordered one to see if it would meet my needs. It was a lifesaver for me the last several years of my employment with the Government and enabled me to complete a twenty-five year career.

OTHER DEVICES

A CHI machine is electrically operated and has a footrest for both feet. A timer allows the user to determine how long the machine will be on. Most people use it for ten minutes twice a day. It was designed by a chiropractor and provides the body with a fish like motion to exercise all the organs in the body.
A foot peddler allows me to move my legs up and down, as if I was walking, only from a sitting position. This is small, compact and easy to take with us in the motor home. It helps me to simulate walking in inclement weather.
I have a bicycle exerciser which is small and can be used sitting down to obtain the motion of bicycling. When it is placed on a small waist-high table, I can use it to exercise my arms.

CHIROPRACTIC TREATMENT

Because cells are controlled by the nervous system, when any bones of the spine are sublexated or misaligned, it can cause irritation on related nerves. About once a month I can feel my body going out of alignment, which can lead to a fall if I get off balance. My experience has been that when I go in to my Chiropractor for treatment, he aligns my spine so that I have increased balance and well being. I have also had Chiropractic treatment with NET (Neuro-Emotional-Technique). This practice uses questions and testing the body with the technique of Kineseology (using the arm to validate where the problem is located) to determine where the misalignments are and then restoring the system by gentle manipulation. I have had successful experience with this method also. Many studies have been done showing the benefits of

Chiropractic treatment. If you are interested, stop by one of the offices to obtain brochures and check it out.

OSTEOPATHIC TREATMENT

Cranial-Sacral Treatment-Using hand manipulation, an Osteopath holds the neck and head in his/her hands to properly align the skull and spine. I have benefited from this treatment by increased flexibility and mobility of my body.

ACUPUNCTURE

Needles attached to an electric source allow a soothing electrical current to flow into the body's energy pathways so that the vital life force (Qi) flows freely. A licensed Acupuncture Therapist or a trained M.D. inserts the needles with a gentle twisting motion in the body's energy pathways which removes energy blockages. Sometimes the needles are first heated in an herb and then inserted into the body's meridians or pathways with a twisting motion. The patient lays in a relaxed state while the painless treatment, which usually lasts 20-30 minutes, takes place. My personal experience with Acupuncture is described in Chapter 8. There is no doubt that the Acupuncture treatments saved my life by allowing me to get off the steroids after being on them for thirty years.

BODY WORK

A variety of techniques working on or with the body to align, strengthen, to help remove blockages and balance it, are available. Some of these are Yoga, Fieldenkras, Hellerwork, and Rolfing. One needs to investigate and try out to see which one, if any, are best suited for a particular body. Some of the techniques are more gentle than others. It is best to know and really listen to your body and consult a doctor before going into a strenuous bodywork program. I had success with a gentle yoga program twelve years ago but would not consider it under my present circumstances. I believe the exercises I do on my own, rather than a group sponsored program, better suit my needs now.

MUSIC

Pachellbel's *Canon* is used as a background for Hypnotherapists, Massage Therapists, doctors, such as Osteopaths, Chiropractors, and others interested in complimentary techniques and have found it slows breathing and heart rate with a rhythm of approximately 60 beats a minute as it creates harmonic vibrations with a calming effect. Exercise instructors and fitness experts, on the other hand, use music with a different beat, which is more physically stimulating and exciting. Music as been used for centuries to help people's mood. The Bible records how David played his harp to lift King Saul's depression.

CURRENT RESEARCH SHOWING BENEFITS OF MUSIC

Cornell University Researchers have found that music has a deep emotional impact on the brain's limbic system, which can evoke peace, sadness, fear, joy or awe. The University Hospitals of Cleveland, Ohio, have reported the boosting of patient's immune system from a single 30-minute music therapy session. At the Georgia Baptist Medical Center, researchers reported that playing lullabies with the heartbeat of premature newborn infants was so beneficial that they were discharged as much as two weeks earlier than infants who did not receive the music.

At the Center for Biomedical Research in Music at Colorado State University in Fort Collins, Colorado, researchers found that walking speed was improved 25% when music was used with therapy in treating people with Parkinson's, stroke and cerebral palsy as compared with walking speed improvement of 10% in people who received conventional therapy. Patients undergoing bone marrow transplants at the University of Rochester in New York produced white blood cells earlier with music assisted relaxation therapy, than those patients who did not have the music therapy. (*Natural Health* Mag., March 2004)

SOUND

Sound has been used for centuries to help people heal. Monks have used chanting to help them "tune in" to the Creator. Chanting actually changes breathing and emotional states. Vocal toning, by itself, or in conjunction with hypnotherapy is being used to help people heal. The bell has been used to sound assemblies and atop churches to bring people to worship. Many churches, such as ours, have a group (bell choir) that is trained in using bells to play different hymns. Quartz crystal "singing bowls" have a deep resonant tone and the larger ones actually produce a vibration throughout the body. Gongs, chimes, and tuning forks have all been used to help Alzheimer patients improve. Drums are being used more in drumming circles to boost the immune system. Studies conducted at the Meadville Medical Center's Mind-Body Wellness Center in Pennsylvania showed that there was an increase in the number of infection fighting immune cells found in the bloodstream of drummers.

Flutes, harps and other musical instruments, used by themselves or in groups produce a "connectedness" besides a calming effect and a "losing of self" in a state of harmony.

QIGONG

Qigong is a 5000-year-old Chinese Healing Art and a newly revitalized science, using the pure energy of gentle movement, sound and visualization so healing can take place on the physical, mental, emotional and spiritual levels. Clinical research in China over the last 25 years has shown a 90% success rate on over 2,000,000 patients and has treated over 185 diseases. Attending a Qigong Healing Circle (adult education) where a group of people participate which amplifies the sound and vibration is the best way to get started.

COLOR

Color has been used in interior decoration for years to adapt the mood of the user to the particular purpose of the scene and can be used in healing to alter stress and bring calmness or allow for more energy if one lacks motivation.

RED

I'm sure everyone has heard of the expression, "seeing red". When a person says this, he/she is really expressing anger and so it is not surprising that the color red is associated with anger and passion. High Blood Pressure has as its main contributor, stress and anger, and the color of blood is red. Red is physically stimulating and energetic as well. It is associated with the root energy center for balance and security.

ORANGE

Orange is a vital, warm color; in its golden state it is the color of the sun that indicates consideration, self-control and thoughtfulness. With a brownish tinge, it lacks vitality. It is associated with the navel energy center and the gonads.

YELLOW

A golden yellow is cheerful, and indicates health and well-being, as well as a good mentality to easily learn. If the yellow is ruddy, it indicates timidity. It is associated with the adrenal glands or solar plexus energy center.

GREEN

Green with a dash of blue indicates healing; a growing vitality (the color of plants, grass), a strong, friendly color. With more yellow it indicates deceit. It is associated with the thymus and the heart energy center.

BLUE

This color is the essence of spirituality and indicates contemplation and tolerance. It is associated with the thyroid or throat energy center and has to do with the will and choice. Green with a dash of blue or blue by itself is good for release of stress.

INDIGO

This color indicates a search for the truth, wisdom, discernment and is associated with the pineal gland or what is known as the "third eye" energy center.

VIOLET

This color is affected by how an individual uses it; for the highest good, with positive choices, it can have creative energies, strength of character, good mental ability and judgment. This color is associated with the pituitary gland and crown energy center. It seems to interconnect the nervous and glandular system.

ART

People with an illness have used art therapy to express their emotions concerning their illness as well as their recovery. Whether it be watercolor or other forms of painting, sculpture, carving, pottery or other ways of creating art, this is a useful medium for healing. Onlookers also benefit as they gain not only an appreciation for the artist as well as the work but receive an emotional insight and understanding into an expression of another self that can not be told with words or any other way. This is also part of the process of healing.

WRITING, POETRY

Writing or journaling one's pain is very cathartic and healing In the process, one can find a meaning and make sense of what has happened or what is happening. One technique is to write down all your negative emotions and then toss the paper into a fire and watch it burn. Fire is used as a symbolic act to purify or transform; therefore it is like releasing the negative emotions and having them transformed. Writing one's life story down involves healing as well as creating something and sharing.

It provides a legacy of one's life. Poetry is also used to express one's feelings, whether sad or glad, as there are always others who can relate to what is being said, but do not know how to express it in words. Many times it is used to inspire others Writing music falls into the same category.

In Appendix, "A" I share some of my poetry.

HUMOR

Humor helps one focus on something else besides the disease or pain, and in doing so, releases the pain and negativity. (One cannot laugh and still be negative-two mental states can't be held at same time). In Proverbs 17:22, we learn, "A merry heart doeth good like a medicine." It helps bring into healthy action muscles, nerves, the cardiovascular system and parts of the body that need exercising and gives us balance. Norman Cousins, former editor of *Saturday Review*, talks about how humor helped him recover from a collagen disease that caused him a great deal of pain. In his book, *Anatomy of an Illness*, he says, "I made the joyous discovery that ten minutes of genuine belly laughter had an anesthetic effect and would give me at least two hours of pain-free sleep. " He used old films of the Marx Brothers, Candid Camera videos, etc. and lost himself in laughter. It helps us cope and change our perspective so things don't seem so awful.

APPROPRIATE AND INAPPROPRIATE HUMOR

However, when using humor with other people we need to exercise caution, because what one sees as funny, another person might consider an insult. The rule of thumb is to listen to what another person says, and see if they take things lightly or if they are more serious. Also, we need to think twice about what we say around a person with a terminal disease. Some things can be humorous; other things can sound cruel. For example, a group of my friends and I were out with another friend who has a terminal disease. When we took my friend home, I asked her husband how he was, and he replied, "Oh, I was OK until you brought her home." I know that remark had to have hurt her. Sarcastic humor was totally inappropriate here. What she needed to hear would have gone something like this, "Well, I'm fine now that the Love of my Life is back."

TURN THE INSULTS INTO HUMOROUS RESULTS

When someone says something to you that could be considered an insult or that might ordinarily hurt your feelings, turn it into a laugh. It takes practice, but you can do it. Don't respond right away, be calm, take a deep breath and silently ask God to help you see the remark in a lighter way. Then in a lilting voice, respond, not in kind to hurt, but turn the remark around to be funny. For instance, when I gave a workshop to supervisors at NAS Miramar, I was in the middle of answering questions about the workshop material (something serious), when the Commanding Officer walked in. Soon. He raised his hand and I said, "Yes Captain?" Then he said, "Nancy, is that a wig you have on?"

Well, the question was personal and I could have been embarrassed by it, or said something inappropriate, which could have been bad for my career and I could have made a fool of myself in front of all the supervisors who respected my work.

However, after a short pause, I said, "Only my husband and hairdresser know for sure." Well, that broke the tension and everyone laughed, including the Captain.

INCREASE YOUR HUMOROUS LIBRARY

Tom has helped me to appreciate more humor in my life. He is always twisting words around to get various meanings and I never know what he is going to say to the waitress/waiter when we go out to a restaurant. One waitress had a terrific comeback that I will never forget. Tom made some smart remark and she said, "I think we're going to have to decaffeinate you." Well, we all had a good laugh over that one.

I now laugh at things that used to get me angry. For instance, one time we were camping at a Thousand Trails Campground, Lake of the Springs, where there were wild turkeys. I had not noticed them eating on the blueberry bushes, but found out soon enough. A group flew up in a tree above me where I was sitting relaxing and reading a good book. All of a sudden I received a shower of blueberries all over me and realized the turkeys had decided to use that tree as a porta potty! Well I rushed in the motor home, took a shower, washed my hair and washed my clothes. However, this incident has provided much fodder for humorous storytelling around the campfire with other campers.

There are various techniques to help one increase their humorous library. Look around you...what objects have odd shapes or remind you of someone or something in your life that once was painful, scary or uncomfortable? How can you turn this into a remark that can make people laugh? What stories in your life can be turned into something humorous? Remember the funny remarks of others.

GOD'S CREATION

God has created natural forms of healing power, such as nature and animals as well as helping humans create forms of healing power, such as music, etc.

ANIMALS (PETS)

We love watching the birds out in the wild and also at home listen to their singing. I love watching any kind of animal, wild or domestic. We enjoy our times at the Zoo and Wild Animal Park. Who has not observed the brilliant colors of the Macaw without intuitively knowing that kind of beauty can only be created by God! Of course, our little Shih Tzu, Tao, is truly a gift from God, and we enjoy him every day with his antics and captivating face.

LEARNING FROM ANIMALS

The following is an email from a friend of how we can learn from animals to have a balanced lifestyle and enjoy life.

SOME GOOD ADVICE!

If a dog was the teacher you would learn stuff like:
When loved ones come home, always run to greet them.
Never pass up the opportunity to go for a joyride.
Allow the experience of fresh air and the wind in your face
to be pure ecstasy.
When it's in your best interest, practice obedience
Let others know when they've invaded your territory.
Take naps.
Stretch before rising.
Run, romp, and play daily.
Thrive on attention and let people touch you.
Avoid biting when a simple growl will do.
On warm days, stop to lie on your back on the grass.
On hot days, drink lots of water and lie under a shady tree.
When you're happy, dance around and wag your entire body.
No matter how often you're scolded, don't buy into the guilt
thing and pout...run right back and make friends.
Delight in the simple joy of a long walk.
Eat with gusto and enthusiasm. Stop when you have had
enough.
Be Loyal. Never pretend to be something you're not.
If what you want lies buried, dig until you find it.
When someone is having a bad day, be silent, sit close by
and nuzzle them gently.

NATURE

Nature is very healing. Try matching your breathing to the
rhythmic sounds of nature, the wind, the trees, and especially at the
end of the day when all is quiet, breathe deeply and find the breath
of God, as you say silently to yourself, "Breathe on me breath of
God".
    I have always felt closeness to God when I have been out in
nature. It first began when my parents took me camping as a child
and I used to fall asleep under the stars. As I am writing this, we are
camped on our property in Murphy, Oregon. We are surrounded by

trees-cedar, douglas fir, pine, maple, madrone, oak and lots of undergrowth, including new trees, growing at all different lengths, wild blackberry bushes, ferns, wildflowers, small rocks, dropped leaves and fallen logs. Further down the gradual slope of the land closer to the river, one finds lots of large rocks, moss, more trees, poison oak, sword fern and other growth. Some days we see deer go up and down our property as they obtain water from the Applegate River.

It is interesting to listen to the different songs of the birds as they communicate with each other. It sounds like a bird orchestra at times. We also like to see them perch at the top of a real high tree and then circle around a distance and come back to the same tree, as if they were marking their territory.

I will have more to say about animals in a section further on in this chapter. We go for a walk about sundown and watch the sunset over the winding river. It is truly a gorgeous sight to behold and makes me so grateful to God for the privilege of being here.

Coming from Idaho, I have always loved mountains. They remind me of the majesty of God. Snow has always reminded me of the purity of God, and rain and waterfalls have always reminded me of washing away impurities, cleansing and renewal through Christ. The sun has always reminded me to be cheerful, to smile, to have a positive attitude, and to pass blessings on to others. The blue skies and a gentle breeze seem to indicate, "smooth sailing" or "have fun hiking or walking". I have always loved the big puffy shape of clouds and they help me to relax.

FOND MEMORIES

Flowers have always fascinated me with their splash of colors, both pale and brilliant, and unique shapes. They can be so delicate and small, such as wildflowers, or big and robust like a sunflower. My mother loved to grow iris so when we came to California she brought some bulbs from Idaho along with her and planted them by the walkway to our house in Point Loma. They were huge blooms in pretty violet and white shades and the delicate fragrance was heavenly. She also grew beautiful roses. The perennial message, "stop and smell the roses" really needs to be acted upon in this busy world with so much stress.

A couple of deep breaths (unless one has allergies) into a rose can do wonders for your day! I was again privileged to be in the Horizon Group where our leader, Jean Kenneally had an unbelievable rose garden and no wonder! For many yeas she was President of the Rose Society and she was the one who furnished yellow and white roses to decorate the church pews at our wedding. When I first learned from a phone call that my father had passed, I went to the rose garden in Balboa Park and found solace.

OUR OREGON PROPERTY ENCOURAGES REFLECTION

The green trees provide me with a calm and peacefulness that is indescribable. As the sun shines on the leaves the green turns different shades and as the breeze blows gently through the branches, it seems to whisper a gentle melody. They come in all shapes and sizes, like human beings. There is an old oak tree on our property that has lots of gnarls and bumps and has a twisted trunk. It has a hole in the middle that looks like an eye, with a snout similar to a nose, and below it, an opening like a mouth. When we first got this property 25 years ago, it was barren at the top with no leaves and looked like it was about to die, but Tom and I were both fascinated with it. When our road was put in we asked the crew not to cut this old oak down and they couldn't understand why. Since the sun has been shining on it, during the ensuing years, it has blossomed out at the top and it is full of green branches and leaves. We think it is even more beautiful than it was 25 years ago. It seems Tom and I saw a lot more inner beauty and potential to this tree than the road crew did. It means a great deal to us both symbolically and spiritually. It is very much like my life with all the twisting and scars (burls) from the Arthritis and surgeries but somehow my parents, God and Tom saw the potential and this love turned "my scars into stars" as Dr. Robert Schuller says.

You can hug a tree and somehow feel the comfort of God hugging you back. As I sit and look at the trees, they remind me to listen...not only to them and all of Nature, but to go within and listen to my Inner Self.

MORE REFLECTIONS FROM NATURE

The rivers have always reminded me of the continuous flow of life. If we flow with the river of life and "let go and let God" we flow smoothly. If we try to go against the flow of life or God's will, we experience resistance and difficulties. The lakes represent clear waters, but when we throw a rock into the lake, it causes ripples, which upset the clarity of the waters, just as when we toss around negative emotions, it has a rippling effect on us and others around us. The ocean reminds me of the tides and how we must be watchful not to get caught in the "undertows" of the ocean or of life. The desert too, has its unusual beauty with its unique rocks, clear nights and curious formations of dunes. Particularly in the Spring when the desert wildflowers come out with their splash of color, it is beautiful.

The seasons have special messages for us too. Fall helps us to make preparations, not only for winter, but also for events in our lives. Winter is a time for the Holidays (along with stress management practices), family gatherings and reflections. Spring is a time of renewal and sowing, not only in the garden, but also in our life (mending fences or misunderstandings from the past). Summer is a time for recreation and enjoying nature. The sunrise indicates a new beginning, a fresh start with God's forgiveness of the past and a day with opportunities to share God's abundant love and life. The sunset indicates peace and harmony at the end of a day with God. I think of the song my mother used to play on the piano by Carrie Jacobs Bond, "When I Come to the End of a Perfect Day"..."and I sit alone with my thoughts." This is a time for reviewing our day with God. What peace there is in silence. Many times Tom and I sit outside watching the dusk turn into evening, as the shadows of the trees become silhouettes against the night sky. At a certain time, the crickets come out with their chirping. Then the moon comes out. In its fullness, I think of how God lights the way for us, even in darkness. The stars remind us of God's great expanse of creation and what little specks we are in comparison, but His love for each one of us is just as great. It reminds me of the song, *How Great Thou Art* .

OTHER SUGGESTIONS AND RECOMMENDATIONS
TO AID HEALING

Many tapes, magazines and books are available to aid in one's healing. I have included a list of some I have used in Appendix for your benefit.

DISCLAIMER

Because each person is an individual and individual bodies can react differently, it is recommended before trying any alternate or complementary remedies or before using any of the methods or remedies suggested above, that each person talk to his/her own personal doctor or health practitioner. Part of healing is taking responsibility for one's own choices and not blaming others if things do not turn out the way one had hoped for or expected.

A CHRONICLE OF MY HEALTH HISTORY

I am chronicling my health history to show how God has amazingly pulled me through a multitude of health challenges. I know I would not be alive today if it wasn't for the prayers of untold friends and by the miracle of God.

Born Sept 4, 1935.
Tonsillectomy and Adenoids out 1941.
Finger joints became enlarged...first doctor said it was growing
        pains!!
Diagnosed with Rheumatoid Arthritis approximately March 1946.
 Doctor said he didn't know what to do. Searched for other doctors.
Condition worsened... weight of a sheet caused me to cry out with
        excruciating pain.
Finally, placed on medication, which helped, but doctor left town.
        Became worse. New doctor prescribed Gold injections but
        had to be taken off due to adverse reaction.
Went to the Rinehart Clinic in Oregon for treatment approximately
        1949. Help lasted approximately one year, then I got worse.

Doctor in 1951-2 told me I would never finish school, work or
      marry and urged parents to put me in a Crippled Children's
      Home, which my parents didn't accept.
      Became so bad I had to drop out of my Junior Spring
      Semester and have home tutor.
Hospitalized summer 1952 with Cortisone treatment in L.A. Felt
      better and finished my Senior High School year.
      Became worse due to adverse reactions of Cortisone
      (convulsions, hallucinations, etc.). Hospitalized December
      1953. Taken off drug immediately and shock to my system
      caused me to almost die. Had my First Near Death
      Experience. After six months, placed on Steroid ACTH,
      which allowed me to live a fairly normal life.
1966 fell and broke left pelvis and fractured right hip...hospitalized.
1971 had Gallbladder and Appendix out.
1974 had Hysterectomy.
July 1976 had my first artificial joint surgery...right knee.
      Treated by Homeopathic Doctor.... became better.
1983-4 treated with Acupuncture for chemical, environmental, and
      food allergies. Started gradual process (nine months) to be
      taken off Steroid ACTH due to adverse reactions...almost
      died Second Near Death Experience.
November1984 had my left knee surgery for artificial joint.
Surgery 1985 (Spring) for right wrist to be surgically frozen.
December 1986, extremely painful case of Shingles.
From 1987-1988 had surgery every 3-4 months Both shoulders and
      both elbows surgically replaced with artificial joints, left
      thumb joint had pin and right arm pin surgically removed.
Surgery 1996-left artificial hip implant.
Surgery 1997 right knee redone second time.
September 1998-Flesh-Eating Bacteria. Hospitalized.... treated with
      Antibiotics. Given 1% chance of living. In and out of life and
      death for two weeks. Had Third Near Death Experience.
      October.... first skin graft (80% successful).
      November...second skin graft (100% successful) Took
      almost two years to recover.
May 1999-left knee surgery redone second time.
January 2000-had pneumonia...was able to be treated at home.
2001-diagnosed with Osteoporosis...taking medication.

June 2002 fell off second step of motor home, back flipped seven feet and landed on a gravel pad. Fractured right pelvis and had mild concussion to the head.

April 2003 fell and broke left upper arm in between implants. Wore splint for three months until bone healed. Started taking prescription medication Forteo (injection) to rebuild my bones and in one year my bone density had increased 17%.

May 2003-Outpatient Colonoscopy...diagnosed with Colitis.... taking medication-Nexium and Colazal

December 2003-Catscan of nose. Diagnosed with chronic sinusitis

September 2004-Fell on face, skin lacerated and peeled back on left hand. Taken to E.R., treated-five stitches above mouth, skin put back on hand, given CScan and MRI. Neurosurgeon diagnosed Cervical Myleopathy.

October 2004-Underwent Sleep Study and was diagnosed with Sleep Apnea. Standard treatment of CSC mask did not work. Treatment with Homeopathic Remedy successful.

CHAPTER 11

AMAZING GRACE MATTERS

MY MIRACLE RECOVERY FROM FLESH-EATING BACTERIA

Hymn: Amazing Grace

Scripture: "For by grace are ye saved through faith." (Eph 2:8)
"Though I walk through the valley of the shadow of death, I fear no evil; for Thou art with me; " (Psalm 23:4)

TAKING ALONG GRACE ON OUR JOURNEY

Everyone, at some point in their journey, will face a crisis that is frightening, confronting, challenging or in the realm of the unknown. Some call this crisis point, "The Dark Night of the Soul". It is at this time that the grace of God carries us through. I am reminded about the Footprints Poem when God carries us.

FOOTPRINTS IN THE SAND

One night I dreamed I was walking along the beach with the Lord.
Many scenes from my life flashed across the sky.
In each scene I noticed footprints in the sand.
Sometimes there were two sets of footprints.
Other times there was one set of footprints.
This bothered me because I noticed that during the low periods of my life
When I was suffering from anguish, sorrow, or defeat,
I could see only one set of footprints.
So I said to the Lord, "You promised me, Lord,

That if I followed you, you would walk with me always.
But I noticed that during the most trying periods of my life
There have only been one set of prints in the sand.
Why, when I have needed you most, you have not been there for me?"
The Lord replied,
"The times when you have seen only one set of footprints
Is when I carried you."

By Mary Stevenson
(Born 11/8/22 Died 1/6/99)

"MY DARK NIGHT OF THE SOUL"

On September 28, 1998, I woke up delirious, couldn't get up by myself and blistering sores were breaking out on my right wrist. Three days earlier I had been diagnosed with the flu; the doctor told me to go home and rest. Now, my husband, Tom, quite alarmed, knew I had something else and called E.R.

At first glance, the E.R. Doctor suspected a bacteria infection but in order to determine the exact source, ordered a multitude of tests combined with antibiotic treatment. Before long, my left arm was involved. As the sores rapidly spread up both arms, the skin turned black and fell away from my arms revealing the loss of soft muscle tissue underneath and extreme bleeding.

At that point, the doctor suggested amputation of both arms, but Tom said he had faith that I would survive without the amputation. Three days later, the doctors gave a definite diagnosis of flesh-eating bacteria (Necrotizing Fasciitis) from a culture that was grown by taking a sample of serum from my sores the first day of hospital admittance. The doctors gave me a 1% chance of living because the disease spreads so rapidly and I was first misdiagnosed as often happens with this mysterious disease.

Tom was told that evidently I had been near someone with a strep throat and as they coughed or sneezed, their respiratory droplet invaded an open sore on my right elbow. The strep a bacteria, once inside the skin of my arm, started eating the flesh underneath the skin and multiplied as it ate. I was in and out of life and death for two weeks.

A catheter was surgically implanted in my chest, so I could have blood transfusions and multiple antibiotics, including vancomycin, as a last resort. I was given a total of 9 pints of blood, which had to be perfectly matched with mine because of my antibodies from the Rheumatoid Arthritis. It took 86 pints of blood to do this. When Tom discovered I was being given morphine as well, he had it stopped, so I would not become addicted, as some patients have done. At one time, my blood sugar level fell below a person with a diabetic coma. The antibiotics caused a fungus in my mouth and throat, which caused extreme difficulty, and pain in eating so I had to be fed through the nose.

In the meantime, Tom had called our church and the parish nurse was at his side, praying with him and supporting him throughout the initial ordeal. He set up a prayer network with our church, relatives and friends. Our church ministers were there at different times praying for me also.

"Whatever you ask for in prayer, you will receive if you have faith." (Matthew 21:22)

Occasionally, I became conscious, and thinking it was my time to go, prayed for God to give Tom the strength to live a happy life without me. I have no fear of death, because of my faith and since I had lived a victorious life over Rheumatoid Arthritis for 55 years, with 7 artificial joint implants, (2 of them done twice), allergies, shingles, a multitude of health challenges, and almost died twice before, I felt God was calling me home.

I had been blessed with a wonderful husband for 28 years then, and didn't want him to go through any more pain with me, plus I was just so sick, I wanted to let go. However, God had different plans for me. After two weeks, I became quite conscious and realized I was still alive. So I asked God if I was supposed to live, to give me the needed strength to get through the recovery process so I could function again.

I continuously said, "I can do all things through Christ who strengthens me" (Phil 4:13). Knowing that the Holy Spirit is the great comforter, I continually relied on spirit for strength to manifest in my immune system.

A plastic surgeon was called in to evaluate my arms for the prospect of skin grafting. He swabbed what was left of my arms with silvadene. The first graft took place seventeen days after my hospital admittance and was 80% successful. Skin was grafted from my thighs to replace the lost skin on my arms, but the surgeon was unsure how many surgeries would be needed in order for the grafts to take. I was in the hospital a month when they allowed me to go home providing a hospital bed was set up and home care nurses came in twice a day to rebandage my wounds. The surgeon scheduled the second graft a month after my first one, but I had to be admitted to the hospital several days before, because as the home care nurse was taking off my bandage one day, some of the first skin graft came off with the bandage, and the artery started to bleed. I went into shock a the nurse put pressure on my arm and Tom called E.R. I had my second skin graft two days later. The night before surgery, one of the nurses came in with a young man and his guitar who asked if he could play some music for me. Of course, I was delighted! He played all four verses of the hymn, "Amazing Grace", and I knew at that moment that the next day's graft surgery would be successful. It was like God telling me that everything would be okay.

The doctors were extremely surprised that the outcome was so successful. They said, that, "barring any unforeseen events, no more grafts would be necessary" and I thanked God for answered prayers. After six more days, I was discharged and allowed to go home providing I would follow the home nursing schedule for re-bandaging twice a day.

Then three months later, the bacteria showed up in my right knee. I had more antibiotics given to me at home through my chest catheter but I became allergic to many of them. This was especially dangerous because of the possibility of the bacteria going inside my knee implant. We prayed some more and the bacteria mysteriously disappeared.

Due to my long bed therapy, my left knee flared up and three months later I underwent a left knee surgery to replace part of my artificial knee implant. During this time, I was really learning the lesson of patience!

Before the doctors could take out my chest catheter, it took two graft surgeries, nine months of laying on my back with my arms bandaged and outstretched on pillows, very painful exercise therapy to learn to walk again, another knee surgery, eating lots of nutritious foods and supplements since I had lost so much protein, using natural therapies, such as massage, homeopathy, herbs and flower essences.

Everyday I cleared my mind to release negativity, reread my favorite Bible passages, and constantly used positive self-talk to affirm my recovery. I listened to my hypnotherapy tapes to release pain and regain functions. Every breath was a prayer for my body, mind, emotions and spirit to be better each day.

With my catheter out, we got permission from the doctors to take a motor home trip, even though I was still bleeding under my left underarm. Since Tom had worked with the surgeon from the beginning and knew how to take care of my wounds, the surgeon trusted him. We took a three-month trip to the Pacific Northwest and I came back a new person.

Being out in nature has always been very therapeutic for me. The lush green forests, the snow-capped majestic mountains, the sound of a rushing river, the hypnotic splash of water over rocks as the sun dances in and out of the trees or the roar of a waterfall has always been like God pouring out his healing power on me. On the way back home we were fortunate to see an ad about the sale of a litter of Shih Tzu puppies, eight weeks old. I had always wanted a dog and know God brought this special puppy to us. We named him Tao. He is a wonderful healing aid and has delighted me with his enchanting expressions and playful attitude. He is extremely intelligent, creative and sensitive to the way I am feeling.

It took another six months before my left underarm stopped bleeding. One night, as I felt something stick me, Tom took a magnifying glass and discovered that a fold of new skin had grown over some staples that had not been visible before because a big scab was covering the area. The scab finally fell off so that the staples could be seen. My surgeon had me come in and under a local anesthetic; he cut the skin fold and removed the last of the approximately 400 staples that were used in the skin grafts. That was a year and a half after the diagnosis of the bacteria. As the doctors said that my body was free of the bacteria, they admitted that it was a miracle that I survived without amputation. My surgeon and his staff labeled me "the miracle woman".

I still have physical, emotional and mental residues and scars, but I have learned to turn them into stars by giving presentations of my miracle recovery and sharing my story of hope to others who need encouragement from devastating physical illness or disease.

Note: For every person who survives this disease, 7-8 die from it. I truly believe it was through the grace of God that I am still alive today. Apparently, I have more work to do on this earth.

What is Flesh-eating Bacteria?

Flesh-eating bacteria is medically called streptococcus pneumoniacoccus, Type A or scientifically known as Necrotizing Fasciitis. This bacteria can end up in fat, muscle, lungs or in the bloodstream. Depending on its location and a person's susceptibility its presence can lead to anything from septic shock to organ failure t flesh-eating bacteria.

How does one get the disease?

A person with a skin cut is first exposed to someone who has a strep throat. It can be at a mall, a restaurant, or anyplace where you can be around people. The person having the strep throat coughs and the bacteria is airborne.

Flesh-eating bacteria most commonly enters the body throug sores, cuts or other breaks in the skin. The minute it enters the cut it goes to work and starts eating the soft tissue under the skin. The bacteria multiplies as it eats away the fat, muscle and soft tissue.

The symptoms are most commonly a run down feeling and may involve fever, vomiting, or swelling of the limb involved. It is often misdiagnosed as flu, chronic fatigue syndrome or arthritis. It is important that a person sees a doctor or ER immediately. The problem is that it is difficult to diagnose until the bacteria breaks through the skin so you can see visible blisters or sores or discoloration of the skin and by then, it is almost too late because the skin just drops away and there is very little left underneath the skin. Even then it can mimic other types of bacteria and thousands of dollars worth of tests need to be done in order to verify the correct bacteria.

Treatment

Often amputation of the limb(s) involved is recommended to prevent the spread of the bacteria. Combinations of antibiotics are used immediately. The problem is that the bacteria are getting resistant to many of the antibiotics used. Also, people who have had to be previously treated with antibiotics due to infections or surgery become allergic to antibiotics. The most powerful antibiotic is vancomycin and research is going on to develop newer antibiotics as well.

Prognosis

Survival is good if the disease is correctly diagnosed immediately and the antibiotics are effective. Skin graft surgeries are needed for the infected areas and depending on how the skin grafts take, there may be many surgeries needed over a period of time. Blood transfusions are also needed, as there is a great loss of blood. Also the patient loses a lot of protein and needs to double or triple protein requirements. Recovery time varies but where the disease takes hold and the person survives, it usually is a minimum of nine months of very painful treatment. A lot of people do not live due to the fact that they are not diagnosed properly or get treatment right away. Many survive only because they have amputation.

Prevention

Make sure all cuts are properly cleaned and treated and even then there is no sure-fire prevention. People who have never been sick a day in their life and have a cut can still get infected.

CHAPTER 12

RELATIONSHIPS MATTER

Scripture: "Thou shalt love the Lord Thy God with All thy
Heart, and with All thy Soul, and with All thy Mind.
This is the First and Great Commandment. The
second is like unto it: Thou shalt love thy neighbor as
thy self..." (Matt: 22: 37-39).
"Be kindly affected one to another with brotherly
love." (Rom 12:10)

Hymn: In Christ There is no East or West
Blest Be the Tie That Binds

TAKING ALONG RELATIONSHIPS ON OUR JOURNEY

The most important relationship we will ever have is with
God, His Son, Jesus Christ and the Holy Spirit, so we will take them
everywhere we go.

In our relationships with others, we may perceive good and
bad relationships, but even the bad relationships have important
things to teach us. It may not appear as such at the time, but upon
review, everyone we come in contact with, helps us to grow
spiritually. No one comes into our life by accident...everything
happens for a reason. We often find faults in others that help us
become aware of the same fault in ourselves. When this awareness
occurs, it is an eye-opener, which can help us release some
inappropriate behavior so that we can become a better person. The
bottom line is that we all need each other. Some give us the love and
support, as well as the prayers that we need along the way. Others
provide guidance and learning. Still others provide the important
friendships we need to discuss and process the events as we go
along our journey...and we do the same for others. We are all
interconnected in a strange and wonderful way as God uses each one

of us to help one another find our way back to Him, so that our relationship with God may be made more perfect. And, therefore, as Christ taught us we are also to love one another, which is the most important aspect in relationships.

COMMUNICATIONS

Communication is probably the second most important aspect in relationships. Communication is not just the words that are said, but the gestures, tone and pitch that are used. It is said that words make up only 7% of communications. My mother said, "Sometimes it is better to leave some things unsaid". She was a wise person. We need to think of the consequences before we speak, as words can hurt. I'm sure everyone knows of someone who talks constantly and almost never stops. That is one-way communication. Some of the happiest times Tom and I have had is when there is unspoken communication. I remember when we had only been going together a few months and were visiting my mother at the cabin in the Cuyamaca Mountains, Tom and I were taking a night stroll. The skies were so clear and the stars were shining brightly. We laid down in the middle of our private road, and held hands as we just looked at the stars and the beauty of the skies.

Two-way communications is where there is an equal amount of exchange between the parties and listening takes place. Throughout life sometimes we are learners and sometimes teachers. If we find out we are talking too much and not learning from others, it definitely means we need to listen more instead of talking. Another thing we need to remember is that men and women communicate differently. Women socialize and go into detail more in their conversation. Men like straight answers and bottom lines, without a whole lot of detail. Men do not like to ask directions; women do.

ACTIVE LISTENING

Active listening is when we repeat back to the other person what they said using different words, to make sure we are understanding what they said. It would go something like this:

Wife: I think we are getting in a rut staying home every night and I'd like to do an evening out.

Husband: So, you're not satisfied to stay at home with me anymore? What's the matter...I'm not good enough for you? (Not OK response)

Active Listener Husband: What I hear you saying is that you need a change from the evening routine of staying home and want to go out.

Wife: Yes, we haven't been out in ages and the change would be good.

Active Listener Husband: So, you think going out would be good change and so do I. Let me know what nights are good for you and I'll check my schedule so it'll be good for both of us. Then I'll make reservations. Do you want to pick the place or do you want me to?

Oftentimes, if we are tired or not thinking what we say, we can become defensive or "hear" something that the communicator did not intend to communicate.

This is what happened above when the husband made the "not OK response". Another point is the wife could have phrased her first remark differently. Instead of "I think..." and "I'd like to do..." the better phraseology would be, "What do you think about an evening out?" or "Do you think we get in a rut by staying at home all the time?"

One of the best books on how to communicate with others using the proper ego state is *Born to Win*, by Muriel James and Dorothy Jongeward, showing how Transactional Analysis (TA) can help us identify games people play in communications as well as show us the consequences of these games if we don't know how to stop them or step out of them. "The Blame Game" is one of blaming others for one's own mistakes rather than taking responsibility for behavior of one's own making. This can set up a pattern of denial, which results in a loss of friends as well as an unhealthy mental attitude and lack of spiritual growth.

KNOWING OURSELVES

If we are going to relate to others in a positive way, we need to know ourselves. What kind of a person are we? Are we more of an introvert or an extrovert? Are we shy and withdrawn or are we a loudmouth that always wants to be the center of attention? What are our strengths and weaknesses? What kind of self-talk do we use and what is our "inner critic" saying? Do we see ourselves as victims or always wanting to control the action? Neither role is good for a healthy relationship. Do we need to make some improvements? How can we do this?

MADE IN GOD'S IMAGE

We are all children of God, whether we acknowledge it or not. We are made in His image and yet are all individuals with different gifts, talents, strengths, weaknesses and lessons to be learned. We have a mind and soul encased in a body. How we develop those talents, gifts, strengths and deal with our weaknesses determines how well we learn or lessons. By receiving guidance from God as we begin our journey, developing ourselves as we continue, taking along what matters, we grow spiritually, learn our lessons, become blessings to others, loving, forgiving, celebrating, enjoying life and at the end of this life's journey, passing on to a better life beyond.

THE PROCESS OF BECOMING

As we journey through life we are always in the process of becoming. Hopefully, it is for the better, and by the end of our journey, we would like to be at our highest and best, having learned most of our lessons.

PERCEPTIONS

How we perceive others, is in large part, determined by our habits, beliefs and values. So, if our habit is to socialize with only our own race, faith, economic class, etc. our perception of anyone outside of that will be "tainted" or not true. If our parents were prejudiced and taught us to hate certain groups of people, our perceptions of those people again will not be real. We need to remember the song, "You Have to be Taught to Hate", from the musical show, "South Pacific", and become aware of the need to change our values and programming, if that is the case. As a follower of Christ, we are called upon to see (perceive) the love and beauty within each person and to treat each person with brotherly/sisterly love. We are called upon to even love our enemies Again, I was blessed by the teaching of my mother to draw a huge circle to include everyone, even when others might draw a circle to exclude me. The motto of our church is "Open Minds, Open Hearts and Open Doors". No one is ever excluded and all are made welcome.

JUDGMENTS

We often get caught up in judging other people by their behavior. We need to distinguish between the person and the behavior. Everyone needs to be loved and forgiven. God already loves and forgives us and wants us to change our negative behavior to positive behavior. However, we need to love and forgive ourselves and ask God to help us become aware of and find ways to change our negative behavior. We also need to be loved and forgiven by others. Others need to exercise patience and support us as we learn to change our behavior as well.

RELATING WITH LOVE AND FORGIVENESS

The Bible is our guidebook, showing us how to live through the life of Jesus Christ. If we look at the two great commandments, we are to (1) Love God and, (2) Love our neighbor as ourselves.

192

We love God with all our hearts, mind and soul through giving thanks, prayer, praise, worship, reading the Scripture, confession, communion, by listening to His guidance, seeking His will for our lives and carrying it out. We love our neighbors by being God's messenger or minister to them, forgiving 77 times 77, and by measuring our behavior with the standard of behavior set forth by Jesus Christ. We need to look at the gap and find out what keeps us from operating at the same level of behavior as Jesus.

THE EGO

The dictionary defines ego as the self; the individual as aware of himself. In psychoanalysis, it is thought of as that part of the psyche, which consciously controls the impulses of the id. Spiritually, it is known as the "willful self". It is usually the ego, our willful self, that is full of sin, guilt and fear, and does not allow us to see God's redeeming love and grace.

CATEGORIES OF RELATIONSHIPS

There are all kinds of relationships.
GOD, JESUS CHRIST, HOLY SPIRIT
This is the most important relationship and allows us to have healthy relationships with everyone else as long as we stay connected to their love and power. Through this relationship we receive Agape or total unconditional love and forgiveness, grace, the pattern of behavior we need for all of life's experiences and the strength and power to carry out this pattern of behavior. Out of this relationship we experience the church as a family relationship, to pray for and care for each other and newcomers as they come for fellowship.

FAMILY

We are born into a family which forms our habits, beliefs and behavior. As we mature we learn to make choices and at a given age, determine what habits, beliefs and behavior we want to carry along with us and which ones we want to leave behind. While in the family relationship, we usually find one or more members with whom we do not get along with on a continuous basis.

Some are really adversarial relationships and others are just bothersome. However, these relationships help us to test out the water and learn to relate appropriately before going out into a society where we may have to get along with more difficult or challenging people at school, work, marriage and life's experiences.

Our parents provide us with the faith we need to make the right choices through our life's journey. If one has not been blessed, as I have to be raised by parents of faith, one is disadvantaged from the start and must forge ahead in search of a faith to live by.

However, as wonderful as my parents were, they were not perfect since no parents are. As I grew up, I had to look at some of the information I received from my parents that was faulty, if I wanted to leave behind some of the programming that is not helpful or positive in relating well with others. This information had to do with prejudice, particularly of some religions and races. I have now discarded that information and while I was working for the Government even worked in programs to help others become aware of prejudice and help them release biases that had been passed on from their parents. As much as we love our parents, we need to rationally look at all beliefs that have been passed down to us as well as all our parents' behaviors to determine if they are in accordance with the model of beliefs and behavior that Jesus gave us to follow. If they are not in accordance with that model, we need to discard them.

FAMILIES WE MARRY INTO

When we get married, we have another family we relate to. Just as in our birth family, there may be some relationships that come easily and are more comfortable and others that are more of a challenge, such as the traditional mother-in-law/daughter-in-law rivalry, which was my particular challenge. Some personalities are like oil and water and no matter how hard one or both parties try to get along, there is always an edge of uneasiness.

Old school values (shoulds and shouldn'ts) conflict with new viewpoints and ways of doing things, such as, the role of women in society and marriage, etc. Each party tries to convince the other that their "way" of doing things is right.

When I discovered this was to be an ongoing challenge, I fervently prayed for God to help me. The lesson I learned is that it is better to, "listen" in their presence and then go home and carry through with one's own beliefs. However I found out that it is easier said than done. I must admit I was not the success in this area that I wanted to be. I asked for forgiveness and found loving unconditionally, sometimes from a distance was the best. My intent was to always have the best turn out for both of us.

STRANGERS

We come in contact with total strangers every day of our lives. It is up to each of us to have a smile on our face and initiate appropriate pleasant conversation to make each person's day a little brighter. We will never know the positive impact we can make on others by showing them we care with a smile.

FRIENDS

I have found that my relationship with my friends has been an invaluable blessing in my life's journey. As the youngest member of my family, I have seen my parents and some of my siblings pass on and the comfort and friendship I have received from my friends is unsurpassed. Also, during the times I have been sick, my friends have supported me in so many ways. I hope I have served them as well, in listening, helping and just being there for them. We have shared so many times of joy together as well...the memories flood my mind with fun and laughter.

I have kept in touch all my life with two of my friends that I have known from the age of five years. One passed away several years ago but the other one still lives in San Diego. I have a circle of friends from Junior High and High School that I dearly love and are like family to me. I have friends from college, from church, from various places of work, from different organizations, from motor home clubs, and strangers we have met at campgrounds, on our

Oregon property and elsewhere. I am extremely blessed to have so many dear friends in my life!!!

The Angel eyes Cards have an Internet site that has a poem about friends that I would like to share:

FRIENDS ARE LIKE ANGELS

Our friends are like angels, who brighten our days.
In all kinds of wonderful magical ways.
Their thoughtfulness comes, as a gift from above.
And we feel we're surrounded by warm, caring love.
Like upside down-rainbows, their smiles bring the sun.
And they fill ho-hum moments, with laughter and fun.
Friends are like angels, without any wings.
Blessing our lives, with the most precious things.
Author Unknown-

HOW TO KEEP YOUR FRIENDS

1. To have a friend, BE a friend. (Be friendly) When people had trouble pronouncing my maiden name (Troendly), I told them that it rhymed with friendly, as our dad had reminded each one of us to say. It seemed to have stuck.
2. Stay connected. Make the effort to keep in touch by phone, letter, email, sending cards on special days or just to say thank you for being my friend. Return calls promptly.
3. Always thank people for being who they are. Accept them as they are. Love them and forgive them.
4. Keep your address and phone list up to date. If you lose track of people, try to reconnect through the internet or other ways.
5. Be interested and stay interested in your friend's lives.
6. Listen to their stories and problems.
7. Help your friends wherever you can. Be willing to share any information that can help but don't force your ideas or opinions on them.
8. Respect the privacy of friends when desired.

9. Always call before dropping by to visit. Never intrude or outlast your welcome. Always pay your fair share and be willing to treat.... never munch off people.

10. Be a blessing to others and they will be a blessing to you.

CASUAL OR SOCIAL

We are introduced to other people by our friends, or we meet people at parties or social gatherings. Some of these will be relationships that will come and go, others may last. However, nothing ever happens by accident. Always learn something from each one.

PROFESSIONAL

Our career or jobs bring us into contact with a variety of people. I learned never to talk negatively about anyone I worked with, as I never knew who would hear it next. It is wise to be respectful and appreciate the contribution each person makes to the whole. Team work and cooperation is very important. I learned to always do my share and more and always have a smile on my face when I walked in to work each morning, no matter how much pain I had. Many of my professional relationships have become my life friends; others faded away. I got along well with nearly all of my supervisors, except one or two. On my desk or cubicle, I always kept a picture of Tom as well as our Oregon land or some pretty place where we had vacationed, and when things got too bad, rather than getting into an argument, I would just look at my pictures and say to myself, "This is what I am working for" and keep quiet. I also would use the phrase, "This too shall pass." It worked and now I look back and found out it really was worth it as we are enjoying our property and retirement

INTIMATE

Intimate relationships provide the best opportunity for spiritual growth. Tom and I have always had God at the head of our relationship and have kept prayer as a constant companion in our daily lives. The best human relationship I have ever had is with Tom. We have appreciated and praised each other's strengths and have encouraged and supported each other as we worked to change our weaknesses into strengths. We both have a conscious desire to never verbally undermine the other in public or in private. We are definitely soulmates. We have always accepted each other as equal individuals and never use power plays. In fact, in our marriage ceremony, we asked our minister to include these words from Gibran that, "Your mutuality should never destroy your individuality."

Traits needed are love, forgiveness, patience, trust, respect, release of blame, judgment and ego, acceptance, understanding, appreciation, kindness, willingness to listen and take responsibility for one's own thoughts, words and action. I will certainly admit that I have not always exhibited the above traits, but both Tom and I always have the best of intentions and know that love and forgiveness will prevail. We have not always agreed, and in fact we have had some serious arguments, where one or the other walked out of the house. However when emotions cooled down, we were able to come back and learn from the situation and each other. We never let the anger keep us apart at night. Our joys far outweighed our sorrows and pain.

KEYS TO A HAPPY RELATIONSHIP

Research psychologists at The Family Foundation Project at the University of Washington in Seattle, headed by John Gottman, discovered four keys to a happy relationship. 1. Learn to calm down when communication becomes difficult. 2. Learn to speak and listen non defensively (speak without blame and listen with empathy) 3. Validate your partner (acknowledging partner's point of view, accepting appropriate responsibility and apologizing when you are clearly wrong). 4. Practice, practice, practice the other three points until they become "second nature". Let your partner know what's right instead of what's wrong the majority of the time and continually tell and show each other love.

MARITAL LOVE AN EXTENSION OF GOD'S LOVE

For me, the love two people share in a marriage is an extension of God's love. One has to be continually aware of the other party and work towards combining the needs of both without neglecting a need of the other party. In the total plan of the universe it helps to "Let go and let God." Pray, Pray, Pray!

THOUGHTS ON RELATIONSHIPS

I believe we are all here to both teach each other and listen to/learn from each other. I consider us all God's messengers. Some people show us by their lives what not to do and other people show us by their words and actions how to live. Jesus is the perfect example of how to live one's life. It is always good to remember the Golden Rule and ask ourselves the question, "What would Jesus do?" By releasing judgment and having love, compassion and forgiveness for all of God's creatures and creation, we are really showing that we love God.

Chapter 13

CARETAKING MATTERS

Hymn: This is My Father's World

Scripture: Love one another as I have loved you (John 13:34
Do unto others as you would have them do unto you
(Matthew 7:12 and Luke 6:31)

TAKING ALONG THE ROLE OF A CARETAKER ON OUR JOURNEY

Caretaking begins with our parents taking care of us, and as we grow and mature we learn to take care of ourselves and take responsibility for our lives. However, we all have a responsibility for taking care of each other (in the sense of having compassion, concern, and doing what we can to help when asked), the Universe and all the creatures therein. We do not own anything; we are merely caretakers or stewards for as long as we are on this earth. All creation belongs to the Creator.

FAMILY

Growing up in a family can be a blessing or full of trauma if it is a dysfunctional family. However, life is full of challenges and we are here to learn our lessons. Some lessons have to do with family or relationships; others have to do with health, etc. It's not what challenge we face, but how we face it. Do we face it with courage and strength from Christ or do we allow the situation to control us through fear? We teach each other things and some times we learn how to do things that are positive and some times we learn how to do things that are negative.

We must take responsibility for discerning through prayer, how to correct negative behavior and faulty parental programming to a more positive and appropriate behavior and programming.

Sometimes we need professional help to do this. However, there is a life lesson in all of this, such as forgiveness. Many of the sibling rivalries fade as we grow and mature. It is important to have a sense of humor in looking back and seeing some of the silly things we did to annoy each other. The fun in family gatherings, sharing and supporting family members through joys and sorrows are some of the things that make up the wonderful memories of life. I again have been blessed with such wonderful parents and family.

MARRIAGE

The caretaking of a marriage is very important. In the first place, before one can know and understand another in an intimate relationship such as marriage, one needs to know and understand oneself. Love, faith in God, commitment and prayer are the foundations of a lasting marriage. Respect for each other, honesty, understanding, two-way communication, growing together, a willingness to compromise and learn from each other, fidelity, sharing, having fun and supporting each other "through sickness and health, joys and sorrows", are all important aspects. Our marriage has been tested as much or more than any other because of my health challenges. Our faith in God, prayer and love have made our marriage last. Allowing emotions, cruel words and arguments to get out of control can undermine the relationship. Always be the first one to forgive. When children enter the picture there is another factor, which I will not address, since we did not have any. As far as I can see, any issue or factor (including children), in which one spouse or the other, takes a one sided position, can lead to trouble. In these cases, a professional counselor or therapist might be needed.

Tom and I have had our share of arguments, like any other couple, but we have never let the sun go down without making up. We have complemented each other and supported the other when that was needed. I was always encouraged by my parents and Tom seemed to need that same encouragement from me, so whenever he started a new job or challenge in life, so I was there to encourage him in a new undertaking. Tom has a great sense of humor and I needed that to help me "refocus" my life from the seriousness of pain. Humor is very healing. Each of us had certain issues that we had to work on as lessons of life. I have learned to have more patience and Tom has had to release his ego, because it takes real humility, compassion, and love, for a man, particularly, to take on the role of caretaking. I have been blessed beyond belief to have this man as my husband, and I thank God each and every day.

When we first got married and for the first fifteen years, I did the cooking, cleaning and washing, besides working full time. However, with all the surgeries and health challenges I have had since then, Tom has taken over these duties, without complaining. I have limitations that I don't talk about, but suffice it to say, without Tom, I would need a full time assistant. I help do whatever I can and when I can because I am extremely grateful for this "Earth Angel" as I call him. There is a song I learned when I was young that we used to sing around the fire at the Camp Fire Girls camp. It is called, "Tell Me Why". The words are as follows, "Tell me why the stars do shine, tell me why the ivy twines, tell me why the sky's so blue and I will tell you just why I love you". "Because God made the stars to shine, because God made the ivy twine, because God made you, that's why I love you." Tom and I still sing this song around the campfire when we are camping. I truly believe God made us for each other and that we are Soulmates.

THE ROLE OF FRIENDS AND GROUPS

Being kind to others is the first step in friendship. It is important to take good care of our friendships. We can support each other in multitudes of situations and crises, besides the joy and sharing that comes from having special friends.

I had always been taught that it was the inside of the person that was important and not the outside. In the first grade, one of my best friends was a girl with a cleft lip. A lot of the other kids used to make fun of her and the way she looked and talked. It made me angry and I got into several arguments with the kids on the playground that taunted her. I taught her the saying, "sticks and stones will break my bones, but names will never hurt me." I knew deep down, though, that no matter how brave we thought we were, that it really did hurt her feelings. Her mother used to thank my mother for teaching me to be kind and a good friend to Velma. Velma's father was in the military and when they moved, I lost contact with her. I have often wondered what happened to her and many times have sent up flash prayers for her.

One of the things my mother taught me was, "There was person who made a circle and drew me out, but God and I had the will to win. We made a circle that drew him in." This is paraphrase of words from Edwin Markham, but I like my mother's way of saying it the best.

I have always been fortunate to have many friends and even though there were those who shunned me when I got the Arthritis, there were many more who have supported me throughout my life.

Throughout this book, I have shown the love and friendship that came from my school friends, not only as I was growing up, but that have continued up to the present, my college friends, the friends I made through the different organizations I belonged to, the friends I met through church, work, and everywhere I go. New friends are continually added, particularly those we meet traveling. I cherish each and every one of them. It seems God has especially blessed me with innumerable wonderful friends to help compensate for my health challenges and I am extremely grateful.

NATURE

Hymn: FOR THE BEAUTY OF THE EARTH -John Rutter

For the beauty of the earth, for the beauty of the skies, for the love which from our birth over and around us lies; for the beauty of each hour of the day and of the night, hill and vale and tree and flower, sun and moon and stars of light; Lord of all to thee we raise, this our hymn of joyful praise.
We honor the Creator when we honor the creation.

Scripture: "The earth is the Lord's, and the fullness, thereof."
Psalm 24:1

We must never forget that every part of nature is and was created by God. We talk about "owning" property, but it is only a temporary gift from God enabling us to enjoy as long as we take good care of it. We are stewards or caretakers of all that surrounds us. When we upset the ecosystem by too much development in an area where specific animals use to obtain their nourishment, they will turn on us.

We need to have a healthy respect for all nature and value all species so that there is a right sharing of all resources for all of God's creatures.

The following was included in "Reflections" by Ardath Rodale in a Prevention magazine. It hit a chord of resonance within me and I wanted to share it with you also.

"May all I say and all I think
Be in harmony with thee,
God within me, God beyond me,
Maker of the tree"

A Chinook prayer

As Ardath Rodale's last sentence said, "Reach out with tenderness to touch the trees, the earth, and all living things."

ANIMALS

Tom and I are not vegetarians, but we are not hunters. We do not own a gun and do not believe in killing animals for sport. We believe in protecting endangered species but are not active protesters. We pray a lot for what concerns us. We enjoy going to the zoo and just enjoy watching animals in the wild or domestic animals as well.

As I said in the chapter on healing, all nature and all creation is tremendously healing and I can sit for hours and "just be" mesmerized in the beauty and wonder of God's greatness. It is in nature that I most feel a "oneness" with God and all creation. As caretakers of this great beauty we need to preserve it so future generations can enjoy this same feeling of being close to God.

ORGANIZATIONS

Tom and I belong to and support with our money, the Nature Conservancy because, as stated in the Spring 2003, issue of their magazine, page 23, it says, "The Nature Conservancy recognizes that it is saving the landscapes 'of our hearts, our souls, our very being.' and that these places sustain and enhance our lives spiritually." The Conservancy takes the money that is given by contributors to buy land that is crucial to supporting our ecosystem and preserves it for the future.

THOUGHTS ON CARETAKING

1. We need to remember that everyone and everything is a precious creation of God's and if we say we love God, we need to take care of and love everyone and everything He has created.

2. We need to be AWARE of our thoughts, words and actions towards everyone and everything in order to properly love and take care of them,

3. We need to have a living faith, so that our lives totally reflect the love and caretaking that Jesus had.

CHAPTER 14

FRUIT OF THE SPIRIT MATTERS

Hymn: In my Heart There Rings a Melody

Scripture: "But the fruit of the Spirit is love, joy, peace, long
suffering, kindness, goodness, faithfulness,
gentleness, self-control." (Gal 5:22,23)   (Also
meekness, temperance....patience, mercy, kindness &
forgiveness)
  In Colossians 3:12, 14f, we find, "Put on then,
.......compassion, kindness, lowliness, meekness, and
patience......And above all these, put on love, which
binds everything together in perfect harmony
......And let the peace of Christ rule in your hearts."

TAKING ALONG FRUIT OF THE SPIRIT ON OUR JOURNEY

As we look individually at each one of these virtues, they
become more than words. Throughout our journey, we will be
presented with many situations and opportunities to integrate these
virtues into our personality. Sometimes we will fail but invariably
the same or similar situations come up again and again until we
learn the lesson, which gives us many chances to practice until we
"get it" right.

LOVE

Christ gave us two great commandments about love:
"You shall love the Lord your God with all your heart, mind and
spirit", and the second is like unto it, 'You shall love your neighbor
as yourself". (Mt. 22:37,38; Luke 10:27). This is again reflected
when Christ told us to serve others, "Inasmuch as you have done it
unto the least of these, you have done it unto me." (Mt. 25:40).

The way I love God is by seeing Him in all creation and loving and appreciating all creation by taking care of it and loving and serving others. There are many times I fail at this, but I seek out His guidance and strength to help me do better. I must confess, my greatest lack is a "lost opportunity". When I review my actions at the end of a busy day, I find there were many times when I could have done something for others and I missed the opportunity because of the busy times in which we all find ourselves these days...or I had three choices facing me at one time and I missed the greatest chance to serve others because I chose something else over it. However, our God understands the human weaknesses and loves us anyway...and because of this great love for us, we continue to love.

JOY

"The fullness of joy is to behold God in everything."
Julian of Norwich, fourteenth-century English mystic

I see everything and particularly nature as a reflection of God and when we were on our trip to the Australian rain forest in 1992, I was so spiritually moved that I wrote a poem, called "Reflections of Oneness", and I share my joy of this poem with everyone in Chapter 16. Our guide took us to a fig tree that had been there since the time of Christ. It was a gigantic tree that was intertwined with other trees and vines. It was awesome and filled me with a joy and inspiration that could only be expressed in a creative work such as a poem!!!

Yes, the colors of flowers, especially in spring, the sound of a waterfall splashing on the rocks, the deep beauty of a forest, the glory of a sunrise or a sunset, the chirp of the birds, Tao's (our Shi Tzu) playful eyes, as well as the wonder on the face of a child's first view of something all make me rejoice. There is a combination of love and joy when I look at Tom. Whether we are talking or not, just having his presence with me fills me with joy and makes me realize that God brought us together.

I am the kind of person for which tears come easily. I have tears of sorrow when others are hurt. I also shed tears of joy when I hear about a Good Samaritan, people helping others to recover after a tragedy such as a fire, etc. And I shed tears of joy when I see

207

something beautiful, such as a work of art or hear masterpieces such as "The Messiah". The "Hallelujah Chorus", I believe, is one of the most, if not the most, beautiful piece of music ever written. The greatest joy for me is knowing that Christ is my Lord and Savior and the "Hallelujah Chorus" expresses or symbolizes for me the praise and majesty that I feel when I hear this music.

"Rejoice in the Lord always; again, I say, Rejoice." (Pps 4:4)

PEACE

My greatest peace comes when I am in meditation in our Japanese sun house Sacred Center or out in the stillness of nature and feeling this "oneness" with God and all creation. All I feel is love and beauty and a desire to share this feeling with others. However, all too often this peace is shattered when I go out into the real world and the business involved in getting things done trigger human emotions when things are not done "just right" and the flow of words to explain to others what needs to be done to correct the problem does not come out in the polite and compassionate way that is in keeping with the "inner peace" that I had just a short while ago and is now shattered.

Or after coming out of meditation with this feeling of connectedness, I encounter the blaring headlines of violence in the newspaper or hear on TV of another drive by shooting or the latest crime report, it is experienced as hurt from within self. All I can do is pray that God will help me understand so that I may again have this state of peace within to help radiate it out into a troubled world, that I might be an instrument of God's peace and have this state of peace on a more continuous basis, even in the midst of confusion and chaos.

"Let the peace of God rule in your hearts." (Col. 3:15) "The peace of God which passeth all understanding, shall keep your hearts and minds through Christ Jesus (Pps. 4:6,7)

LONG-SUFFERING

As we grow in our faith we are tested in many ways, sometimes to the point of suffering greatly and to know that we can always lean on Christ for strength and receive comfort is most gratifying. By understanding that everything has a purpose, we can come to know that we are being molded into a more spiritual state that can be used by God as a help and a blessing to other people. When this happens, we are partaking in a small way, of the load that Jesus took upon Himself for our sakes and hopefully becoming more like Him.

KINDNESS

The characteristic of being friendly, benevolent, thoughtful is how kindness is defined in the dictionary. I have always thought that being kind to one another was a necessary and almost automatic part of living. This is what I was taught by my parents and have done my best to carry out in my life. In Chapter 17, I explain further how being a blessing to others and being thankful for the kindness and consideration shown by others to me has been a blessing in my life.

GOODNESS

Goodness is the state of being generous. It is important that we share what we have with others who are not as fortunate. That includes our time as well as our money. When I was younger and had more physical strength, as a member of our church college age group, I enjoyed going down to Mexico to visit the orphans at La Casa de Esperonza. I remember one time we brought a group across the border and took them to the zoo. Besides having fun ourselves, the smile on the kid's faces was all the reward one needed.

We just got back from a walk on our neighborhood park with our adorable Tao. The mother of some kids came up and asked if it was okay for her kids to pet Tao and of course we said "yes." Tao loves everyone, particularly children, and he is very gentle. As the kids petted him they squealed and giggled. It was such a pleasure to see their smiles that came from our sharing our love with them.

FAITHFULNESS

The act of keeping faith, or being loyal and dependable to one's faith is the definition from the dictionary. We are tested many times in life, through our own personal experiences or through the things that happen in our government, or in the world. We need to keep in mind, again, that no person or government is perfect, and we do not live in a perfect world.

However, we have a perfect God and must remember He is always in charge, holding out His hand to us. Whether or not we understand or agree with what is going on in the world, we must never give up our faith and continue to pray. Also, when we recognize imperfection in others, or in the world, it is a chance to practice forgiveness, as we remember our own imperfection and how God forgives us. Most importantly, never let go of God's outstretched hand, as He is always there to love us and help us.

GENTLENESS

Gentleness is the state of being polite or refined and treating everyone in the same manner. It goes along with kindness. "Let your gentleness be known to all men..." (Phil 4:5)

MEEKNESS

Meekness is the state of being patient; not inclined to anger. It is not being passive to the point where we are used as a doormat. However, we have the responsibility to learn how to communicate to others in a polite and courteous way, so that they understand what we consider appropriate and inappropriate behavior. (Convey our high standards without appearing "mightier than thou")

Meekness also involves patience. I remember when I had the flesh-eating bacteria and my arms were kept bandaged and laid straight out on a pillow for nine months, I couldn't bend them to help myself. Sometimes a fly would light on my forehead or buzz around me, and if Tom was busy, I just had to have patience and transcend the frustration until the fly went away.

TEMPERANCE

Temperance is self-restraint in conduct; as well as using moderation in terms of appetites, such as eating, drinking alcohol, etc. My parents taught me politeness and appropriate behavior. They continually reminded me of the Golden Rule, and as much as possible, I have tried to carry it out all my life.

Fortunately I have been blessed with not being able to eat too much, as I get sick. I never smoked and drank alcohol only in small amounts and then it was in celebration of a birthday, etc. Too much alcohol, as well as too many medications, literally makes me sick. However, I know of people who are not as fortunate and are addicted to food, smoking, gambling, medication, etc. We need to have compassion for these people and at the same time encourage them to get the professional help they need.

INNER CRITIC

Many people have an addiction or lack manifesting some of the fruits because they do not love themselves enough. There is an "inner voice" or critic that comes from the past programming of a parent, friends or cultural programming that says, we do not look right; we do not have the body shape that is glamorous, beautiful, etc., so we try to diet and end up gaining more weight. We need to love ourselves just as we are.

MANIFESTING THE FRUITS

Jesus said, "By their fruits you shall know them." (Matt 7:16-18)

How do we manifest the fruits of the spirit? Only when our spirits are united with God's spirit, can we manifest the fruits. The more time we spend with God in prayer, meditation and loving others, the more consistent we are in our behavior and words in carrying out a practical application of our beliefs. In all our experiences in our daily living, treating others like we want to be treated. In other words, by carrying out the Golden Rule every day of our life. By encouraging and enabling others who are weak and helping, never impeding anyone's growth in a positive way. With God's help, this takes a lot of self-monitoring...paying attention to what thoughts are beginning to form in our minds, what emotions we are feeling and listening to our bodies.

If we find any negative thoughts, feelings or tensions, taking steps to cancel, release them and relax, asking God to forgive us and replace all negatives with positives. We need to make sure we are in a right relationship with God before we can be in a right relationship with others. We need to analyze our intent and purpose behind each word and action to make sure it is pure without any hidden motive. It is always good to ask ourselves, "What would Jesus do?"

Seek opportunities for the greater use of love, faith and hope in being a blessing to others. The more this is done, the more one will experience the fruits in their life and the more joyful energy one will have to expand their life in seeing new opportunities for love.... and it will keep on building. Positive action builds more positive energy with which one has to take more positive action. It is a self-fulfilling prophecy; just as negative words and action build a self-fulfilling prophecy for a negative life.

CHAPTER 15

PEACE MATTERS

Hymn: In Christ There is no East or West
    Let There be Peace on Earth

Scripture: My peace I give unto you (John 14:27)
        "and the peace of God which surpasses all understanding,
        will guard your hearts and minds through Christ Jesus."
        (Phil 4:7)
        "Now may the Lord of peace Himself give you peace
        always in every way..." (2 Thes 3:16)

TAKING ALONG PEACE ON OUR JOURNEY

If we honor and believe in the "Lord of peace Himself", it seems we ought to be walking on the path of peace and really living the life of peace.

There are so many aspects to peace just like there is to love. It seems one needs inner peace before any other peace can come. "The aim of our pilgrimage is to be transformed from within that we might perceive reality in a new way, experience the world in a new way, and live our lives in relationship to the world in ways that God's will might be done and God's Kingdom come."

John Westerhoff

Then we can be an instrument of peace within the family, with neighbors, with the country, with people of other races, religions, ("But why do you judge your brother? Or why do you show contempt for your brother? For we shall all stand before the judgment seat of Christ." – (Rom 14:10) and then world peace. "If it is possible, as much as depends on you, live peaceably with all men." (Rom 12:18) This means even your enemies. "If your enemy hungers, feed him; If he thirsts, give him a drink; (Rom 12:20). "Do

213

not be overcome by evil, but overcome evil with good." (Rom 12:21)

"If we have no peace, it is because we have forgotten that we belong to each other."

Mother Teresa

Someone asked Mother Teresa why she never protested war and her answer was that she lived her life for peace, not war.

I have not always been the kind of instrument for peace that would have liked to be. Sometimes it seems so elusive, particularly with the world situation. But, it has always been this way and I am convinced there is a better way than war and violence. If we can put a man on the moon, and produce the lifesaving technology and communications technology we have nowadays, we surely have the minds to come up with peaceful solutions to world problems. We are confronted continually with the rationality of a "Just War". Every since 9/11, "revenge" has been the cry and the security of the homeland; our nation has been in the forefront of the news.

War has never solved anything and it seems to be self-perpetuating the more we turn to it as a solution. When we use war to attain peace, we create more people that are willing to sacrifice their lives for their "cause" and create more wars. "We" become like "them". Since we are all interrelated, we are really declaring war on ourselves. As Pogo in the comic strip said, "We have met the enemy and it is us."

ROOTS OF WAR

The U.S. NEWS AND WORLD REPORT Magazine (April 26, 2004), issued a Special Report on "The Roots of War" by Thomas Hayden. The author asks a question, "Can humanity ever escape its age-old legacy of battle?" On page 50 of that issue, he writes, "...there is ample evidence that previously 'warlike' people can rapidly become peaceful, if the causes-both ecological and cultural---underlying the battles are removed. The Vikings, forced into raiding parties by a population boom in the 9th century A.D., terrified Northern Europe for centuries, but no one now fears a visit from the Danes. Even in the New Guinea Highlands, where tribal warfare routinely claimed the lives of a quarter of all males, peace soon followed a governmental ban on warring in the 1960's.

He continues, "If the latest news from the baboon front is any indication, ending war really might come down to just giving peace a chance. In a paper in the on-line journal *PUBLIC LIBRARY OF SCIENCE*, scientists report that one group of the primates in Kenya seem to have broken with a tradition of aggressive males terrorizing the rest of the troop. After the fiercest animals died of disease, a more peaceful culture took hold-and has persisted for nearly 20 years, even after new males arrived. The transformation contradicts everything researchers thought they knew about the baboon society. Maybe it holds a lesson for the rest of us too."

PERCEPTIONS DIFFER

Our present administration's view is that the U.S. will spread freedom to Iraq and the Middle East. The view of all the Middle East is that the U.S. is Imperialistic and is forcing our way of life on them. Perceptions are different but even in the United States, the President is losing the support he once had for being in Iraq. At this time (June 2005), the United States is one of the most hated countries in the world and most believe the United States was the aggressor in invading Iraq without just cause. We need to start rectifying this image by changing our policies before much longer, or we will leave a legacy of violence.

DESTRUCTION IS PART OF THE PRICE OF WAR

This destruction was done in WW II but it shows what can happen in any war. A US military base in Babylon, also used by the Polish government for operations in Iraq, has caused the destruction of many artifacts of ancient Babylonia, once known as "one of the wonders of the world."

A QUESTION OF PEACE AND JUSTICE

As part of the solution to peace, we need to deal with the matter of justice. As Martin Luther King said, "Peace is not the absence of conflict but the presence of justice." (Spirituality & Health-June 2004, p. 47) The dictionary defines justice as fairness; reward or penalty as deserved; the use of authority to uphold the law equally.

HOW CAN PEACE WITH JUSTICE BE ACHIEVED WITHOUT WAR?

1. Wherever we see injustice, take some corrective nonviolent action.

    a. Examine our own prejudices, racial, religious and nationality thoughts, feelings and behaviors and take steps to eliminate injustices in our own lives.

    b. Pray for peace with justice

    c. Be a part of an organization that stands for peace and justice.

    d. Write letters and make telephone calls to those in power that can take more action.

2. Support Conflict Resolution, Mediation, Counseling in all situations.

3. Live a life that models peace, love and justice and teach others to do the same.

4, Attend classes on peace and read books on peace.

Tom and I attended an all day class at our church sponsored by the San Diego School of Christian Studies and given by the Claremont School of Theology on "Practicing Peace". The class was based upon a book edited by Dr. Ellen Ott Marshall, *Choosing Peace Through Daily Practices (Pilgrim Press, April 2005)*. I would highly recommend getting this book.

NONVIOLENT COMMUNICATION

Marshall Rosenberg is the founder of the Center for Nonviolent Communication. He lives in Europe but travels the world teaching nonviolent communication and mediating conflicts in such places as Palestine, Israel, Russia, Serbia, Croatia, Ireland, Rwanda, Burundi, and Nigeria. In an article from the San Diego Union by Mark Sauer, Staff Writer, on October 14, 2004, Rosenberg is quoted as saying that nonviolent communication is "the way of thinking, communicating and using power that helps us connect to one another in a way that we enjoy contributing to one another's well being. It's an attempt to live in harmony with certain values." He goes on to say that, "everything human beings do is for good reason...to meet needs." When he enters a country as mediator in a situation, he begins by talking about needs and requests a leader from a specific tribe or group to start talking about the situation in terms of needs. The first sentence may come out as an angry accusation at the other side but Rosenberg, repeats the sentence by reframing it to include the word "needs" and asks for clarification. The need may be for safety, for food, for land, housing, equality, etc. The next step is to see how the needs can be met without violence, such as bartering or trading to make for a win-win solution. War usually starts as a power move to get more land, etc or revenge for what another country has done to the other country or its people.

Violence comes from being taught to hate, by observing power plays by bullies or larger countries on those weaker or smaller people or nations. Rosenberg says, "No culture is violent. Our nature, I'm convinced is compassionate...The work of Margaret Mead and Ruth Benedict shows that ...there are many cultures that never had much violence until they were encroached upon and their natural culture destroyed."

All the Religions of the world advocate peace. In the U.S., since 9/11,the Muslims seem to be getting a bad rap. There is an internet forward that is making the rounds of e-mailers, which indicate all Muslims believe in a Holy Jihad against all unbelievers of their faith. This statement is absolutely false. In a gesture of understanding after 9/11, Tom and I attended a friendship meeting between people of all faiths at the Muslim Community Center of Greater San Diego and found a warm welcome from the Muslims. A Presentation of their faith was given with a question and answer period following. Then we had a social time of fellowship and Tom was talking to one of the teachers who gave him a copy of the Holy

Qur'an. Tom has been reading it since then and has found many similarities with our Bible as far as teaching love, friendship and morality.

We need to have the vision of peace foremost in our minds. We need to have more people see that peace is a result of praying for peace, thinking peace, feeling peaceful within, relating in peaceful ways and every peaceful action taken as a step towards peace. In other words, we must be committed to living, as Jesus would live in this world today

My goal at this stage of life, is to continually talk peace, and act peacefully in all my relationships. It may be an elusive goal, one that I may not see in my lifetime. It is like the goal Robert Browning talks about, "Our reach should always exceed our grasp, or what is there a heaven for?" Jesus certainly wants us to resist evil, but not by using violence. Unfortunately, violence has become a way of life in the United States. As Walter Wink, professor of biblical interpretation at Auburn Theological Seminary in New York City states, "I believe that the world is ready to embrace nonviolence both as strategy and as a way of life. Nonviolence has never been more relevant. The world has never been more ready." (Spirituality and Health, October 2004, p. 63

I am convinced this is the goal Jesus wanted us to achieve. He continually talked about "the Kingdom of God being within us", and that we are called to live a life worthy of this Kingdom. Just close your eyes for a second and imagine Jesus standing in front of a crowd that includes you. His magnetic eyes seem to look right through you as He says, "Blessed are the peacemakers" (Matt: ***

LET THERE BE PEACE ON EARTH AND LET IT BEGIN WITH ME

MY THOUGHTS ON PEACE
WHERE DO WE GO FROM HERE???

Do we continue to war with those countries who have a different form of government in the belief that we know what is "best" for their people, with those countries who have nuclear power, with those countries who have terrorists? How can we ever be certain that every country is free of terrorists? Where do we stop? Consider the mindset of fear that terrorists may once again invade our homeland and revenge for 9/11 that has beset our nation. When do we start treating the Muslim world with respect and the fairness that is implicit in the Golden Rule?

Are there enough people in this country that are willing to trust God to be in charge of things and follow the behavior model set forth by Jesus to love rather than a philosophy that says the Geneva Convention Treaty is outdated and we must lower our behavior to that of the terrorists themselves?

The choice is ours: Love over fear, forgiveness over revenge, and peace over war as Jesus taught us or the other way around? What is your choice?

WORDS TO HEED

"Wars are not acts of God. They are caused by man, by man-made institutions, by the way in which man has organized his society. What man has made, man can change."

Frederick Moore Vinson in a speech at Arlington National Cemetery on Memorial Day, 1945

There is no way to peace ----peace is the way.

A. J.Muste, quoted in Pacifist and Prophet

If you want to make peace with your enemy, you have to work with your enemy. Then he becomes your partner.

Nelson Mandela, Long Walk to Freedom

I dream of giving birth to a child who will ask, "Mother, what was war?"

Eve Merriam, Peacemaking: Day-by-Day

Nothing will end war unless the people themselves refuse to go to war.

Albert Einstein, interview with G.S. Viereck

Peace is based on a respect for life, the spirit of reverence for life. Not only do we have to respect the lives of human beings, but we have to respect the lives of animals, vegetables, and minerals...The way we farm, the way we deal with our garbage, all these things are related to each other.

Thich Nhat Hanh, Peace is Every Step

Why of course, the people don't want war...But, after all, it is the leaders of the country who determine the policy and it is always a simple matter to drag the people along, whether it is a democracy or a fascist dictatorship or a Parliament or a Communist dictatorship. Voice or no voice, the people can always be brought to the bidding of the leaders. That is easy. All you have to do is tell them they are being attacked and denounce the pacifists for lack of patriotism and exposing the country to danger. It works the same way in any country.

Hermann Goering, quoted in Nuremberg Diary

Peace demands the most heroic labor and the most difficult sacrifice. It demands greater heroism than war. It demands greater fidelity to the truth and much more perfect purity of conscience. The Christian fight for peace is not to be confused with defeatism.

Thomas Merton,
Courage for Truth: The Letters of Thomas Merton to Writers

It isn't enough to talk about peace. One must believe in it. And it isn't enough to believe in it. One must work at it. Justice cannot be done for one side alone, but must be for both.

Eleanor Roosevelt, "Voice of America" broadcast
November 11, 1951

CHAPTER 16

CELEBRATING LIFE MATTERS

Hymns: How Great Thou Art,
Praise the Lord
Count Your Blessings

Scripture: "In everything give thanks, for this is the will of God in Christ Jesus for you."(1 Thes 5:18)

"Rejoice in the Lord always. Again I will say, rejoice!" (Phil 4:4)

CELEBRATING GOOD TIMES ON OUR JOURNEY

When we visited Vancouver Island, B.C. in 2000, we stayed five days in Victoria, as there were so many things to do. While we were there we went to a concert at the University of Victoria produced by the Good News Choir, called CELEBRATE GOOD TIMES. The director, Louise Rose, wrote in the program brochure,

"I know there are those for whom celebration is almost always difficult. You might say...what about those whose family history is riddled with unpleasantness. What about those who face health challenges? And what about those who are terminally ill? What about those who are grieving, recently separated or divorced? What about those who are losing or have lost their sight, a love, a dear friend, their hearing, mental capacity, mobility?

I respond that each of us will face adversity. Sometimes that adversity will be devastating. Whatever adversity comes, I believe there is always somewhere in life where celebration can occur.

Celebration is necessary. Perhaps some celebration is even mandatory. I ask you to consider being present to celebration in your life during the brief time we spend together in this place. Perhaps a place to start is simply to celebrate the fact that you are here."

Thank you, Louise Rose, for those beautiful thoughts. They convey my thoughts and feelings exactly. The messages in the songs of "Celebration", "People Get Ready", "Feeling Groovy" and "Stand By Me" were truly uplifting and I will never forget that evening of celebration with you and your choir.

CELEBRATION IN MY LIFE

FAMILY CELEBRATIONS

Despite the fact that I have had many physical challenges in life, I have always enjoyed celebrating. Our family celebrations were always special...I will never forget our holiday gatherings with my mother playing the piano and all of us gathered around singing hymns. During W.W. II we usually had servicemen around to share our delicious meals as well. Every Sunday we always went to church, and when I was older we would bring servicemen home and then had our meal together. Birthday celebrations were special too. There were not a whole lot of gifts, but it was the occasion and celebration that mattered. I loved the camping trips with my family too.

When my folks moved to their mountain retirement cabin in Julian, everyone drove up there for the family celebrations. Celebrating my parent's 50th Anniversary (1917-1967), a year before my dad passed away, with the whole family there was a truly fun and memorable experience. When my dad passed away in 1968 and again when my mom passed away in 1975, the loss was deeply felt but what we celebrated was the legacy of love they gave us.

There were several reunions my sisters and I shared after that. One was my Uncle Lawrence's 98th Birthday and the other one was the sister reunion at Lake Tahoe in July 1989. That was the last time we were all together as Mary passed away the next year. Edith passed away in 1999. Now, the four of us that are left get together on a one to one basis on vacations or trips, as it is too hard for some to travel.

CELEBRATIONS WITH FRIENDS

Just mention briefly as these are documented under "Stretching my Wings"
China Lake with Verna, Kay, Esther, Mary Jane to Yosemite 1959
Trip to Hawaii 1958 with Claudia, Mexico 1960 with Judy
Trips to East Coast & N. Y. 1965 Pat Barrett, San Francisco with Pat Barrett (1962) Ellen (1967) Danni Burton, Ellen Orient 1968

HIGH SCHOOL REUNIONS

5th, 20th, 30th, 40th. I served on the Reunion Committee for our 50th Reunion.

CELEBRATIONS WITH TOM

Tom feels the same way about celebrating. When we got married, it was a celebration. It was not a big wedding, in fact I only had one attendant but 200 people attended. It was a celebration of friends and family, although my mother was in the hospital but she wanted us to go ahead with our scheduled plans. The reception was held in the church social hall and right afterwards Tom and I went to the hospital to visit and celebrate with my mother and sister Edith, who had stayed with my mother while the wedding, took place.

Each year we celebrate our "Meetaversary" (the day we met, July 27), our "Askaversary" (the day Tom asked me to marry him-Midnight Dec. 31st), and every year we celebrate our Anniversary by listening to a record of our wedding ceremony and again reciting our vows to one another, as well as lighting an Anniversary candle that was given to us (with Lilly of the Valley aroma), and again looking at our photo album. Of course we celebrate birthdays, holidays and everything we can think of. We love to travel, go to concerts and just have fun. Tom jokes that when he gets up in the mornings, looks in the mirror, and sees a reflection of himself, he knows that he's alive and he celebrates!

For me, every day is a celebration of hope for a wonderful day. I will admit I have had some days when I didn't always feel this way, but the grace of God has helped me to turn that around.

Tom and I celebrate life by just having each other around, praying and worshipping together, with relatives and friends, through music, art and museums, laughter, by playing with our doggie, Tao, through the beauty and wonder of nature, by talking or being silent, discussing issues, by growing together, by learning and reading, by traveling, going to the zoo, the beach, and by having fun in just about everything we do. It is important to have time apart as well.... time to spend with others, do things you need to do, errands, time to create and time to be alone with your thoughts. As Gibran said, "let there be room for spaces in your togetherness"

HOW WE HAVE FUN

Tom and I enjoy all kinds of music and concerts. Our first date was to the San Diego Symphony Summer Concert. We go to as many concerts as we possibly can afford. Our church presents a concert one a month with our choir, The Masterwork Chorale, other well known choirs from around the world, soloists, symphony members, organists, etc. My favorite is and always will be Handel's "Messiah". We enjoy classical, light opera, musical shows, New Age, Spiritual, country, jazz, etc. Artists we have seen and particularly enjoyed are John Denver, Yanni, Yo Yo Ma, Celine Dione, Sarah Brightman, Josh Groban, Charlotte Church. In my younger single days, I was able to see Ella Fitzgerald, Segovia, Carlos Montoya, Trini Lopez and the Tijuana Brass, and others.

TRIPS AND FUN

Zoo, Wild Animal Park, Sea World, camping...Roaring Fork and Frying Pan in Colorado. Best fishing

224

TRIP TO FIJI/AUSTRALIA/NEW ZEALAND/HAWAII-NOV/DEC 1985

Tom and I had always wanted to see the beauty of New Zealand as we had heard the Fjords were a great deal like the ones in Norway. Tom and I joined the tour group in Los Angeles on November 20, 1985. Upon crossing the International Dateline we lost one day en route. In the afternoon of our first day in Fiji, a wonderful sightseeing tour took us through Nadi native villages, a cultural center, shopping and the countryside. The next day a cruise ship took us to Castaway Island (one of a number of small islands that surround Fiji). We changed into our swimming suits at the beach resort and had a delightful day in the sparkling sun, the 73 degree water and beautiful white sandy beaches. A delicious smorgasbord lunch of native delicacies and fresh fruit was served. After returning to Nadi in the early evening, we got ready for a native feast of food and dancing (similar to a Luau).

The next morning our flight was to take us to Australia via Auckland, New Zealand where we would have a flight transfer. As it turned out we were delayed in Auckland for 12 hours due to maintenance problems and the airlines provided us with rooms and meals at a very nice nearby hotel. After arriving in Sydney, a train ride took us to Featherdale Wildlife Park, where we had the privilege of holding a koala. This was one of the delights of my life! They are very precious animals and we need to protect their survival. The next morning on a boat cruise around Sydney Harbor, we viewed historic waterfront homes, the Opera House and other sites. After lunch a minibus sightseeing tour took us through Sydney and the Southern Beaches, stopping at the historic "Rocks" area and other places.

The next day (Nov 26) we flew to Christchurch, New Zealand, where a bus took us across the Canterbury Plains to Geraldine, a picturesque country town, before entering MacKenzie Country where hundreds of sheep roam the hill. We were able to visit a sheep farm, where I had the delight of cradling a little lamb in my arms. On the 27th, we drove over Burke Pass to Lake Pukaki and finally ended up at Mt. Cook National Park. This pristine natural scenery is enough to take one's breath away. That evening, a Gondola Ride took us to Skyline Restaurant for our Thanksgiving dinner. The view from our window made us feel we were on top of the world and the food was delicious, including kiwi cheesecake and a whipped creme desert. On the 28th, a coach drove us across the Lindis Pass, to Lake Wanaka, Cromwell, and the rugged Kawarau Gorge, ending up in Queenstown, where we stayed at the Lakeland Regency, on Lake Esplanade. I was extremely impressed with how clear the lake water is. One could see fish as far down as the bottom.

New Zealand is very environmentally conscious. Queenstown is a delightful place, which borders the beauty of the lake, and has tall alpine-like forested mountains surrounding the town's quaint shops. The next morning's tour was to the Cattledrome, where all kinds of cattle and sheep were on display. It was a great education! Then on to Coronet Peak, where the panoramic view was awesome. We learned about the history of Arrowtown, viewed Lake Wakatipu and ended a wonderful day with a ride on the Kingston flyer, a vintage steam train.

The next day was one of the highlights of our trip - an excursion to Milford Sound! We traveled through the beech forests of Eglinton Valley and into the rugged grandeur of the Hollyford Valley before reaching Milford Sound and then a small boat took us through the majestic Fjords. It really does look like the pictures one sees of the Norwegian Fjords. On the boat cruise we saw fur seals, small penguins and multitudes of waterfalls. At Te Anau we stayed at the Fjordland Motor Lodge and viewed a most magnificent sunset before retiring for the night.

The next day included a full day of travel to Dunedin, known as the "Edinburgh of the South Pacific", where we visited the stately residence of Olveston. Again, the next day was one of traveling back to Christchurch to spend the night before our early morning flight the following day to the North Island capital city of Wellington.

Arriving in a terrible wind and rainstorm which had so much force it almost pushed us down the airplane steps, we got right on our coach. Just then the storm broke and we were able to take a tour of the city and its picturesque harbor. The afternoon was spent driving through the countryside to Palmerston, where we enjoyed a short sightseeing tour of this city before continuing through the Manawatu Gorge, to the city of Napier, which is full of flowers and gardens.

On our way to Lake Taupo the following day, we went through rugged sheep country and were stalled for some time by a traffic jam of what seemed like thousands of sheep crossing the road. We all enjoyed the time to reflect on how important sheep are to the life of this country. There is a lesson here - take time to be good stewards to all of creation; the animals, plants, the earth, the environment, including our part to create clean air, not pollute, etc.

Near Lake Taupo we stopped to see Huka Falls and the surrounding area. We took a pathway above a river gushing through a scenic gorge encased with lush ferns and trees. As the river widened, it flowed more calmly as it seemed to now be a part of the surrounding beauty instead of passing it by so fast. It reminded me of a parallel of how we live sometimes, as we rush through life so fast, that we fail to really appreciate and be a part of the present moment.

When we slow down, open ourselves wide to the beauty of the present moment, we become calm and God reveals to us many things we often overlook. We continued on through Wairakei where we had a short tour through a Geothermal Plant and ended up in Rotorua, where Natives use the steam coming from the ground to cook over the rocks. Since we had the afternoon free, Tom along with four other men rented two boats and went fishing. They came back with three huge rainbow trout (enough to feed 30 people). The hotel chef prepared them for breakfast the next morning and it was enough for a nice serving of fish for each person in our tour group

That day was full of wonderful sightseeing experiences, including the visit to a Maori Village, the Arts and Crafts Institute,

227

the Agrodome (where all breeds of sheep were displayed and we observed the shearing process), and Rainbow Springs. In the evening we enjoyed a Maori feast and concert (called Hangi). The Native dances were delightful and the singing sounded like a chorus of angels. That evening at our Hotel, Tom and I enjoyed a wonderful hot springs bath before retiring for the night.

The next day we traveled to the Waitomo Caves, where we took a boat through the canals of this world-famous Glow-worm Grotto. We found this to be most fascinating as the little creatures lit up our way through the otherwise dark cave. That afternoon we stopped at the Te Awamutu Rose Gardens, which were spectacular. We continued on through Hamilton and arrived in Auckland by early evening.

Our travels the following day led us through seaside resorts, townships, to Kawakawa and then to the picturesque Bay of Islands, where we saw abundant waterfalls, and lush scenery so beautiful, it almost takes your breath away.

We rose early the next morning for an exciting coach trip to Cape Reinga, which is at the very tip of New Zealand. The coach then took us to the beach, where we went shell hunting and found some most gorgeous samples. Then on to what was an extraordinary treat, since we live on the Pacific Ocean side of the U.S. - we viewed the meeting of the Pacific Ocean and the Tasman Sea. On the way back, we stopped at the Wegener Museum and the Waitangi National Reserve with its many Maori carvings contributed by all of the tribes of New Zealand. This was formerly the official British residence where the Maori chiefs signed the Treaty of Waitangi in 1840, settling the property dispute. The display of ancient papers and exhibits was a treasure house of Northland history. And speaking of history, as we returned on our journey, traveling next to the shoreline, we happened to see a group of Maoris in their Native Dress with a War Canoe.

The bus driver stopped so we could get some pictures but asked us not to speak to the Natives (we understood some friction still existed between the Caucasians and the Mari's due to the

British appropriation of Native property much like what we did to the American Natives). Since Tom and I are interested in other cultures and people, he went up and started talking to the Maori Chief, and found out what was happening. They were having a dress rehearsal of the next day's historic event when they would welcome voyagers arriving on a Polynesian canoe which would really be a recreation from the past to signify the first arrival of Maori Polynesian ancestors to New Zealand soil from Hawaii. The Maori 80-man War Canoe was to go out in the water and meet the Polynesians as they prepared to land. Just then the Maori Chief left Tom to start the dress rehearsal. We were fortunate to see this amazing rehearsal as the commands were issued by the Chief and the oarsmen, in a precision-like fashion brought their oars down and then up as they rowed out to sea.

We arrived back at our hotel relishing the memories of being at the right place at the right time for a once in a lifetime event.

The next morning we packed to go to Auckland to catch our return flight to the States via Hawaii. We will never forget this wonderful travel experience.

TRIP TO AUSTRALIA, SEPTEMBER 1992, (23 days)

I had become involved in the study of flower essences and when I found out the 3rd International Conference of Flower Essences was to be held in Sydney, Australia, Tom and I jumped at the chance to go. Every since our trip in 1985, we had wanted to go back and see more of Australia and this was our chance! Since we had taken a tour before, we wanted to do it ourselves this time and some dear friends who knew what we were looking for referred a travel agency to us. Our travel agent turned out to be a lady who had lived in Australia when her husband had worked there and she knew all the "right" places to send us after we told her what we wanted.

We flew from San Diego to L.A. where we boarded a Qantas flight that took us to Australia, and from there we had a few stops at different airports to change planes. We finally arrived in Tasmania 32 hours later.

LAUNCESTON; WILDLIFE; CRADLE MOUNTAIN LODGE

We rented a car and drove to Launceston where we stayed at a country club with a lovely swan swimming on a pond in front. The next day on the way to our destination we stopped at a Wildlife Park with kangaroos, wallabies, koalas, wombats and Tasmanian devils. We actually held a wombat, koala and petted a Tasmanian devil as the caretaker held it. This animal is a story in contradictions. It is very ferocious and carnivorous and yet the fur feels like silk thread. We arrived at the Cradle Mountain Lodge, a scenic mountain resort with cabins and a lodge where we shared communal meals. It had snowed which made the beautiful scenery even more beautiful. We even built a fire in our fireplace that night. The wildlife was fascinating. An Australian wild cat was in the woodpile outside our cabin. We also saw a furry possum (which is totally different from those in the U.S.)

OUR VISIT TO TASMANIA ENDS

We went on through Stratham, Queenstown, Silver Hills (where we saw the land stripped of trees and totally barren, almost like a bomb had devastated the area. It showed us what happens when we are not good caretakers of the land). We saw other places where clear cutting had occurred and it was a real lesson on the eco-system as we saw some dead skinny animals that needed the vegetation to survive. Then we drove on to Hartz Mountain National Park for the day (which was like going through an enchanted park with huge Eucalyptus trees that had been there forever) and to Hobart for the night. The next day we turned in our rental car and took a small plane to Portland on the mainland.

AN AUSTRALIAN SHEEP RANCH

In Victoria at the Grampians National Park we saw aboriginal rock paintings and then drove on to the Glensia Homestead, where we stayed with an Australian family at their sheep ranch and ate at the table with three other couples staying there.

MELBOURNE AND FAIRY PENGUINS

We drove on to Melbourne and stayed at a Bed and Breakfast Inn. The shopping market they have in Melbourne is covered with a big tarp and goes on and on for about a mile and houses all kinds of merchants where one can get tremendous bargains. Needless to say, we didn't miss this one! South of Melbourne on Phillips's Island we saw the fairy penguins parade in from the ocean in the evening.

SNOWY MOUNTAINS

The next day we drove through the Snowy Mountains, which took so long that we had to spend the night at an alternate lodge, which had been referred to us in case the snow held us up. However, the drive was worth it as we saw miles and miles of pristine snow, which looked like a winter wonderland.

CANBERRA

Our next stop was Mariner's Lodge at Bateman Bay, where we enjoyed walking along the seashore. We went on to Canberra where we stayed at the Forest Motor Inn and saw the most awesome Botanical Gardens ever as well as the Ginninderra Falls. We were sightseeing in our rental car, when we lost our way, and all of a sudden found ourselves riding down the middle of a racecar track. Thank goodness here were no races going on!

PETTING A JOEY IN THE POUCH

Australia has public rest rooms due to the wide open spaces where one can drive for great distances without seeing anything but wildlife. At one of these stops there happened to be a herd of kangaroos. One of the females was carrying a baby in her pouch. I know these kangaroos are strong and can kill with one wallop, but that didn't even enter my mind at the time, as I had no fear whatsoever. My intuition took over as I was fascinated and had an inclination to pet the Joey. I started talking to the mama just like she was a person and asked for permission to pet her Joey, and if this was not agreeable to her, she was to give me a negative sign. I walked very slowly towards her, talking in a very respectful voice. She stood straight up as I approached. I reached my hand slowly towards the pouch and petted the Joey's head. It was very soft. I then backed away very slowly; thanking the mama for the wonderful privilege and telling her what a beautiful Joey she had produced. We went on to see the Rehwinkel's Animal Park, where we roamed among the animals, through the natural bush land, and gardens by the lakes.

BLUE MOUNTAINS

The next day we traveled on to Bathurst and saw the Blue Mountains where we took a tram that went so fast from such a high distance to a low area that it seemed our eyeballs would pop out. However, we saw some waterfalls that were spectacular. We stayed at the Jenolan Caves House, a hotel built atop a cave, which we toured. The flowers were spectacular, Eighty percent of the species and thirty percent of the genera of Australian flora are found nowhere else in the world.

FLOWER ESSENCE CONFERENCE

The Conference was held Friday evening, Saturday and Sunday, September 18-20, 1992, in Manly Beach, a picturesque beach resort near Sydney. Leading researchers and flower essence practitioners around the world, which offered a rich diversity of theory and practical application, held workshops and Seminars. We learned so much about the ability of flower essences to resolve negative emotions and beliefs and their ability to heal at the physical level as well as deeper levels, such as the sub-conscious. At the

Friday evening session, a group of Aboriginal Elders spoke to us and explained how their ancestors had passed down the information of how the flower essences are used to heal and how they, in turn, had the same experience of healing with the native flowers. I was so enthused that I decided to take the intensive training to be held in the high sierras in July 1993 with the Flower Essences Services. As explained in Chapter 7, I did so and after a six month research documentation of my work, I became a Certified Flower Essence Practitioner.

CAIRNS

We flew to Cairns and stayed at the Silky Oaks Lodge where we had a beautiful Swiss-like chalet with a balcony overlooking the river, in a Far North Queens land National Park in the middle of the Daintree Rain forest. Flowers and wildlife were in abundance. This place was like paradise! Every day we went on an individual tour. One day we took a Daintree River Cruise, where we saw crocodiles, then visited Mossman Gorge and Port Douglas before returning to Cairns. The next day we took a tour to the Great Barrier Reef and those so inclined went scuba diving. It was awesome to see the underwater beauty. A full day touring the Atherton Tablelands on the scenic train journey to Kuranda was in store for us the next day. In Kuranda we attended an Aboriginal Dance Theater by the Tjapukai Dancers, which was not only educational but also aesthetically enchanting. On the way, we passed spectacular waterfalls and tropical plants. We saw Dinner Falls, Crater Lake and Milla Milla Falls. On the way back, we cruised on Lake Barrine with full commentary by our guide as we passed some 500 species of trees and wildlife, which abound along the shores.

Our favorite trip was a wilderness safari in a 4-wheel drive vehicle, in the Daintree Wilderness Rain forest, where growth is so dense it has been intact for 135 million years. Our guide took us to a fig tree, which was larger than our home and was in existence at the time of Christ. I was so awed that as soon as I got back to our Lodge, I wrote a poem, which reflected my feelings as I saw this beautiful majestic tree. It symbolizes the majesty, love and oneness, which come to us from our Creator:

POEM-REFLECTIONS OF ONENESS

AS I STAND HERE UNDER THIS MAJESTIC TREE, I FEEL
THE VIBRATIONS OF MILLIONS OF YEARS OF BEING ONE
WITH NATURE AND WITH THEE.

MY LIFE IS ENTWINED WITH ALL LIVING THINGS BEFORE
ME, ALL LIVING THINGS IN THE PRESENT AND THOSE IN
THE FUTURE, AS THE ROOTS OF THIS TREE ARE
ENTWINED WITH THE TRUNKS AND ROOTS OF
OTHER TREES AND VINES.

I LOOK TO FIND THE TOP OF THE TREE AND FIND IT IS SO
HIGH IT HAS BECOME ONE WITH THE SKY. I LOSE ALL
SENSE OF PROPORTION AND DIMENSION TO MY BODY AS
I MELT INTO THE WONDER OF THIS MOMENT.

I HEAR THE BIRDS, THE SOUNDS OF OTHER ANIMALS
AND THE WATER GUSHING OVER THE ROCKS. THE SCENT
OF FLOWERS AND LEAVES AFTER THE RECENT
DOWNPOUR OF RAIN SURROUNDS MY BEING WITH
CLEANSING AND FRESHNESS.

I REALIZE I AM ONE WITH ALL AND THEE, AND WE ARE
ALL ONE IN THEE-REFLECTIONS OF ONE ANOTHER AND
REFLECTIONS OF THEE,
　　　　　AS IS THIS MAJESTIC TREE.

By Nancy T. Burk

The next day we reluctantly departed for the return trip back
home, never forgetting this once in a lifetime trip to a "land down
under" full of enchanting creatures, flora and fauna and wonderful
surprises each day.
zabaglione with marsala
Prawn and apple in lemon mayonnaise
Filet steak mushroom sauce

TRIP 1993 TO NORTHERN CALIFORNIA AND OREGON

We camped on our property in Oregon, saw sister Charlotte and family in Dallas, Oregon and sisters Edith and Carol and husbands. On the way back we stopped at a California State Park where Birney Falls is located and due to the heavy rainfall, the falls were the fullest they had been in some time.

TRIP TO CANADA, JULY 1995

In 1995, after Tom retired from Qualcomm, We immediately took off in our motor home for a three-month vacation. On the way to our Oregon property we saw Nancy's sister Edith and her husband Carl. Then we stopped to see Nancy's sister Charlotte and her husband Bud and other relatives in Dallas, Oregon. We traveled two months in Canada (mostly B.C., Jasper national park, lake Louise and Banff). Some of the highlights included Butchart Gardens, a ferry trip from Port Hardy on Vancouver Island to Prince Rupert on the mainland where we saw glaciers and beautiful scenery (about 600 miles), lots of wildlife including moose, elk, deer, bear, rocky mountain goats and bald eagles. In one campsite a bald eagle flew into the tree above us and stayed for some time, then soared off - what a sight to behold! We spent one night 500 feet from the foot of a glacier but were nice and toasty in our motor home. The scenery was spectacular-trees all over, sub alpine meadows where wildflowers were profuse. At Mt. Revelstoke one of the forest guides even asked Nancy to give a mini workshop on flower essences. We saw many, rivers, lakes, waterfalls (our Christmas postcard was taken by Bijou Falls in B.C.) We went into Hyder, Alaska and went up the Alaskan highway to ft. St. John but turned around due to bad weather.

We came back into the states via Idaho and camped in many of the campgrounds Nancy's parents took her to as a child, such as Sugar Loaf Island on Cascade Lake where Tom caught 2 steel heads and a number of rainbow trout. We spent several nights at Sun Valley and saw Elvis Stojko and other stars at the ice show as well as a jazz fest and our friend Joe Fos, who plays the piano in the lounge at the lodge. In Oregon we spent some time at Union Creek campground and then went to our property where we found lots of delicious ripe blackberries to eat.

CAMPING TRIP TO NORTHERN CALIFORNIA, OREGON, WASHINGTON 1996

Just five weeks after my artificial hip implant surgery; we took off on our vacation and saw Mt. St. Helens in Washington, saw sister Charlotte in Dallas, Oregon and then camped on our property, as well as camping with friends Mary and Cecil Wade. We saw the Daffins and Huckabys on the way back in Grass Valley, California.

VACATION TO HAWAII (MAUI) 1997

On our trip to Hawaii in 1978, tom and I saw all the islands except Maui, and we had always wanted to go back and see this island. So in March, we decided to go since we had an opportunity for a free condo in Oahu for three days and then we flew on to Maui where we rented a car and toured the island. We really enjoyed the drive up to the volcano Haleakala and going through Iao Valley. The lush beauty of the drive to Hana with waterfalls, flowers and ferns around every corner provided many backgrounds for taking pictures We really took our time and just relaxed, taking in all the beauty of this wonderful island,

TRIP TO OREGON, AND IDAHO 1998

This trip included our property and favorite places in Oregon as well as going to Idaho. We went directly to Idaho and camped along the Salmon River, Then we went to Sun Valley and saw Joe Fos at the Lodge and the Ice Show with Surya Bonalei (sp?) and a lot of other ice Stars.

The most memorable time was at Bonner's Ferry, where we got the last campsite available as they had a re-enactment of pioneers crossing the Snake River in covered wagons. Everyone was dressed in 1890's clothing, Native American guides led the group and the crossing was as historically correct as it could be. One wagon was even caught by the swift river currents and tipped over, but the occupants, including an Idaho Senator were soon rescued.

On the way back to our property, we stopped at an Oregon campground where we met some terrific people, Carol and Terry Richards, who were camped right across from us. On the back of their motor home was a sign, "Heart transplant in '89, spending my extra time". We got acquainted and they joined us later for a campfire songfest of hymns. Terry played the harmonica and Carol had an electronic keyboard, as she played the piano for the church they belonged to.

We had a wonderful time and the next morning we took down names, addresses and phone numbers and departed on our separate ways. They were going east to La Grande to see Carol's mother and we were heading west with the next planned stop at Paradise Campground, McKenzie Bridge (one of our favorite campgrounds). As it turned out McKenzie Bridge is where they lived.
`We arrived at Paradise Campground, got our site and I was sitting in a chair outside when this minivan drove up and this young lady with two kids got out. She came up to me and said, "Are you Nancy Burk?" Well, I was stunned to say the least, because I didn't recognize her. It turned out she was Carol's daughter, Denise and Carol had called her from La Grande, telling her what kind of a motor home we had and to go to the campground and find us. Carol wanted us to use their other car, while we were camped there, so we could go sightseeing and not have to use our motor home and move it. Here we were, being offered the use of a car and the owners didn't even know that much about us .We were honored to think that Carol and Terry trusted us that much. We followed Denise back to their property and picked up the car, which we used with great care. We

went to their church on Sunday before we returned the car and left on our way.

That was the start of a beautiful friendship that continues to this day. We enjoyed camping with Carol and Terry on several camping trips after that. Terry passed away in 2000 and Carol remarried Jim Lauman in September 2002. I regret we could not attend the wedding but I was laid up with my broken pelvis at the time.

TRIP TO NORTHERN CALIFORNIA, OREGON AND WASHINGTON 1999

We love traveling in our 1998 class a motor home (Rexhall Vision, 26 feet). It has a queen size bed, large shower and raised toilet to accommodate my joint implants as well as rails inside and out to help me. As soon as doctors gave their permission we were off - left June 16 and got back Sept. 16. Traveled around northern California, (Big Sur area where we honeymooned in 1970), Oregon and Washington.

We were camped at the thousand trails campground in Leavenworth, Washington and were just coming back from a walk when we saw this couple trying to get in our motor home. It turned out they had just bought a Rexhall Vision, just like ours and mistook our motor home for theirs. Well we got acquainted with Trudy and Bob Roswald and have enjoyed meeting them at different campgrounds and the Rexhall Rallies every since. In fact we ended up camping next to them at the La Conner Thousand Trails campground.

On the way back to our Oregon property, Tom was able to get some fishing done. We saw relatives as well as went to concerts and fairs. For my birthday in Oregon tom got me an adorable Shih Tzu puppy (we named him Tao) that was born in June. He was 8 weeks old when we got him and he loves traveling. We both love him and he is a great therapy aid!

The manufacturer of our motor home (Rexhall) have a rally every year in Lancaster, Ca, where their plant is located. It is held at the fairgrounds and we planned to go and meet friends that we became acquainted with on our summer trip and camp next to them. We camped on the grass with a shade tree overhead and the temp was 75 with a nice breeze. We had a terrific time, met so many new friends. Rexhall treated us royally by having a maintenance crew check each rig's appliances for free, having workshops and seminars, and along with the club's officers provided fabulous food and parties. Tom even won a $50 Rexhall jacket and he even got me one like it.

CELEBRATIONS IN 2000 INCLUDING SIX MONTH TRIP TO EAST COAST

In February we spent 5 days at the ABH Hypnotherapy conference in Irvine and the last of February spent a week in Las Vegas at the Monte Carlo hotel. We were there with lots of friends to celebrate the retirement of Orlin Stansfield. His wife, Barbara gave him a tremendous party at the Bell Agio and needless to say we all had a great time. Tom and I went to see the great Tommie Tune musical at the MGM Grand and the David Cassidy musical at the Rio.

In March we settled our income tax, made preparations for traveling (forwarding of mail, maintenance checkups for us and for motor home, etc) and April 15 took off in our motor home with Tao, our Shi Tzu, for a 26 state, 6 months trip.

At our first stop in Tucson, AZ we visited with Shirley (H.S. Chum) and Bob Miner and had a delicious southwestern brunch. In phoenix we visited with Pat Barrett and had a wonderful surprise from her sister Geri who was there visiting as well. (Both H.S. Chums). We stayed a week in Verde Valley, AZ at the Thousand Trails Camp, and took a 4-hour train ride into the canyon country and attended a chuck wagon BBQ dinner and western show at the "Blazing M" Ranch. We went to Prescott to visit with Carol (college chum) and Jerry Munford and attended Maundy Thursday service at

239

the Methodist church where Carol is co-pastor. Easter Sunday we got up early and went to sunrise service where Carol delivered a wonderful sermon. Then we had breakfast with their family and went to the 9:30 service. Our stay in Arizona ended with a beautiful drive to Sedona and Flagstaff.

In New Mexico we stayed at a state park for a week in Albuquerque and visited with Marie Stockton, daughter, Darbi and grandsons Sawyer and Tanner. Sawyer (4 yrs) is a very precocious, little "man" and way ahead of his age. We got a kick out of him providing us with details on things we were not aware of. We spent 6 days visiting Barb (H.S. Chum) and Larry Germain and celebrated our 30th anniversary with them. Barb and Larry (both are retired nuclear physicists) were wonderful tour guides and took us to old town, to the Albuquerque natural museum, Bandalier national monument where we saw a pueblo village, Los Alamos (1 week before the terrible fire) and spent a whole day in Santa Fe where we saw cathedrals, art galleries, museums and went from one shop to the next wide eyed and entranced with the beautiful collectibles. We saw a huge rose quartz geode that must have weighed 100-150 lbs and cost $8,000. We brought it back with us (the photo, I mean). They also took us to a chamber music concert and to the Albuquerque symphony whose guest was yoyo ma (one of our highlights). We enjoyed eating all kinds of Mexican foods fixed in a variety of ways. Barb and Larry's home overlooks Albuquerque and has a beautiful view. They are collectors and the visit to their home was a cultural and artistic education and celebration in itself. Our last day we took the scenic tram ride to Sandia Peak.

Next came Texas and miles and miles. Our first nice visit was to Medina Lake, a TTN campground where there were lots of deer. Tao and the deer kept eyeing each other. From there we went to San Antonio to see the Alamo, tower, the beautiful riverwalk and sunken gardens. We then went to Fredericksburg and saw the LBJ ranch and in Austin saw Lady Bird's wildflower garden. At wild basin we went to a great all day music festival where every couple of hours different artists were featured playing their guitars and singing. We were at the TTN lake Conroe campground, near Houston when we got word that mom Burk had passed away. The

240

manager at lake Conroe was very understanding and said we could leave our motor home there while we went back to San Diego.

We rented a Pontiac Grand Am with air conditioning and cruise control and took off with our little dog. Days Inn allows pets and we were able to make it to San Diego in 2 1/2 days.

Mom Burk had lived a good long life (92 years) and at the time we left in April was living by herself. After the memorial service the whole family had a big celebration of her life at the Boathouse. Tom was executor of the estate and since there was a trust he was able to take care of most of the estate division within two weeks and we then left to go back to Texas to pick up our motor home and go on with our trip. We celebrated Tom's birthday in Texas and went through the top of Louisiana. We had previously planned to go to New Orleans and Disneyworld in Florida but because of going back to San Diego had to cut 2 weeks off our previous itinerary.

We stopped in Vicksburg, Miss. And went to the national military park. This is a very historic place, which turned the tide in favor of the union forces during the civil war. We saw many beautiful ante-bellum mansions, one of which had a cannonball still embedded in the wall. A plantation owner was having a big ball when the union forces snuck up and surprised them. We were struck by the beauty and opulence of the mansions and their interior furnishings while still abhorring the lifestyle, which allowed the rich owners to have their mansions at the expense of human beings being enslaved. We also took a boat cruise on the "mighty Mississippi".

In Alabama we stopped at Looney's Tavern and saw an outdoor musical about an historic event, which depicts the drama between the southern mountain people and the rich plantation owners over the secession issue. The next day we visited De Soto Caverns and saw a beautiful underground laser show. Then we visited De Soto Falls State Park and the picture on our Christmas card was taken at De Soto falls in northern Alabama.

Throughout the northern part of Georgia there are beautiful state parks and waterfalls. Among those we visited or stayed at were: Amacalola Falls, Anna Ruby Falls, Tallulah falls, Toccata Falls and Twin Lakes. A wonderful visit with Nancy's relatives, Paula and Bob Daffin and their daughter Oksana, topped off our stay in Georgia. We traveled through South Carolina but didn't have time to stay there, as we wanted to reach Burlington, North Carolina, in time for Nancy's sister Ruth's birthday.

Ruth and Cal Pollard's son Harold and his wife, Louise, hosted a marvelous birthday party for Ruth at their home with the whole family in attendance, except their daughter Nell, who was in California at the time. Of course Ruth, Cal and daughter Gayle were there and we saw Harold and Louise's daughters Tucker and Elizabeth and Ruth and Cal's other son, Scott and his wife Pat as well as Tucker's boyfriend and Louise's mother. We enjoyed three days with Ruth, Cal and Gayle. While there we stayed at the Greensboro campground and lost our awning to heavy rain (5 inches of rain in one hour), but we ordered another one and had it put on in Virginia.

Our next stop was Virginia Beach, VA. We stayed at a state park and it was the first time Nancy had seen the Atlantic Ocean. We saw some outstanding sunsets. We visited the Association for Research and Enlightenment (A.R.E.), The Edgar Cayce organization where Nancy ran into one of her San Diego fiends who was there attending the annual congress. Nancy had a wonderful reflexology treatment while we were there as well. Then we went to the Chesapeake Bay TTN campground and had more rain.

After a night at the Westmoreland state park we went to the very pretty Bull Run county campground, which is close to Centreville, Arlington and Fairfax Station, where Nancy's Niece Barbara Palmquist lives. We had a grand time visiting with Barb and Ed and one day they had us over for a great family dinner and we saw daughters Tara and Tracey, her husband Drew and little Emma (a little over 1 year old at the time). We were there for the 4th of July and saw some tremendous fireworks with Barb and Ed. A ride in the Blue Ridge Mtns. completed our stay.

Then on to West Virginia where we stayed at Bluestone Lake and in Kentucky stayed at Cumberland falls state park. We saw some of the Smoky Mtns. And stayed at Norris dam, where we saw an Appalachian village and center. What beautiful scenery surrounds this part of the country!

Then we went on to Oak Ridge, Tennessee, Where we stayed with Orlin and Barb Stansfield and saw Joyce Stilwell (friends who used to live in San Diego). Our dog Tao had fun rubbing noses with Joyce's two dogs. Barb and Orlin took us to the Oak Ridge lab, where Orlin used to work and sightseeing around the area.

Of course you haven't lived until you've eaten at the Cross-Eyed Cricket Restaurant. We had a fun filled day at Dollywood, seeing shows, shopping and eating.

Then we had to leave for our 3 day reservation at the KOA Opryland which included camping, one night at the Grand Old Opry, a buffet lunch on the General Sherman Showboat and cruise on the Cumberland and a tour of Nashville. We spent two nights at Loretta Lynn's Campground and Ranch and saw her colonial mansion, "Coal Miner's Daughter".

Then on to Arkansas where we spent the night at Fort Smith lake state park. We spent the next night in Hot Springs, Ark and woke up to weather that was 110 degrees with 100% humidity. Needless to say, it didn't take us too long to pack up and head north. We were on our way to Eureka Springs when a wind wave going about 90 miles an hour hit us and lifted our motorhome right up and put it down in the next lane. We were on a country road and thank god there was no other traffic. Trees were falling everywhere but God was with us. It lasted about 20 min. And then stopped suddenly.

Arkansas is one of the best places to find quartz crystals and so we bought some more. We got settled in our campground in Eureka Springs and stayed there for 4 nights. We saw some beautiful botanical gardens, took a tour around the city, took a train ride and saw Pine Mountain Jamboree. However, the highlight was the outdoor passion play and watching "the potter" while he made

243

clay vases at the same time he told the story of the "Master Potter Jesus'.

On the surrounding grounds, there is a chapel, which has artifacts and furnishings donated by every single denomination from around the world, a museum, which has every kind of Bible from the Guttenberg Bible on, and another building with sacred art. The grounds are continually being expanded to include a lot of old and New Testament scenes. It is set off by a 60-foot plaster of paris statue of Christ called "the Christ of the Ozarks" which overlooks the valley. On Sunday we went to church at the Thorncrown chapel in Eureka Springs. This area is a "must see" for anyone traveling near here.

We spent a night at Bull Shoals River Campground and then on to Springfield, Mo. Where we stayed with longtime friends, Darlene and Bob Wilson. (Darlene was the matron of honor at our wedding). We celebrated their 31st wedding anniversary with them. They gave us a tour of the whole area and then took us to Branson where we had a dinner cruise (delicious prime rib) and terrific show on the "Branson Belle".

One day we went to Fantastic Caverns, which are the only underground caverns to drive people through by jeep and carts. Then what is a summer without a good old fashion country Missouri fair? We had a terrific time.

We traveled through Illinois and went to Milwaukee, Wisconsin, Where Tom grew up. We saw his old home, school and the lake where he used to ice skate in the winter. It had been 38 years since he had been back here and he found a lot of changes.

We then went to Kenosha where we visited with Margaret and Jorge Placentia, friends who used to live in San Diego. From there we went to Pine River Wisconsin where we visited Dorothy Burk, Tom's sister-in-law and her son Jim, his wife and children. While living in Wisconsin, Tom had always wanted to visit Wisconsin Dells but never did, so we decided to make up for it. We spent a whole day taking two boat cruises so we could see the upper and lower dells and both of us thoroughly enjoyed the unique rocks and scenery.

We stopped in Zumbrota, Minn. To see Art and Bev (Nancy's H.S. Chum) Olson and had a wonderful visit. Then we went on to Bloomington, to see Earl (Tom's Brother) and Evelyn Burk. They took us to a delicious Italian restaurant. The next day we finally got to see the mall of America that everyone has talked about so much. It is Disneyland, Legoland, Camp Snoopy, eateries, music and shopping all in one.

After we got back it was good just to relax and enjoy talking to Evelyn and Earl in their nice home. That night we got to see their son Jeff and his children, Connor and Jack. While there we stayed at a nearby campground and at 11 pm our last night, the campground host came around and asked everyone to go to the storm cellar immediately. Nancy had just gotten undressed for bed, so hurriedly we got her clothes back on, took our doggie and spent the next hour huddled together with 80 people. Then we got news the tornado had landed 20 miles to the east of us so we could go back to our motor home. Another adventure to add to our experiences!

We got to South Dakota at the same time as the biker's were holding their annual rally at Sturgis and found ourselves surrounded by 600,000 motorcycle riders. Nancy even got a Harley t-shirt to prove it. It was really interesting! We saw the badlands and Nancy had never seen Mt. Rushmore and found it a most awesome sight. We drove through the state park, saw lots of buffalo and wildlife and camped at the lake nearby. The next day we traveled through the rest of South Dakota, Nebraska, and a corner of Wyoming to reach Colorado.

In Colorado we drove through beautiful mountains and scenery and camped at Canyon land state park. Our first visit was near Denver, to see Jim Bates, (a hypnotherapist friend) and his family. We stayed at Castle Rock campground, near Colorado Springs. The next night we stayed in Pike's Peak National Forest and then to Buena Vista to see our friend Penni Evans. We had a wonderful visit and had fun eating out at different places even though it was raining a lot. We drove through historic Leadville and camped at lake Granby in the Rocky Mountains

Then on to Wyoming, camping at Riverton after seeing lots of open range, Prairie Dogs and Antelope. We camped at a national forest camp near Yellowstone where a black bear was clearly visible to us all. The ranger pointed out that we should keep all our food, etc. Inside. The firefighters were camped at the campground across the road and you could hear the helicopters with fire retardent taking off day and night.

The next night we stayed at Tower Falls Campground in Yellowstone after driving around the upper circle seeing lots of beautiful falls, scenery and wildlife. Then we went out the east gate as we had plans to visit friends in Powell. On the way we drove through a part of Montana where rangers were closing campgrounds due to fire danger. In Powell we saw Verna Rogers and sister Bernita and Esther and Steve Nemeth. Nancy used to work with Verna and Esther for the navy at China Lake back in 1957. It was a fun reunion.

The next day we went back to Yellowstone and took in the lower circle viewing the geysers and spending the night at canyon campground. The south gate had been reopened after the fire danger was quelled and we were able to drive through the Teton's where some campgrounds were still closed and you could smell the thick smoke as well as see some of the fires still burning across the lake. In Jackson Hole we saw the musical big river and went to a Chuck Wagon BBQ Dinner and Western Show.

In Idaho we headed for Sun Valley where Joe Fos and his Trio were playing at the Sun Valley lodge and we had tickets to the ice show where Alexei Yagudin, 2000 world champion and Sasha Cohen, U.S. Silver medalist were featured along with many other ice skating professionals. Joe and his trio played for the buffet dinner that preceded the ice show. When he saw Nancy come in he started playing "happy birthday" for her. (We were there over Labor Day weekend while Nancy celebrated her big "65".)

In the Sun Valley parking lot a big motor home pulled up alongside us and tom got to talking to the people, it turns out they were from Boise and knew Gene Sullivan, Nancy's cousin that she had not seen in 50 years. They gave us the phone # and as we drove through Boise stopped and saw Gene and his wife Joni. What a reunion!

Then we went on to Oregon, stopping at the TTN campground in Bend. The next day we arrived at our beautiful property in Murphy in time to go to the last summer concert at Riverside Park. The next day we saw our friend Mary Wade and went to dinner at one of our favorite places, "the Applegate Ranch". Then we took off 5 days to Stewart State Park, Union Creek and Elk Creek so Tom could fish and he caught some delicious trout. We went back to our property and went out with Mary Wade again to another dinner favorite, "Si Casa Flores". Tom had missed his glasses and we looked all over the motor home. He had a dream that night that they were at Elk Creek Campground where he fished in the Rogue River, so the next day we went back there. The campground host said the glasses had not been turned in so Tom went to his fishing spot and there they were - in his glass case floating in the Rogue River. The chances of that happening are second to none! Two days had gone by - what a miracle we found them!

Then we headed north and camped at Delta Campground, Cougar Reservoir, a beautiful spot. From there we went on to another one of our favorites - Paradise Campground near McKenzie Bridge, where we visited with our friend Carol Richards and her family who had us over for a delicious dinner. While there, we went to the Community Church where Carol is one of the pianists for the service. We went on to spend 2 days at Detroit Lake, where Tom caught more fish.

On to Washington where we stayed at TTN Chehalis campground and then Lake Pleasant, near Seattle, where we attended the Hypnotherapy conference and heard Michael Newton, well known therapist and author. After the conference we met Sharon and Sam Sullivan (Nancy's other cousin that she hadn't seen in 50 years) for a dinner reunion. Then we went back to Oregon and stayed at Salem where we rented a car and visited with Nancy's sister Charlotte in Dallas for several days and took her out to eat, etc. We spent one last night at our property in Murphy and were blessed to see a deer on our land before we left and regretfully said good-by to Oregon until next year.

We finally crossed the border into Ca. where we spent one night at a campground by Shasta Lake. Then on to a TTN campground "Lake Of The Springs" which is close to relatives at Grass Valley. We saw Carl Daffin, Nancy's brother-in-law, who had just had knee surgery and was in the hospital and stayed one night with Carol (Nancy's sister) and Don Huckaby. They have a very scenic view of the area from their balcony and it was nice relaxing out there. While in the area, we went out to dinner and visited with Carol and Ray Beckett. Nancy worked with Carol for the navy back in the early 1960's. We hadn't seen either of them since our wedding in 1970.

Joan (Nancy's cousin) and Larry Brady let us put our motor home in their driveway while visiting with them for several days in Sonoma. Larry is the perfect tour guide as he is a limousine driver and knows the best restaurants and the history of the area from way back. He took us for a wonderful wine tour where we had an unparalleled view of the beautiful rolling hills and valley. Nancy hadn't seen Joan for about 40 years and this was the first time we had met Larry, so there was a lot of catching up to do.

Then it was on to TTN campground Soledad Canyon where we had arranged to meet Trudy and Bob Roswald, friends we met at a TTN campground in Washington last year and who have a motor home like ours. We went on together to Lancaster for the 5-day Rexhall International Motor Home Rally. We had a great time with Trudy and Bob and seeing friends from the rally last year like Ron and Judy Planck and making new friends as well. The club did a wonderful job as did Rexhall in making sure there was plenty of seminars and tips on motor home traveling, food, and fun. We all had a blast at the "splish splash bash" theme party where we all acted like we were in our second childhood. More fun !!!!!

Well we finally arrived home (we traveled 15,000 miles) to find it safe and sound, thanks to good neighbors and relatives who checked on it while we were gone. We are still in the process of sorting out things we got while gone (we have 28 rolls of film and about 30 videotapes).

Sometimes we get tired of the sorting so we go off and relax. We saw "Thoroughly Modern Millie" at the La Jolla playhouse and Joe fos came into town for a 3 weeks engagement as the lounge pianist at the "Hollywood Star and Grill". We saw him with friends, Marilyn and Bill Kneeland and Carol and Ed Blum, a number of times, including his birthday party where about 150 people were crowded in to celebrate with him and birthday cake was provided for all. The music for the evening included soloists from the opera, starlight, S.D. Symphony and a young prodigy, a 14-year-old male who played both the piano and the violin. You could hear a pin drop he was so amazing!

This year our guidewords were: "we trust in God, we listen to God and we take guided action from God". Many times on our trip we weren't quite sure what to do or which direction to go because of weather, conflicting information or schedules. We held hands and prayed and the right answer always came.

TRIP IN 2001 TO B.C.
ON THE WAY UP

We spent three wonderful days with Judy and Jim Vaughan in Fortuna where we met 14 wonderful people and had a great ham and turkey meal. When you are in a city or town it is such a reward to meet some of the local residents. All of them had warm wishes for us as we go on our way. Jim drove us to all the surrounding towns as far north as Trinidad where we stopped for a snack of shrimp and soup. It hit the spot. On our way back we saw McKinley Ville, Samoa & Eureka.

Then on the way in Oregon, we stopped to visit my oldest sister, Charlotte and help her celebrate her birthday at her daughter and son-in-law's home.

We spent the next night in a campground in Port Angeles and then took the ferry to Victoria. The good news is 66 cents U.S. = $1 Canadian

IN VICTORIA

We spent five days in Victoria, staying at the Fort Victoria Campground and did the entire tourist things plus. Walked around the downtown streets went to the Empress Hotel, Royal British Columbia Museum (this is a great museum, a must on any trip) spent a day resting and at night we went to Saanich at the University of Victoria for a most wonderful music night of celebration. There were over one hundred people in the choir and nine in the band. Sunday we visited Butchart Gardens. All the flowers were in bloom except the roses so we will have to go back again on our return to Victoria and see the roses, but the rest of the flowers were so beautiful that it keeps one busy seeing as much as one can. Up north here the sun sets around 9:15 or so and the sky is still blue at 10:00 PM. The weather is cold at night around 10°C but up to 20°C in the daytime.

TO NANAIMO

We spent the night at the Rondalyn Resort between Ladysmith and Nanaimo. The next morning we drove to Nanaimo and stopped at the Living Forest Oceanside Campground. Nanaimo is the second largest place on the Island and they have a Wal-Mart, Costco, Home Depot but no Safeway. The weather was around 23-24°C with a slight breeze.

We went shopping and stopped at the bakery for a Nanaimo bar, and found it was just so delicious that we had to share the recipe with you that we found in a brochure.

NANAIMO BAR

Bottom Layer
1/2c. UNSALTED BUTTER (EURO-STYLE CULTURED)
1/4 c. SUGAR
5 tbsp. COCOA
1 EGG, BEATEN
1 3/4C. GRAHAM WAFER CRUMBS
1/2C. FINELY CHOPPED ALMONDS
1C. COCONUT

Melt first three ingredients in top of double boiler
Add egg and stir to cook and thicken.
Remove from heat. Stir in crumbs, coconut and nuts.
Press firmly into an ungreased 8x8 pan.

Second Layer
1/2c. Unsalted butter
2 tbsp. & 2tsb cream
2 tbsb. Vanilla custard powder
2c. Icing sugar

Cream butter, cream, custard powder and icing sugar
together well. Beat until light. Spread over bottom layer.

Third Layer
4 squares semi-sweet chocolate (1 oz each)
2 tbsp. unsalted butter

Melt chocolate and butter over low heat. cool.
When cool, but still liquid, pour over second layer and chill in
refrigerator.

By Joyce Hardcastle

We would make some slight changes to this like sweet milk chocolate, less coconut, different types of nuts, and maybe cream cheese in place of the custard filling.

GOLD RIVER

Since we left we have been to Gold River (at the west side of the island) there we learned about the history of native peoples, the Nootka and the Tribes were the Mowachaht/Muchalaht. The Yuquot project, in 1966, conducted by 2 men of Parks Canada documented archeological evidence of continuous habitation of these tribes for a least 4,300 years. Yuquot (friendly cove) is the site of this evidence, which proves that this area was inhabited long before the arrival of the first Europeans. The innate wisdom of these peoples and how they lived off the land but in harmony with it, their villages and how they constructed their houses, is really very interesting. It appears they have an Asian or Mongolian origin.

From Gold River we saw Buttle Lake and stayed at Strathcona Provincial ark (Ralph River). The incredible beauty of the blue lake against the background of lush green-forested majestic mountains, some that are still snowcapped is awesome. It presents one with an opportunity to not only take a camera picture but also a mental picture to bring back to mind when one is stressed by the challenges of city life.

STAMP RIVER PROVISIONAL PARK.

It is Tuesday, 26 June 2001; I am sitting in our campsite. amidst the lush green forest with ferns and undergrowth surrounding us.. A meandering path of about 25 feet leads to the Stamp River so the sound of the water rushing downstream can be heard from where we are. The river water is very clear and you can see the rocks on the bottom. The sunlight splashes varied colors of light over the many types of foliage, and as you watch, a different canvas is portrayed as the sunlight begins to dance between the clouds. The tree branch that once received the brilliant light is now in the background and another bush has moved to the foreground to take its place in the light. The beauty that God has created for us in nature never ceases to amaze me. I pray every day that humankind will take care of this special gift so that the generations that come after us are able to enjoy it as well.

Tonight after dinner Tom and I will have one last walk around the campground with our little dog, Tao and then sit down to enjoy singing around the campfire with Tao on one of our laps. Sometimes we roast marshmallows or just listen to the sound of the crackling fire as the scent of burning pinewood drifts through the air.

There are only 23 campsites in this park and when we pulled in yesterday, we got the last vacant spot along the river. As we walked around the park to view the rest, we noticed we have the most beautiful site here. God has blessed us again!

MIRACLE BEACH

We arrived on wed eve June 27 and are hunkered in here for 5 days. The Canadian independence holiday is July 1 on Sunday, and if you don't get a campsite early, you don't get one. We will leave Monday A.M. For the Campbell River area. This provisional park is beautiful with an old growth lush forest surrounding a beachfront to the ocean. It is named miracle beach because in 1930 a fire started in Victoria and burned all the forest northward for about 150 miles-this particular community prayed for the fire to stop and it did-right at the door to this place and the community appropriately renamed it miracle beach. It has about 200 sites (with lots of room), asphalt roads, lots of amphitheater programs and a nature house. As with all the provisional parks, they furnish free firewood, so we have a campfire each night.

Tao met a little Shih Tzu puppy 3 mos. old and it reminded us of how small Tao was when we first got him. We became acquainted with the "parents" of the little Shih Tzu (pepper) and coincidentally, they are the campground hosts at miracle beach. Also syncronistically, they are named Don and Carol (just like my Sister & her Hubby) and this Carol's birth date is Sept 4th (the same date as mine) they are a little younger but the last night invited us to campfire at their site & met some more friends of theirs. We exchanged addresses & phone #'s since she has a sister in Oregon and who knows, we may meet up with them in Oregon sometime.

CAMPBELL RIVER AREA

Now we are at a private campground with amenities in a forested area close to Campbell River, a wonderful place for wildlife and fishing.

REVISITING BUTCHART GARDENS

We spent sat. Night at Butchart Gardens again, only this time, since it was at night and later in the summer, they had the most awesome fireworks show I have ever seen in my life (both ground show and sky show) we've seen the capital 4th on TV & last year saw in person (close to the Manassas battlefield in Va.) fireworks which up until now we thought were the best, but the Canadians outdo them both.

Stories are told with music to match what goes on with the fireworks, which include dancing waters fully illuminated with different colors. Just when we thought we had seen it all they came out with something else more spectacular. They had a kaleidoscope ground show which kept unfolding into different geometric designs and colors and a sky show with many rockets exploding into spinning scrolls, stars and different designs in all shades of colors that I had never before seen. We had bench seats with backs and sat on pillows as well so we were very comfortable. We got there about 5 pm, had dinner in their restaurant, went around some of the gardens again and heard an Irish musical group with instruments in terrific concert before the fireworks started at 10 pm (all this for about U.S. $12-$14)

God works in mysterious ways-earlier Tom put his chair in the fireworks area to save a place for my scooter while we listened to the concert in another area. When we went to the fireworks area, someone had moved his chair and so we moved to the next section with seats just as good or better. Seating was on a graduated hillside so no one's view was blocked. We were right behind a family who's wheelchair bound daughter Holly, had Parkinson's and Huntington's Chorea-her hands kept moving all the time in a rather spastic way (I'm not sure of name & spelling but I have heard of it-a brain disease where the immune sys. Goes haywire & attacks brain functions). Her father started talking to us about my scooter & that led to discussions about my health challenges and how God helped me. God led me to go over to Holly, hug her and give her hope & encouragement about God's love & healing. I gave her a kiss on the forehead as she left. Holly's father said she would remember that all her life. Earlier I had noticed another woman across the aisle stare at her with a frown and disgusted look on her face like she wasn't fit to be out in public view. (I have seen that look many times from people who do not understand disabilities and I have felt the hurt as people often looked at me that way) I was glad God placed me there to show holly that she is loved by God and other people including us and has every right to be there. It is sort of a reminder to each one of us-"there but for the grace of God goes I".

Goldstream Provincial Park

Well, Sunday we stayed at Goldstream Provincial Park and took the ferry. From Sidney B.C. To Anacortes.
Some impressions about our Canadian visit: we had our Vet give Tao a comprehensive exam and had him groomed just before we left San Diego. Both of them should have caught the fact that his rear toenail was growing inward (the nails were supposed to have been trimmed as well but were not & we didn't find it out until we left); however, it took a Canadian vet to fix it all up. Being out in campgrounds, it could have gotten infected as it had turned into a nasty wound & was bleeding. (When your pet hurts, you hurt too). Tom & I had been talking about the fact that even on Canadian soil you don't feel quite at home because you aren't familiar with their laws, etc and the concern that if something happened (accident or sickness in a strange place) what would happen. It is the "unknown fear" factor. Well, we sure learned that lesson-that sometimes it is the Americans who don't have the right answer or way & others do.

Another thing we learned is that Canadians have an image that every American carries a gun around all the time and some are afraid to visit the USA as a result. They also think most Americans go around destroying the environment and feel that the USA is currently leading the world down the wrong path environmentally and in other ways. By our actions and our words we tried to let them know otherwise.
Some trivia re currency: a Looney is a one-dollar coin with a Looney bird on the back. A Tooney is a two-dollar coin with Queen Elizabeth's head on the front and a bear behind (no pun intended by

us as this was how the Canadians put it) the smallest in paper currency is a $5 bill.

Also pedestrians have the right of way so if you are a motorist, be very careful, because they don't yield. There are also signs blinking "prepare to stop" when a light is about to change warning you to slow down-we found this very helpful, particularly for us tourists. The police stand in the middle of the highway or at a traffic light taking pictures and mailing the ticket out. Since they are on foot it isn't easy to see them so watch your speed. This brings me to another hint, since the speed limit is in km/hr and most USA cars have miles per hr. Prominently shown on the speedometer and km/hr in lighter print on the inner scale, I found this hard to read and had to remember the various speed conversion. I think the next time I will make a conversion card and tape it along side the speedometer.

BACK IN THE U.S.A.

It is 7-10-01 and we are camped at La Connor, Wash (a Thousand Trails campground). The 1/2-hour ferry ride from Victoria was very interesting (through the San Juan islands which are very picturesque and we stopped temporarily at Friday's harbor). We are really enjoying camping in one place for a week after traveling so much in B.C. Our campsite overlooks a point on the Rosario Straits and we see the most gorgeous sunsets through the trees and over the water. The campground had a BBQ salmon & steak dinner on sat night that was really great.

ON TO OREGON

Well, we are "on the road again" on the way to Oregon to Bend Thousand Trails campground. From there we will do the Cascade Lakes loop highway.

We camped at Twin Lakes and Crane Prairie but no fish. Two years of drought in Oregon has taken its toll. Well they are finally having rain now, so we'll see what happens. Last night it rained hard. So what do you do when you camp in weather like that? Well we read, then snuggled up and listened to our romantic music cassette tape of Roberto and Joe Fos, then took a hot shower & went to bed. Ah, thank God for motor homes.

Here we are at lava lakes where there is supposed to be good fishing-Tom will find out soon. I am sitting here looking at the ripples on the lake, as the sun sinks slowly behind the mountain. Tom is out on the dock fishing. We were lucky to get a campsite right on the lake-the weather is nice & sunny now. Tao has been chasing the chipmunks wherever we go-he is so adorable and amuses us so much with his antics. Tom thinks he is a little Tao spirit inside a doggie suit and I agree.

Tom caught his fish so we are all happy!
The next day we drove over to Madras for the Rexhall pre-rally to the FMCA rally in Redmond and had lots of fun and good food

Now on to Sweet Home for the Country Music Jamboree. About 7,000 people are in attendance. All the proceeds go back into the Community. We had a big delicious breakfast for $3.00 cooked by the people at the Senior Center there. Our campsite was nice & big on soft grass & we had access to the concert area through a back gate just a few feet away. We could see real well from our concert seats. Our camping neighbors were all so friendly. The group "A Sleep at the Wheel" performed and were they ever good! The lead, Rob Benson did all verses of "El Paso" & it was almost as good as hearing the original by Marty Robbins. Of course Kenny Rogers is the consummate entertainer, Suzy Bogguss did some terrific yodeling and Lee Ann Womack did her "I hope you dance" with a new one from her CD's that we bought (she autographed it).

On the way back We stayed at our beloved property in Murphy before leaving Oregon and then celebrated Nancy's birthday with the Abshiers in lake Tahoe.

God also provided many opportunities to share blessings and prayers with strangers along the way,who became friends

MOTOR HOME TRIPS IN 2003

We traveled in our motor home to Arizona in Feb. To see some of our friends and camping at the Colorado River (emerald cove). Again in our motor home, taking our summer vacation, starting in may at Las Vegas to see friends and attend the Celine Dione concert, on to Zion and Bryce national parks, our property in Murphy, Oregon, and visiting our sister Charlotte in Dallas, her daughter Mary, her daughter Julie and one month new son, little Riley (4 generations). We saw friends in Salem and then camped at Detroit Lake (Christmas card photo) where Tom caught lots of fish.

Then on to Doug and Julie's wedding where bride Julie and attendants traveled to the wedding via rowboat on the McKenzie River and enjoyed visiting the Laumans. Camped at Thousand Trails Bend, where we saw the Roswalds and then camped at Union Creek campground. In July relatives Jeff and Heidi Burk & kids as well as Lynn & Ed Lesinsky visited us in Oregon. We enjoyed park concerts, eating out and the jet boat ride through Hellgate Canyon on the Rogue River. Saw the Hammond's in Roseburg and then on to Sweet Home for the Oregon Country Jamboree starring Alan Jackson with the Laumans. Left for the coast and enjoyed Florence; Bandon, where we went to a wild animal petting park, the cheese factory and picked wild blackberries at Harris Beach State Park in Brookings. We camped in the redwoods on the way to Fortuna, Ca. To attend the 40th anniversary vow ceremony of Judy and Jim Vaughan, officiated by Carol Munford.

TRIP TO MEXICAN RIVIERA, NOVEMBER 2003 (11 DAYS)

We had heard so many people talk about cruise vacations that we finally decided to take our first one and it was to the Mexican Riviera with seven ports of call. (Cabo San Lucas, Matzatlan, Manzanillo, Puerta Vallarta, Acapulco, Zihuatanajo, and Ixtapa). We enjoyed lots of rich food, wonderful show entertainment and met some wonderful people. We enjoyed Puerta Vallarta and Ixtapa the most.

MY THOUGHTS ON CELEBRATION

Many people are not as fortunate as we are to be able to travel like we do, and one of my relatives happened to mention this to me in a jealous tone. Unfortunately, she wanted to travel without putting in the many years of work that Tom & I did. When I was younger, I used to pray and dream about traveling and so I was quite motivated to work, earn the money and save, so I/We could do the traveling that we do now. Many times I put in long hours at work, and would transcend the pain of the Rheumatoid Arthritis by focusing in on being productive and being a good employee, rather than focus in on the pain that I had and the stress of work.

My point is, that if one has dreams, no matter what those dreams are, when a person is motivated to work, Prays and expects the dreams to come true, they can. Maybe the dream doesn't always come true in the same way a person wanted it, as God knows what is best for us, but it does come true. For instance, God has given me the knowledge, skills and the ability to know how to transcend the pain of the many physical challenges I have faced with diseases, falls, etc., recover and move on to live a victorious life. My fingers are still crooked with the destruction of the Arthritis, yet, I am writing this book on the computer. The joy of overcoming limitations makes the celebration even greater.

So, wherever we are in life, whatever we are doing, we can always find the joy in celebrating. Smell the roses, look at a smile on a child's face, and enjoy the adorable looks from a devoted pet, such as our Tao. Be glad in the things you can do. Find out what opportunities God has for you to be a blessing to someone else. Praying for someone else is a wonderful way to be a blessing. Feel the joy that comes as you find out that person is better.
Each trip we take, we look for opportunities to be a blessing. Traveling and going places are just not means to an end for us. they have a purpose of searching out opportunities to be messengers for God, which makes our journey even more joyful.

259

CHAPTER 17

BEING A BLESSING MATTERS
LORD MAKE ME A BLESSING OR
OPPORTUNITIES FOR RANDOM ACTS OF
KINDNESS

Hymn: Make me a Blessing

Scripture: 2 Cor 1:3-4
>As Paul says.... we are living epistles for Christ, "written not on tablets of stone, but on tablets of flesh, that is of the heart." (2 Cor 3:3)
>"And be kind to one another, tenderhearted, forgiving one another.... even as God in Christ forgave you." (Eph 4:32)
>"Therefore be imitators of God...." (Eph 5:1)

TAKING ALONG OPPORTUNITIES TO BE A BLESSING ON OUR JOURNEY

When the phrase, "random acts of kindness" became popularized, it made me think that if every person, every day, performed one act of kindness without expecting anything in return, it be would wonderful (courtesy is contagious, let's start an epidemic).

I decided to start experimenting with this idea and asked God to provide inspiration to me of how to do this. On my birthday, September 4, 1996, a florist had advertised a dozen roses free to the first 100 people to celebrate a special occasion. Tom and I thought it was a neat idea, so we went down and stood in line to get our roses. We spent the rest of the day traveling around the city, giving a single rose to some people we knew who were not feeling well, others that we knew, like some of my doctors, where we wanted to show our appreciation for their many long hours, others to show our love and friendship, and some to complete strangers we saw on street corners. The bright smiling faces, hugs and unexpected looks that changed into smiles brought a reward to us that we will never forget. We have a nephew, Scott, who every Christmas Eve, buys a single rose for each member of the family - it is a special touch of love.

Every since then, I have looked for and been open for opportunities to share with others and make someone's life brighter. Especially, since having the Flesh-Eating Bacteria, Tom and I include in our morning prayer, for God to make us a blessing to someone today. Sometimes, it is a small thing that we easily forget, but at the moment, has helped someone else.

On our camping trips we are provided with many opportunities. My first camping trip after the bacteria, in the summer of 1999, we drove into a campground, and after getting settled, a man came over, remarking he used to have a motor home like ours but lost it because of financial problems resulting from a terrible job injury. It turned out he had been a firefighter in a winery fire; fell through the roof, causing a concussion.

He also inhaled formaldehyde, which left him with all kinds of medical problems. In the process, his wife left him with many financial entanglements. He was writing his book about faith and wanted to talk to me. We shared a lot and he admitted that before this all happened, he had intellectually believed in God, but through adversity, he had learned to believe in God from his heart.

Several weeks later, at a Thousand Trails Camp, and I was sitting outside the motor home, when the woman in the next motor home came out and said to me, "You know, I have this feeling that I'm supposed to talk with you."

So, I asked her to sit down and we started talking. I asked her where she was from, but she said she couldn't remember since her mind was failing her more and people didn't understand. I told her that God understood; that it wasn't important anyway, and just to talk about whatever she wanted to and I just listened.

Then I had the opportunity to share my miraculous recovery from the Flesh-Eating Bacteria with her, and with tears almost in her eyes, she said, "I really needed to hear that." As she left, she thanked me for accepting her as she was and gave me a hug

One day Tom and I were at a gem show and I was sitting down to rest when a strange gentleman came up to me and said "You're very spiritual aren't you" I said yes and told him about our prayer network and he said "I know God sent me to you would you pray for my wife?" He gave me a card with her name on it "Elsa Hajajos". Even though she passed on after one year, prayers comforted her during this time.

Of course, at this stage of my life, more of my friends are being diagnosed with illness, having surgeries or need prayer for something in their lives. Our prayer network becomes larger each day, but we know God's power for healing and providing comfort is an ever-expanding source. We know from experience, that prayer works, and if you don't have time for anything else, always have time for prayer.

In my earlier days, kids used to stare at my deformed fingers and I would wonder why their parents had not taught them better manners. As I matured in my spiritual journey, I realized this would make a good opportunity to educate others and share with kids how they can help others with Arthritis or other diseases. Tom and I were at the zoo earlier this year, resting on a bench, when a teenage girl walking ahead of her parents, kept staring at my hands. I said, "Hi" to her and something to the extent that I noticed her looking at my hands, said that I had Rheumatoid Arthritis, that others couldn't catch it and asked if she had any questions about it. She then opened up, said she wanted to be a nurse and asked me what could be done for it.

I provided some information for her and ended up saying that the most important factors in any illness or disease are faith, hope and love, and the fact that others care. Her parents had come up in the meantime and heard the end of my conversation and thanked me for explaining in such a nice way to her.

MAKING A DIFFERENCE

I believe Christ is One who made a difference and I believe He calls us to make a difference in our earthly journey. To this end, here are some important prayers, thoughts and ideas that have helped me make a difference in my life and it is hoped they will help you.

MOTIVATION MATTERS

There will be people we meet on our journey that have physical afflictions, addictions or a lot of problems, but no amount of information we give them seems to motivate them. They march to a different drummer and are not interested in any self-improvement or change. But we are not to judge...we listen, love and accept them as they are as well as continue prayer without ceasing. Sometimes tough love or loving interference works. If we plant a seed, hope and pray, that's all we can do -- we may not see the final result but sometimes miracles do happen with these people.

For me, motivation comes from doing inner work...meditating and finding God within, the Holy Spirit, the teacher, and the comforter. Doing what needs to be done, (the exercises, the proper nutrition, releasing the negativity) comes from the strength and power of Jesus Christ. It does take discipline, but I have found if I keep my mind on my dreams and goals and what I CAN DO instead of what I can't do, sometimes the "can't do", things move into the can do category.

LEARNING OUR LESSONS

Everyone in life has one or more lessons to learn. We all need to learn how to have better relationships and deal with our emotions. Others have more physical challenges as well. Others have addictions, control or power challenges and we all need to love and forgive more.

ADDICTIONS

People with addictions suffer from a sense of lacking something in their life.

Some people with addictions have not learned to love themselves and they use the object of their addiction (smoking, alcohol, etc.) to deal with this lack of self-love. Others have never experienced true love and the desire to be authentically loved by someone is their lack. I worked as a Behavior Modification Counselor at one time and a lot of women who were overweight used food to deal with a sexual abuse issue, rather than confront the lack of dignity they suffered from a personal violation.

One man that Tom knew used food to be large so no one would "push him around". With him it was a lack of power. Still others are addicted to being told what to do, can't make their own decisions and suffer from a lack of being able to take responsibility. People who cannot commit to marriage may fall into this category. Taking responsibility for one's own decisions is not always easy, but sorting out the strengths, weaknesses and consequences of each option and asking for God's help builds strength of character. Taking responsibility for one's mistakes takes a lot of courage but one does not build respect by denial or blaming others.

FULFILLING A LACK IN OUR LIVES

By asking for God's help and honestly, searching our inner self to become aware of the lack in our life, addictions can be overcome. Hypnotherapy is a great help in uncovering the answer to this challenge. Once we become aware of the lack, we can fill that void with God's love, rather than food, alcohol, gambling, cigarettes etc. God loves us and Christ's power can give us the strength to do it. I used this strength to learn how to walk over many times and the same strength is there for people to change their addictions. As we learn these lessons, we have more opportunities to be a blessing to others, to love and support them as they make positive changes in their lives.

HARDSHIPS, CHALLENGES AND BLESSINGS

Overcoming life's adversities actually makes a person stronger reports Paul Pearsall, Ph.D., in his book, *The Beethoven Factor: The New Positive Psychology of Hardiness, Happiness, Healing and Hope,* (Hampton Roads, Pub.). He uses the example of the famous composer to cite research dealing with the hardiness of individuals, the happiness that results from a total involvement in life, the importance of finding meaning in one's life, the importance of optimism, and finding ways in which our actions make a difference.

MY LIFE

Using myself as an example, even though I have had a life with many physical challenges, almost passed over three times, and seem to face continual adversities, that I have found a life of meaning, which has made a difference in the lives of others. I have found that I have become a stronger person because I have immersed myself in life, education, work, church, marriage, traveling and celebrating each day, found meaning in Jesus Christ, my Savior and Lord, found optimism keeps me focused on what I can do, always having hope for a better tomorrow and found that by asking God each day to present me with opportunities to be a blessing to others, that my life and actions have made a difference.

GRANDPA MOTLEY'S POEM

I mentioned that my mother's father was a street corner preacher. Well, he also was a self-educated man and among the papers he left was this poem he wrote which has meant a lot to me:

GRANDPA MOTLEY'S POEM

As the early flower of spring
Is plucked by the passerby,
It's beautiful tint and fragrance sweet
Begins to wither and fade and die.

That flower is removed from its place
Where once it admiringly stood.
So with all in the human race
We change into man and womanhood.

So like the flower that grew in the spring

On the sunny hill or by woodland brook,
Your springtime days of child like things
Are to your life a story book.

Your bark is sailing on the sea of life
Where all is changing whirling strife.
May the boatsman who guides the craft
Be wise and dutiful from first to last.

When the voyage is finally ended
And the stormy sea is crossed
May love and joy then be blended
As in the beginning when other hopes were lost.

Then in age and decaying days
A history of life you've surely written
May it be one of lovely ways
And not of hearts and hopes all smitten.

Then when you're old you can smile and say
I made a wise choice in childhood's day.
Then death closes the drama of the day
In a beautiful sunset with it's golden ray.

-Sydney W. Motley

OTHER INSPIRING THOUGHTS

Leo Bulscaglia was a professor who taught a course entitled, "Love 101" and wrote a book called simply, LOVE. He said, "To me, life is God's gift to you. The way you live your life is your gift to God. Make it a fantastic one."

If I can stop one heart from breaking,
I shall not live in vain:
If I can ease one life the aching,
Or cool one pain,
 Or help the fainting robin
 Unto his nest again

I shall not live in vain.
                              Emily Dickinson

Lord, make me an instrument of thy peace,
Where there is hatred, let me sow love;
Where there is injury, pardon;
Where there is doubt, faith;
Where there is despair, hope;
Where there is darkness, light;
Where there is sadness, joy.
O divine Master, grant that I may not so much seek to consoled,
as to console;
Not so much to be understood as to understand;
Not so much to be loved as to love.
Help me to learn that in giving I may receive;
In forgetting self, I may find life eternal. Amen
                              St. Francis of Assisi

CONCLUSION

Despite my physical challenges, I have been blessed all my life with wonderful people and relationships. My grandpa, parents and family, my teachers, my friends, "Miss Jean", our Camp Fire leader and second mother, Virginia Anderson, one of my mentors, and above all, my husband, Tom.

Whenever I have fallen, God sent Angels to lay me down softly. Each time something adverse happened to me, God's Amazing Grace prevailed. It always could have been so much worse. Each time God has given me the motivation and strength to recuperate and come back so I could enjoy my life, my journey. I have lived a wonderful life, obtaining my education, having a career that I not only enjoyed but was able to contribute to a better society and life for others (making a difference), truly unconditionally loving Tom and being loved unconditionally by him in our marriage, traveling together with Tom to such wonderful places and seeing the beauty God has created in nature, being able to experience the joy that Tao, our Shih Tzu, (our Tao Spirit in a doggie suit) has brought into our lives, and living a life of purpose where God presented me with so many opportunities to be a blessing to others.

I thank God for all of this and more ---for giving me a mind that understood the power of mind over matter, the power to overcome, the power of thinking and acting positively and most of all for His Son, our Lord and Savior, Jesus Christ and for His Amazing Grace. It is my hope that I have lived a life worthy of His calling, a life that has truly been a blessing to others along the paths of my journey, making their lives a little easier, better and happier a a result of knowing me. It is my hope that others have seen me as a "messenger" or angel from God.........that they have indeed seen Christ's light shinning through me.

It is my hope that this sharing of experiences of my journey will somehow be a blessing to each of you as you read it and that there will be something that each one can take along on his/her journey that will make it a little better and more joyful. God Bless each one of you.

CHAPTER 18

GOINING WITH GOD MATTERS

Hymn: Handel's Messiah, Hallelujah Chorus

Scripture: PSALM 23

The Lord is my shepherd: I shall not want. He makes me to lie down in green pastures; He leads me beside still waters. He restores my soul. He leads me in the path of righteousness for his name's sake. Yea though I walk through the valley of the shadow of death, I will fear no evil; for thou art with me; thy rod and thy staff comfort me. Thou prepares a table before me in the presence of my enemies; thou anointest my head with oil; my cup runneth over. Surely goodness and mercy shall follow me all the days of my life; and I shall dwell in the house of the Lord forever. Psalm 23

TRIP ACROSS THE U.S. 2005

In order to make this more interesting I will use some of Nancy's E-Mail that she wrote as we traveled on our way. In January of 2005 Nancy came to me saying that She would like to finish seeing the rest of the 50 States. To do this, she wanted to do it in two separate trips. The first leg was in the winter/spring time frame, with the second in the summer/fall time frame. She had made her plans with a map as to where she would like to go and when. Upon review, I though that it would be to much for her since it would be about 7-8 months on the road and we should split it up into two trips one in 2005 and the second in 2006.

When I ask why she wanted to do this all in one year, She replied, "I feel this will be the last time I will have to see my friends and relatives as well as the remaining States". We had just taken delivery of a new motor home in January, and needed to take it out on a shake down cruse to insure all things would work at the start. We went to a local camp ground and worked on our plans for the 2005 trip. Nancy had done a good job planning it all out,

CALIFORNIA, ARIZONA, NEW MEXICO

February 22^{nd,} we left San Diego heading east and we made stops in Arizona, and New Mexico. In Las Cruces New Mexico, we had dinner at Lorenzo's and had Green Chile and Meat Lasagna...UUUMMMMM Good. It was a delightful blend of Mexican and Italian tastes. The bread is a homemade Sicilian recipe very delicious.

In Kerrville, TX at Buckwheat RV Resort and couldn't believe what we saw...A 40 foot motor home carrying a 250-300 lb pot bellied pig, the pet of the owner. Owner was also pulling a 26 ft trailer with Harley plus he had a jeep (from TX, natch!).

Notes: Tom & I never cease to be amazed at the friendliness of other campers & strangers at rest stops, etc. Today we were invited to Pear blossom, Indiana by a man with a motor home at a rest stop here in Texas. Of course Tao is a draw... they all have to stop & pet him, but even passing each other on roads, people wave, honk, and always have a smile. It would be nice if everyone could be just as friendly in the cities, malls and neighborhoods. Tom & I are blessed with neighbors who are this friendly but just a reminder to everyone that this world is made a little brighter by people who smile, wave & recognize others in some way in their daily life.

LOUISIANA

With Louisiana being the first state we had not been to before. We stopped in, Baton Rouge, New Orleans (pre Katrina), and later on the return trip Natchez, and Shreveport. ". We went to the French Quarter; in New Orleans the River walk Marketplace and we also took an afternoon cruise on a Calliope Paddle wheeler up the Mighty Mississippi, The bayous, as well as Lake Pontchartrain were fascinating.

270

MISSISSIPPI, ALABAMA, AND FLORIDA

We where in Louisiana until march 7th and then on to Mississippi, Alabama, and Florida. Three more states that I had not been to Nancy had been to Florida before so she picked up two states.

Our first night in Florida was at an early rest stop in the panhandle, because there was a tornado watch that stopped us from going east and south.

The next day we were on our way again and the next few days we went as far south as Seminole Florida, and had lunch and enjoyment with three other couples from our Alaska tour group. Next we swung northeast to Winter Haven and the Cypress Gardens Adventure Park. We saw ice-skating shows, water-skiing stunts, synchronized shows with swimming, continuous live musical performances, lots of shops, and restaurants. The new gardens with a beautiful, huge waterfall, animal topiaries, flowers, living gardens (which come to life) are wonderful. Now onto Orlando and the Disney world, Epcot center.

We had a delightful time with my niece, Nancy and Ferd, who live in Deland, we went to the Blue Springs State Park where we saw Manatees and babies (awesome).

Next we went to Cape Canaveral for the J.F.K. Space Center. Wow, we saw the Kennedy Space Center and it is awesome to see the real space shuttles and know they were really in outer space. We saw an Imax film narrated by Walter Cronkite, which showed the earth as the astronauts see it. His words were "and here is the magnificent panorama of our home, the earth, in all its splendor." It really made one aware that if the earth is our home, we need to treat it as our home.... to take care of it and protect it instead of destroying it.

We have seen so many lakes in the interior of Florida...it seems that there is water everywhere we go.... little canals at the side of freeways, mini ponds in the grassy areas. We are also told that any of these watery areas can have alligators, and some of the campgrounds we have been to have actually had alligators come through the campgrounds. I thought alligators were relegated to the swampy area around the Everglades, but not so. They are all over Florida.

Back in Orlando, we had reservations at Dolly Parton's "Dixie Stampede". They had horse shows, re enactment of rivalries between the North and the South with actors dressed in Confederate and Union uniforms, ostrich races, pig races, a buffalo stampede, a ballroom that comes down from the ceiling with dancers who re-live an old-fashioned Southern Ball and more.

The next day we went to Holy Land. The Holy Land, you ask? I bet you thought we were in Florida. Well, we are but there is an attraction, just like Disneyworld, called the "Holy Land Experience" in Orlando. They have replicated the Holy Land with buildings just like one would find in Jerusalem. They have exhibits, films, live shows and musicals. We saw a wonderful musical showing how Jesus healed the Roman Centurion's servant, a fascinating exhibit that brings to life the Wilderness Tabernacle and saw a film, "Seeds of Promise" inside Herod's Temple. We were supposed to see another musical depicting the walk to Calvary, the crucifixion and resurrection of Jesus Christ, but we didn't make it in time. We did get pictures of the tomb. The passion play was being given in the evening, but we left because it started pouring. If you get down this way be sure and see this attraction.

We had a stop in St. Augustine where Ponce de Leon discovered the fountain of youth and Nancy was 20 years younger by April fools day.

GEORGIA, SOUTH CAROLINA

Today we passed the state line into South Carolina again and on the way to High Falls Park, we went through Greenville and saw Reedy River Falls. It is right in town with a tiered park around it. One can view the falls from a suspension bridge to get a front view or go down a slanting sidewalk to see the bottom of the falls where there is a large green lawn and people can relax. We had a hard time getting out of Greenville as we kept running into blocks...a bridge tunnel that we couldn't go through since our motor home was too high, much construction that kept us going around in circles, etc. We laughed remembering the song the Kingston Trio used to sing about the MTA and the man who never returned. Well we finally found our way out of Greenville and on our correct route.

We headed for South Carolina to lake Keeowee to see, Bob Daffin, my nephew, his wife, Paula and daughter, Oksana (15 years). We went to the Methodist Church Sunday morning. The afternoon warmed up very nicely so Bob took us on a boat ride around the lake. There was just a gentle breeze to make it a perfect spring day on the sparkling water (this lake is one of the cleanest in the U.S.). We enjoyed the visit and our time with them so much.

If you ever get to Stone Mountain, an attraction just southeast of Atlanta, Georgia, be sure and see the Laser Show, which was created by Bob, who is owner of Stone Mountain Productions. We really admire his creativity with his business as well as what Bob and Paula have done in adopting Oksana, who was in a Russian orphanage until about 8 years ago when she became a part of their family. This is one of those things that God made possible and was meant to be as Julie, Oksana's closest friend, who lives a few houses away came from a Russian orphanage also, which was located just a few miles from where the orphanage that Oksana was in. It makes your heart glad to see how happy these young girls are.

We went to Issaquena Falls in the northern part of South Carolina. They cascaded down for about 7 layers and were about 40 feet high. It is so great to see waterfalls in the spring when they are so full. We traveled through very scenic country and spent the night in Ashville, North Carolina.

The next morning we set out to see the Biltmore Estate. The grounds encompass about 835 acres and the interior of the house reminded me of the Hearst Castle. It is the world's largest house (about 7 or 8 stories high) and something everyone should see if they are in the area as it is like a museum with so much original art and furnishings

NORTH CAROLINA & TENNESSEE

We got into Oak Ridge, TN., visiting Barb and Orlin Stansfield, Joyce Stilwell, Barb's sister and dear friends from San Diego who moved to Oak Ridge about 11 years ago. We really enjoyed our time with Barb and Orlin Stansfield and Joyce Stilwell in Oak Ridge, TN.

GEORGIA

The next day we headed for Atlanta Georgia. We are at the Stone Mountain Campground, near Atlanta, Georgia, to see the attractions and the Laser show, (the one my nephew Bob created). It is the world's largest Laser show and is shown with the mountain as a backdrop. The face of Stone Mountain has a carving depicting the central figures of Confederate History...Jefferson Davis, Robert E. Lee and Stonewall Jackson. The carving began in 1917 and took 55 years to complete.

We went to The Georgia Renaissance Festival (celebrated every year from approx. April 16-June 5, only on weekends) at Fairburn, Georgia. It is very interactive and more fun! The entrance is through the gates of a medieval castle and all the buildings are replicas of the 15th century. Almost everyone, whether an employee of the festival or not, is clothed in costume and everyone speaks in old English. All the locals attend every year and really do their part to make it realistic by dressing up and mingling.

On to the Calloway Gardens (Calloway family of the Golf Club fame). These gardens of 14,000 acres have been open since 1952. The founder, Cason Jewell Calloway longed for a place where man and nature could abide together in harmony. To this end, the Ida Cason Calloway Foundation was set up to provide educational workshops, interactive exhibits and a host of other activities to teach people to appreciate the beauty surrounding them and to take good

274

care of it as stewards of the environment. It is involved with conservation and restorative methods and research on plants and wildlife. It is designed for one to drive around, bicycle through or take walking paths in the interior where many lakes are located to beckon the waterfowl and areas set aside for various purposes of growing flowers (azalea gardens, holly, mountain laurel, rhododendron, wildflowers, etc.). The longleaf oak serves as a peaceful beautiful backdrop for the colorful flowers dressed in their spring colors. There is a butterfly center and a Birds of Prey Show in the amphitheater. There is a golf course (of course!), and various restaurants/eating places scattered throughout which are designed to fit in, in a picturesque setting. It is difficult to describe the serenity one experiences as you sit on a bench overlooking a reflective pond, etc. It really needs to be experienced! If you are ever down this way I urge you to see how nature can make your day.

ALABARMA

We head for Alabama (Birmingham) to see Ives Wooley Ort and her husband Eddie. Ives is my dear friend and classmate from Point Loma High School.

Today we went out sightseeing around Town. First we went to the Civil Rights Institute in Birmingham and relived history through some very meaningful displays and exhibits. We found out that Birmingham is a fairly new city, which didn't exist until after the Civil War. Then we took a drive to see the statue of Vulcan, which overlooks the city and has a great view. The city is built on iron ore left over from the early days that was spent in mining. We ended up by seeing the beautiful flowers in the Birmingham Botanical Gardens and I saw the huge wild Magnolia bloom. It is a serene contrast to the busy city businesses.

MISSISSIPPI

On our way through Mississippi, we went to The Grand Village of the Natchez and the reconstructed mounds they used as a foundation for their buildings and temples as well as a Museum housing the artifacts of these extinct peoples (from 1200 to 1730). Natchez has about 28 restored mansions, of which we saw Monmouth, Magnolia, Rosalie (Head quarters, of Union Army during the Civil War-located by the Mississippi) and a few others. We also saw the Grace United Methodist Church, where Methodism got its start in the Mississippi Territory (founded in 1794).

GOD PROTECTS US.

As we were taking our motor home through the narrow streets of the Historic District, suddenly Tom stopped. I had been looking down at brochures and I looked up to find a power line within 6 inches of my windshield. It was up on Tom's side and had fallen on my side below the height of our roof. Tom carefully and slowly backed up and guided the motor home over to his side with no traffic coming the other way so that we cleared the slanted portion of the power line. We said a prayer of thanks, knowing that God's Angels had told Tom to stop since he did not see the power line until we stopped so we decided to be on our way out of there and head home to San Diego.

NEW MEXICO

Sunday we were in Las Cruces and had dinner at Lorenzo's (Green Chile Lasagna ummmmmm!) Lorenzo has dollar bills all over his wooden ceiling. Customers give him a dollar bill and 2 quarters.... he wraps the bill around the quarters using the Japanese art of origami and flips it up in a certain way and it sticks to the ceiling. About every 3 months he cleans off the ceiling and gives th money to charity. Tom was feeling generous and gave him a ten-dollar bill so we saw how it was done.

Our next stop was Tombstone, Arizona, (The Old West's Most Famous Town). We had heard a lot about it but had never been there. It is a fun mix of history, drama, shopping, eating and tomfoolery. They take you back to the days in the 1880's of Doc Holliday, Wyatt Earp and Big Nose Kate.

We went on to Tucson and had dinner at Pinnacle Peak's with Shirley Bamford Miner and hubby Bob. Shirley was one of Nancy's classmates at Point Loma High School. Than back to San Diego were we had time to rest and restock for the fall trip through the northern part of the U.S.

THE SECOND HALF

It's July 14th and we are on our way North first stop will be Yosemite National park, than on to Grass Valley to see my sister Carol & her hubby Don and leave Fri. for our property in Oregon.

Our night stop after Grass Valley was at Woodson Bridge State Recreations Area, which after the hot day's drive, was a delightful refuge of shaded trees and grass. But Tao enjoyed it the most as he got to romp with Bandit, a black & white Shi Tzu camped 2 sites away. He was close to Tao's age but a little shorter. While his master sang, Bandit was placed close to her face and he started to "yowl" in tune to her song. We haven't taught Tao that yet, but it made Tao quite curious. Anyway we all laughed our heads off as the 2 doggies put on quite a show.

OREGON

The next morn we headed for Oregon. We spent Sat. night on our own beloved property in Murphy, near Grants We went to the park concert in Grants Pass, and had a delightful time.
We will be in Oregon to the end of July and then take off for our trip back east going across the states at the top of the U.S. We expect to hit Maine over Labor Day Weekend and will see the turning of the leaves in New England. We are excited about the many new adventures that await us, seeing friends and relatives, as well as seeing God's gorgeous scenery.

We traveled to Salem, and visited my sister Charlotte, her daughter Mary and husband Gary, and their daughter Julie and husband Jon and their 2 children, Riley and Maddox. (4 generations)

Maddox is just 4 months old and has a continuous smile or laugh on his face along with a twinkle in his eyes.

Wednesday evening we are going out to eat to celebrate our "Meetaversary" 36 years ago. We think of as many things as we can to celebrate these days, but we have always celebrated the evening we met and Tom said his memorable words, "I wish this night would never end". And....the rest is history.

Now it's on to Sweet Home, Oregon and the 13th Annual Oregon Jamboree. It is a camporee, non-stop live country festival that will last FROM FRIDAY TILL SUNDAY. We will see our friends, the Laumans who always come here, so it is a reunion with good people.

Nancy had her picture taken with Jonathon Harris, an up and coming artist. We got his CD with his autograph. We really liked his "I Was Born to Love You".

After Sweet Home, we will leave for our trip back east and probably stop for the night in eastern Oregon. We never know what adventures lie ahead but we are always ready to love and embrace them.

WASHINGTON, IDAHO AND NORTH DAKOTA

We headed East via 395 N and I-90, We had almost 200 miles of dry weedy hills until we hit Spokane. It occurred to me that is what life is like, with its dry weedy or thorny periods in between the lushness of green beautiful and bountiful periods where there is plenty of water. Sometimes the dry thorny periods can be the greatest learning and spiritual growth times. Also, a question to ponder is whether or not we would appreciate the beauty when we came to it without something to compare it to.

We are in Post Falls, Idaho on I-90 E we saw some magnificent Idaho scenery (high mountains, tall trees in a thick forest), past beautiful Lake Coeur D'Alene, and further on, cold streams and rivers by the road and small meadows with yellow

278

wildflowers. All day long it has been hot with blue Montana skies...now I know why John Denver was inspired to write the song about the blue Montana skies.

From The Burks BELIEVE IT OR NOT file: We had stopped for lunch in St. Regis and while we were eating Tom saw a motor home towing a flatbed trailer with a helicopter on it. You never know what you are going to see on these trips. Today we went over the Continental Divide and ended up for the night in Billings, Mont.

We are right in the middle of "Bikerville" as the Sturgis, Harley Rally starts on Mon. The campground and roads are full of bikers. It reminds me of 2000 when we were coming back from our trip back East and we went to see Mt. Rushmore right when the Sturgis Rally was taking place (unknown to us) and we found ourselves in the middle of a million Hawgs. It was an interesting experience and one we wouldn't have traded for anything. I still have my Harley T-shirt to prove I was there. Sometimes bikers get a bad rap but we found them to be great people, just like everyone else.

We are in Medora, North Dakota. What a lot of contrast we saw on the road today! We have followed the Lewis and Clark Trail every since Oregon and history really came alive today at a rest stop where we had lunch. Tom read the marker indicating the fur traders, solely for the hides in this area had killed 40,000 buffalo and since that was the source of food and clothing for the Native Americans it started the Native uprising, which ended in the Battle of Little Big Horn nearby. Tom and I couldn't help imagining how these barren hills were once alive with the sound of Buffalo hooves as they thundered across the plains before this happened. It was hot and dry as we traveled farther on and saw disbanded cabins, one after another left by disenchanted occupants. We saw a hill with a group of about 8 wild horses of differing sizes standing proud and tall in the independent unbridled beauty against the blue sky. What a sight to behold!

I had never been in North Dakota before so Medora held a lot of surprises. It was founded by a French nobleman, Marquis de Mores in 1883, who named the town after his wife, Medora. All kinds of rumors surround his life and his supposed shooting of a man in a saloon argument.

Medora is home of the Theodore Roosevelt National Park, a well as some great entertainment. We attended a Magic, Music and Comedy Review that afternoon that was great. History came alive once more as we saw the play, "Bully", and a one-man show about the life of Teddy Roosevelt. Ray Anderson, professional actor, played the part of Teddy. He even came down into the audience and shook our hand! Do you remember he was an asthmatic and used to be made fun of by kids who called him 4 eyes? He was from New York but when his mother and wife died on the same day, he was deeply grieved and came to North Dakota in 1884 to hunt and heal. He bought a ranch in Medora, literally "found himself" and became a different person, hearty and healthfully robust. He found the large herds of bison gone and the grasslands destroyed. Conservation increasingly became a major concern of his. He acquired the name "Teddy" when he was out hunting and killed a bear. His hunting partner urged him to shoot the cub but he looked into the eyes of the cub and couldn't do it. The headlines hit the papers and from that day on he was known as "Teddy", a warm person.

In Fort Mandan, North Dakota where Lewis and Clark and their group, "Corps of Discovery" met Sakakawea (correct Native spelling-it means Bird Woman) in Oct 1804. I am especially interested in this history as I am a distant descendant of Meriwether Lewis. My father's mother, Harriet Lewis Troendly, came from his lineage.

MINNESOTA

We are in Savage, Minnesota, near Bloomington. We had great visit with Skip and Evelyn (Tom's brother and his wife) at a wonderful Italian Restaurant. The next day, Bev (Beauclair) and Art Olson came up from Zumbrota and we had lunch and wonderful visit. (Bev. went to PLHS, class of '54). It is so nice to be able to see so much of our country as well as visiting with relatives and friends.

WISCONSIN

Today we drove from Minnesota into Wisconsin, Tom's home state. The drive sent us through small towns and rural farmlands, green trees and grassland. The scenery is a very peaceful setting, totally free of urban stress. We even passed a bison farm. It was a slice out of small town Americana of almost a century ago. Homes looked like movie sets of yesteryear, close together with porches and almost every home had a flag waving from their porch.

Folks are very inclusive here. Whether they know you or not, you are made welcome with conversation and offers of food.

We had a gathering with Tom's relatives from his father's side who live around here. Anita, his niece, was here with Stacey, her daughter; Brandi, granddaughter; and Wood, a friend. Then Susie, Anita's sister and Tom's other niece was here with daughters Kathie & Pammi as well as Kathie's hubby and family and Pammi's hubby and family. Anita, bless her heart, provided the food for the whole group all day long. She also gave Nancy a beautiful comforter she had made.

Altogether there were 14 of us during the day and 6 more later on. We had fun looking at the Family Album of pictures and Tao loved it because everybody played with him. That evening, Jimmy Burk, wife Pam and 3 kids arrived and Susie came back with Brenda, her other daughter that Nancy had not met before, for an evening of fun and talking.

Susie has been on our prayer list periodically as she is totally blind now. Susie is a wonderful composite of traits, with a flair and zest for life like the character in the play "Auntie Mame", part comedienne with a sense of humor like Lucille Ball, and an old soul with a great philosophy of life and a lively spirit. Despite her physical challenge, her lack of material abundance and her trials of life, she is an amazing person with lots of love that is evident in all the family.

What a day of fun and visiting (it started in around 11 am and didn't end until almost 10:30 pm) in the country outdoors beauty! It was like the old fashioned gatherings my family used to have when I was a child, growing up and the get togethers we had a the cabin in Harrison Park, near Julian. Thanks to the Burk relatives that made me feel so welcome out here in Wisconsin.

MICHIGAN

Thursday, August 18, 2005 5:20 PM

Today we traveled through northern Wisconsin past (Green Bay) and ended up in northern Michigan, a state neither Tom nor I had ever visited. We are camped in Cedar Rapids in a State Park right on the shores of Lake Michigan, which we can see right from our motor home dining window. We can look across and see Wisconsin on the other side. This park is beautiful with grass and tall trees all around.... a gentle breeze comes from the Lake. We were just backing into our campsite when Tom noticed the picnic table had to be moved. Before he could get out of the motor home, the man across the road had come over to help Tom move the table. Tao had a ball with all his playmates, particularly a 140 lb white pyerionese; it was really quite a mutt and Jeff show. We went out for a walk and when we came back the couple in the campsite on the other side of us was waiting to meet us. She wanted to give us cookie bars for our dinner. The people in the Midwest here are so friendly...always willing to help. A lot of them are from farm roots and are a hardy and full of heart bunch of people.

Today we traveled through the Hiawatha National Forest to Sault Ste. Marie on Lake Superior where we saw the Locks and International freighters around 900 yards long with tug boats and horns. We came on down I-75, over a bridge that was longer than the Golden Gate separating Lake Huron and Lake Michigan with enough cable wire (42,000 miles of wire used to make the cable) contained in tubes to encircle the world 1 & 2/3 times. We ended up in Saginaw Bay.

ONTARIO, CANADA
NIAGARA FALLS

Well, we finally made it to London (Ontario, Canada, that is)! We got into Niagara Falls early enough to see the falls illuminated at night...how beautiful! We saw the falls in the daylight...awesome! Now I know why the Canadian side is better. You have a head on view of the falls
.

We went to the Skylon, a sky tower with an observation top, which showed the falls in all their glory. A beautiful sunny day with puffy clouds topped off the perfect photo op

The musical we attended last night is called "Oh Canada, Eh!" (That rhymes with "hey" and means, "agreed"). It was a wonderful musical comedy with lots of laughs and great singing by the artists. They came down into the audience and a pretty actress came right over to Tom, sat on his lap and sang, "Put Your Head on my Shoulder". Ham that he is, he played right along, gooey-eyed at her.... I even have a picture to prove it. We had a riotous good time.

BACK TO THE U.S.
NEW YORK

Today we drove back across the border and ended up at Lake Cayuga State Park in the Five Fingered Lake Region. This part of the country is filled with many lakes and lots of pretty green trees. Today was a special day of reliving history. We went to Seneca Falls, and, if you asked yourself," What is the importance of Seneca Falls to history?", then I would like to share with you just how important it is. In July, 1848 Elizabeth Cady Stanton, the leader, along with many abolitionist friends of hers, including Quaker women and an African-American male, Frederick Douglas (a former slave and active in the freeing slaves movement) organized and participated in the first Women's Rights Convention held in the

Wesleyan Methodist Chapel, Seneca Falls, New York (no wonder I am a Methodist)! Most churches believed that a woman was to be "obedient" to her husband.... never mind the fact that the law allowed him to whip her. More than 300 women and men attended the convention.

The National Park Service has set up a museum commemorating the event as well as displaying statues of those involved, the history of women's rights and the important declarations of the time. A "Declaration of Sentiments" was presented at the convention declaring, "All men and women were created equal". It demanded equal rights for women in property and custody laws, educational opportunities and participation in the church, professions and politics (at that time a woman was denied these rights). It was just the beginning of a 72-year struggle to gain women the right to vote. Susan B. Anthony met Stanton 3 years late and the rest is history or more appropriately, "her story".
I had my picture taken with Elizabeth Cady Stanton's statue and the Tom & I together had our picture taken with her and Frederick Douglas. It was a great day.

I was reminiscing over the phone with a friend who worked with me when I was Federal Women's Program Coordinator for the Navy about going to Seneca Falls and seeing the Women's Right's Museum. It reminded me of what got me started in the women's movement in the 70's...I ordered some rose bushes from a Nursery in New York and filled out an application for credit. They sent it back saying I had to have my husband's signature even though I was making as much as most men.

One of my friends had just begun her career as a lawyer and Calif. had just passed a law concerning women not having to have their husband's signature for credit. She told me to write them with copy to her as my lawyer stating that if they wanted to continue to do business in Calif. they had to comply with the new law and that my husband's signature was not required. As a result I was instrumental in having them change their credit app so that a husband's signature was not required. I also had to sign a statement for the loan company saying I would not get pregnant in order for my salary to be counted for the app for our home loan. It made me quite aware of the discrimination against women and read "Feminine Mystique" and everything I could get about women's rights. I was quite active, attending NOW meetings, taking MS Magazine and was known as MS Nancy Burk, instead of Mrs. It was a chapter in my life that really helped me contribute toward equality for others.

Well, today we drove through Poland & Norway to the Adirondack Mtns. to spend the night at a State Park at Lake Pleasant. It is lovely through this area.

We are at Ft Ticonderoga and Museum, a National Historic Landmark, at the base of Lake Champlain. This was the site of the first American victory of the American Revolution, won by Benedict Arnold, Ethan Allen and the Green Mtn. Boys. I had my picture taken with the drum and fife regiment dressed, as they would be in the 18th century. The view over Lake Champlain is breathtaking and we had lunch at the restaurant overlooking the lake.

VERMONT

We had a most AMAZING experience today as we visited an original farmhouse (c.1790) built by a Quaker family who was part of the underground railroad movement to provide a sanctuary for slaves who ran away from their plantation owners. The floors were slanted so I had to use caution as Tom guided me through the house. It is now known as the Rokeby Museum, a National Historic Site, located on Route 7, Ferrisburgh, Vermont.

Thomas and Jemima Robinson moved to Vermont soon after its declaration as a state from Newport, Rhode Island. The Robinsons, dedicated Quakers, who lived their faith (active abolitionists, women's rights supporters and peace advocates) provided fugitive slaves with employment and education to start new lives. Four generations of the family lived here to become farmers, authors, and artists as well as advocates for human rights. They were extremely prosperous and used their money to help others. They left an extensive collection of some 10,000 documents and we were privileged to see some original letters, dated 1837, which were carefully preserved by lamination. The records provide history of early Vermont from the 18th to 20th centuries and are available for research study. So much of the underground information was kept secret to protect the identities of the fugitives that researchers are still piecing bits and pieces together to get a better and more accurate picture of the events. Recent research shows Frederick Douglas and William Garrison as frequent visitors who stepped on the same floors Tom and I placed our feet...what an awesome feeling!

Something we learned is that the fugitives ate with the Robinsons and slept in bedrooms upstairs...there were no secret cellars, etc. as may have been used in the South. Quakers who lived their faith and were abolitionists as well inhabited most of Vermont We owe a lot of our current rights to these early courageous people who risked much for the sake of helping others.

On a visit to a Vermont Maple Sugar Farm today, we saw a video of how they get the syrup in April and May and then process i with the equipment they have at the farm. We enjoyed sampling anc buying...homemade maple ice cream ummmmmm good!

NEW HAMPSHIRE

Today was scenic/waterfall/driving day. Unfortunately, the weather did not cooperate and we had rain all day... it started in yesterday and from what the news reports say, it will get worse as the fallout from Katrina gets closer. Thursday will probably be the worst but we have so much to be thankful for (we have been quite concerned about those living in the Gulf area).

The White Mountains are beautiful and have quite a few waterfalls. However, we couldn't see what we wanted as many were inaccessible for Nancy. New England does not make scenic areas as accessible for the physically challenged as the Western States do. But I have learned to focus on what I can do instead of what I can't and just have to pass up those things that aren't do-able.

We had heard the Flume Gorge was something not to be missed but there is a shuttle one has to board that lets you off and then there is a steep 1/4 mile hike to the gorge and nearby there is a gorgeous waterfall. The shuttle has no lifts for scooters/wheelchairs, etc. Since it started raining harder, that let me out anyway, but we parked and Tom did the three waterfalls, taking both a camera picture and the video cam so I can enjoy them vicariously in the comfort of our motor home! (I am so blessed to have him as my husband).

We drove the Kancamagus Highway and the area surrounding it memorializes New Hampshire's famous Native Americans: Passaconaway (Child of the Bear) was a peace-loving chief who, in 1627, united over 17 tribes of New England into the Penacook Confederacy and ruled wisely until his death in 1669. Kancamagus (The Fearless One), grandson of Passaconaway, in 1684, followed as leader of the Tribal Confederacy after his Uncle, Wonalancet, and tried to keep peace between his people and the pioneering whites until English harassments caused war and the tribes scattered to upper New Hampshire or Canada. About 1725, Paugus, (The Oak) was Chief of the Pequawket Tribe, along the Saco River. Later, around 1760, Chocorua, was known as Chief of the Ossipee Tribe, around Conway, and as legend has it died on the summit of the mountain which now bears his name,

MAINE

We drove to Bucksport to spend the weekend with my dear friend and PLHS'53 classmate, Shirley (Horton) Roth and hubby Dave. In my Jr year of High School (because I was so sick) I had to withdraw from attending classes & have a home tutor. Shirley came by my house every day to bring me homework and visit me. I will never forget that kindness as it meant so much to me. One of our goals on this trip was to come to Maine to visit her, as she is like family to me, and also meet her husband, Dave. Dave is just like Shirl, easy-going and lots of fun...what a delight!

287

Shirley and Dave drove us around Bucksport, which is a fascinating place. It is like reading an absorbing historical novel and finding yourself time traveled into the pages. Every house is different with old-fashioned architecture, and it keeps one's head turning back & forth so not one is missed.

Jonathon Buck founded the first mill in Bucksport in 1764 and the town grew to be an important lumber and fish port. After burning by British soldiers, the town was quickly rebuilt and incorporated in 1792. Now petroleum products are offloaded here & U.S. magazine coated papers shipped out.

It is quite a historical town as Fort Knox (no not that one) is located here. Begun in 1844 to protect the upper Penobscot River, the Fort was manned during the Civil and Spanish-American wars but was neither finished nor attacked

Questions of the day: Where to spend the perfect 70th Birthday, what to do and who to do it with?
Answers: in Maine, and a trip to Bar Harbor (having a pina colada and lobster tail lunch, with decadent chocolate cake), Bass Harbor, Acadia National Park and with Shirley and Dave Roth, his sister Mary and hubby Pat and Shirl's sister, Sheila and hubby Ron. What a treat to see Sheila again and meet her hubby, Ron...such a cool guy who fits right in with this crazy bunch of fun people.

The weather was just warm and nice, sunny with big puffy beautiful clouds in the sky and the drive was gorgeous with vibrant green trees and rivers, lakes and finally the Atlantic Ocean. (Shirl calls it God's country). Tom & I had the time of our lives, laughing until we almost cried, shopping at Bar Harbor and taking pictures. An episode with an Italian family who couldn't speak English made us laugh sooooo much. One of the ladies came up to Tom and started talking very fast in Italian (like he could understand). Tom was dumbfounded and just stood there. It wasn't clear if they wanted him to take their pictures, if they wanted to be part of our pictures or if they wanted him to get out of the way. Finally he moved and they started posing and someone else took their picture in the spot where we had been.... I wish it had been captured on video, it was hysterical to watch. It was just the most delightful day, celebrating and having a lot of fun!!!!!!!

Today we drove to Fort Knox and Tom, Dave, Mary and Pat went through the tour while Shirl and I got to the 1st level. The sky was the bluest blue and the trees were the greenest green...what a view we had from the top of the cliff. The river was just gorgeous. We came back and later went to the town of Belfast and shopped, then on to Orono, another town to a restaurant called Margaritas for Mexican food. We haven't had that good kind of Mexican food since Oregon. Tomorrow we leave for Kennebunkport with so many great memories of fun and being with the greatest people ever. It will be hard to leave but...we need to be on our way. Thanks so much Shirl, Dave, Mary, Pat, Sheila, and Ron for making our stay in Maine the very best.!!!!!!!!1

We drove a short distance through the town of Kennebunkport with all its quaint shops but found this big motor home does not do well on these narrow New England streets, so we drove around the town along the Atlantic coast.

It was one of those warm fall days with the sun glistening on the waters. The waves splashed upon the rocks with gusto and made water spray designs against the blue sky. We had been told the estate of G.H. Walker Bush was on Ocean Ave., so we slowly meandered around the beautiful estates, and sure enough, there it was...we recognized it by the pictures we had seen in a magazine. It is on a Peninsula and has 11 acres of pure beauty. It is called Walker's Point. The property came into the Walker family in 1902, purchased for $20,000 from the Kennebunkport Sea Shore Co. by Mr. D.D. Walker and his son, George Herbert Walker. (Grandfather and great grandfather of George Walker Bush.) The senior Walker was a successful St Louis dry goods merchant who summered in Kennebunkport and fished on that property for 20 years

We had turned in at a viewpoint with a sign that said "NO RV PARKING" to take pictures. As Tom was taking pictures these 2 men with dogs came up and started visiting but it turned out to be many questions. We had the motor home door open and one of the dogs was sniffing around and started to come in when Tao growled. When Tom got back inside, we talked and both of us were sure they were Secret Service men. They even told us George and Barbara Bush was at the estate over Labor Day Weekend and took their boat into town to eat and shop.

MASSACHUSETTS

We drove our rented car to Plymouth today and saw the places where this country began. We saw Plymouth Rock, a replica of the Mayflower, a statue of Massasoit, the Native American who helped the Pilgrim's through the first winter, the first church, the Howland House (the only house now standing in Plymouth where pilgrims are known to have lived), the Harlow Old Fort House, and the Forefathers Monument (81 feet). We went to Pilgrim Hall, a museum housing the actual artifacts, clothing and possessions of the Pilgrims. However, it was not Nancy friendly (no ramp for the physically challenged) So we were unable to get in. I was quite surprised, as there was plenty of room at the side of the building to build a ramp.

We drove into Boston today in a rental car, and....not a good idea!!! We drove because the shuttle and trolley that they recommend tourists take are not Nancy friendly (no access for physically challenged). Boston is a maze of streets, tunnels longer than I ever imagined, and toll bridges that cost, cost, cost. We promptly got lost but finally found Bunker Hill, commemorating the site of the first battle of the American Revolution, and the USS Constitution (the world's oldest commissioned warship afloat-a 52 gun frigate that never lost a battle.... nicknamed "Old Ironsides" because cannonballs bounced off her thick, oak sides). We had late lunch down by the Boston Harbor and found our way back home totally exhausted over the experience, we went to bed early, so we could reclaim our sanity.

Then we drove to a place memorialized by Patti Page in a song that goes, "sandy dunes and salty air, quaint little cottages here and there, you're sure to fall in love with"...(you guessed it) Old Cape Cod. Only that song was 50 years ago and today it is quaint huge cottages EVERYWHERE. The once enchanted area of tranquility is now very congested but well worth the drive. The sun shining on the sea is still as gorgeous as ever and the sand dunes very picturesque.

I got to thinking about how I perceived this area as a westerner. Whenever I heard of Hyannis port, I always related it to the Kennedy's and Mass. but never related it to Cape Cod. It was not until we actually took the drive up the Cape Cod Peninsula that it dawned on me that it was a part of the Cape. What they call the "Upper Cape" is the area around Plymouth. The "Lower Cape" is the end of the cape where Provincetown (where the Pilgrims landed) is located and what one thinks of as the real Cape Code as in the song. In between are a lot of towns, some coastal and some not.

Some of the names of the towns are Yarmouth, Brewster, Orleans, Hyannis and its port (where the Kennedy compound is located.... but one can only view it from a distance by boat). There are two islands off the Cape...Nantucket and Martha's Vineyard (I always wondered about that name.... now I know. It was discovered in the 1800's with wild grapes on the Island. The man who discovered it wanted to honor his daughter Martha, and so he named the Island Martha's Vineyard).

It made me realize that in order to really know a place one has to visit it. We perceive things from a distance but don't really get the big picture unless we are actually there. If one thinks about the meaning of that sentence, it is true in more ways than one.

RHODE ISLAND, CONNECTICUT and NEW YORK

Today was a four starter.... starting in Mass, going through Rhode Island Providence), Connecticut (I-95 and past Mystic, New London, where the Sub Base and the USS Nautilus are located, and New Haven, among other places) and ending up for the night in Montgomery, NY. Connecticut does not have any campgrounds at all near the west end where we would be for the night so the nearest one was in rural NY. Tom didn't want to go through the traffic of

NY City (been there, done that) so we wound ourselves around the congestion.

Where are we today? ...We don't know and that's okay.
We're here to experience the beauty along life's high way.
That's sort of how today went. We started from our campground in NY, on our way to New Jersey and found ourselves in Pennsylvania! We got back on our route and took the road that led to New Jersey. After finding out that a bridge we were to cross over had been closed we took an alternate route 521 down New Jersey and wound up in a campground in East Stroudsburg, PA in the Pocono Mts. for the night. Along the way we saw beautiful scenery, a lot of trees changing color here, winding around State Forest and Lake Owasee, meandering roads, small towns, spreading farmlands and some huge plantation looking homes with lots of land.
It was a day of surprises to say the least!

PENNSYLVANIA

We got our rental car and went to the Lancaster Info Center to get brochures, etc. to help us plan our day. This area has towns with strange names that came from the past, either from the usage of phrases that were uttered by pioneers or from the purpose of the town at that time and the name became permanent, through continuous usage by the inhabitants.

For example, the town Bird-in-Hand got its name when two men were traveling and were trying to decide whether to stay in this small place with an Inn or go on to Lancaster as they did not know whether they could find an Inn that was not full. One of them uttered the phrase, "Well a bird in the hand is worth two in the bush" meaning, it's better to be safe staying at the Inn where they were at, rather than being sorry by going to Lancaster and finding no vacancy. So the name "Bird-in-Hand" became the name of the town Another town is named Intercourse. It started out as Entercourse, meaning, where the roads crossed or where connections were made and through spelling error came to be spelled Intercourse; or some have said that the word was used to mean where friends conversed or had conversations.

Well, we had lunch at the Family Inn and Restaurant in Bird-in-Hand and went on to Intercourse to visit an Amish Homestead and see a theatre production of "The Amish Experience". We learned the origins of the Amish, how they were different from the Mennonites and why they choose to live the way they do. There are dozens of varieties of both the Amish and Mennonite groups but they have a common history. Their beginnings (1525) come from a group of radical Christians called "Anabaptists" at the time of the Protestant Reformation in Europe. They wanted a return to the simplicity of faith and practice as seen in the early Christian church in the Bible. The Amish Division took place in 1693. Both groups are Christian and stress that belief results in practice...the differences have been in the interpretations of the practices and how much "worldliness" or technology is allowed in their lives or to what degree they choose to bring it into their lives (lifestyle).

Whenever a group of people wanted to live a little differently than the core group, they split off and started their own living style. The purists are called "The Old Order Amish" who want nothing to do with those outside their culture...they use the horse and buggy, plough their farms by the farmer using his horses without modern machinery, and follow the rules of simple living and hand-made goods and products. Their founder's name is Jacob Amman (1693), thus the followers were named "Amish". Peace is a way of life for all groups and they all refuse to participate in war, much like the Quakers, however, they are different, as they want their privacy respected and are a quiet people. The "Old Order" believe that a man's role and woman's role are completely separate and each has their place.... needless to say the man is the ruler of the homestead. The danger in the "Old Order" is the inbreeding and prevalence of genetic disease. The "New Order" of Amish or more modern believers and Mennonites accept and use technology and mix with people and the world to the degree that their individual faith permits them to do.

At any rate, all of them make beautiful solid furniture and toys from wood, and delicious homemade foods. The great number of farms and home grown markets where one can buy fresh vegetables and fruits are prevalent as is the abundance of restaurants.

We had dinner at "Good 'N Plenty Restaurant" and I must say the adjectives describing the restaurant were quite accurate. We ate family style; at a table set for 16.... bowls of individual foods were passed down the table from the hostess who brought them. First, pepper slaw, chow chow (pickled vegetables), and bread and butter. Then the entrees.... sliced turkey breasts, tender roast beef in gravy, fried chicken, creamy mashed potatoes, chicken gravy, lima beans, corn. Then the deserts of strawberry/rhubarb pie, shoo fly pie Jell-O, chocolate pudding, and choice of vanilla/chocolate home made ice cream or rainbow sherbet.

The name shoo fly pie came about because the women would put the pie (made from molasses and brown sugar with a white and brown uncooked sugar on top) on the window sill to cool after baking, which attracted flies, so she would say, "shoo fly, shoo fly away from the pie" and the name became permanent. I must say the pie is VERY RICH.... two bites are enough for me.

PENNSYLVANIA, MARYLAND and DELAWARE

Today was a three stater.... Pennsylvania, Maryland and Delaware. Our goal of seeing all the New England states has been completed! We decided since we were close to Delaware, we would do it in the rental car. We left early and did a tour of the Herr's Potato Chip Factory, close to the Penn/Maryland border (of course we got free samples). Mr. Herr was employed by Hershey's Candy and married the daughter of his employer in 1946 and they started out with very little to make potato chips.... they moved several times as they prospered, and also as one place burned down. They believed in giving back to the church and now have their plant in Nottingham as well as an Angus Ranch and are known as Herr Foods. We ended up buying a lot of snackies from their store (Jalapeño flavored tortilla chips, dips, pretzels, flavored potato chips and popcorn).

After lunch in Maryland, we drove to Delaware, close to Wilmington. The northern borders of Maryland and Delaware are so similar that it is hard to tell when you leave one state and enter the other. On the way back, we went to Brandywine River Art Museum in Chad's Ford, Pa. near the border. We saw originals of Winslow Homer and many from the Wyeth family, including the famous "Braids" that made known the relationship between the artist and the model, as well as many of the famous Native American portraits, action filled cowboy paintings, beautiful landscapes and still-life's. Also on display were the works of Howard Pyle, Alice Barber Stephens, George Cope, William Trost Richards and many others. It was quite a treat!!!!1 We took Tao with us and he enjoyed his exercise around the gardens of the Museum.

We got back exhausted but fulfilled in more ways than one...what a day!

AND BACK TO PENNSYLVANYA

We left Lancaster for Hershey, PA and toured the Hershey Chocolate World.... got a free candy bar but resisted buying anything as we were full of too many rich foods already. Hershey owns a huge amusement park with roller coaster, etc. and Disneyland like atmosphere, sports complex, entertainment center where concerts are performed & Chocolate World. Chocolate World is where factory tours are given in a ride like one would find at Disneyland (you are put into a cart which makes its way around the displays on an automated track).

"Four score and seven years ago, our fathers brought forth upon this continent a new nation..."
Does that tell you where we ended up today?
Yes, we arrived in Gettysburg, Pa, and went to the American Civil War Museum where we saw wax figures come to life to tell episodes of the prelude to the Civil War. Then we went into a theatre and saw the Battle of Gettysburg portrayed on film and also with action vignettes of wax figures with light flashed on them. We picked up a CD for an auto tour through the battlefield.
If any of you come this way, I would recommend this auto tour tape. It is exceptionally well narrated and makes the tour very interesting,

pointing out the historical facts as well as filling in the grey areas that you don't find in the history books, such as the song "Dixie", the Confederate Anthem, being written by a Northerner and the song, "Battle Hymn of the Republic", the song adapted by the Union Forces as their anthem, which came from an old Southern Gospel hymn.

The auto tour is supposed to take 2 hours but we found it took us 4 hours, as we didn't want to hurry through. The statues and monuments are very well done showing great artwork and the plaques are interesting to read. There is also a statue honoring the Native American Tribe that fought in the New York Brigade. The Peace Light Monument dedicated during the Eisenhower Administration where 1,864 veterans returned to Gettysburg...their average age was 94 impressed Tom & me! We found many lessons for us to learn.

MARYLAND, VIRGINIA

We went from Penn, through Maryland to Virginia, where my niece's family lives in Fairfax Station. Barbie is the daughter of my sister Edith who passed on 6 years ago. She and her husband Ed have two children, Tracey, who is married to Drew (3 children, Emma, James and Matthew) and Tara, who is married to Hugh (1 child on the way).

Barb & Ed took us to D.C. where my sister Edith and her husband James Carl Daffin (we called him "Daffy") were interned at Arlington National Cemetery. Daffy was in the 4th Marine Div, WW II (Iwo Jima, Tinian, etc) All week long we have felt close to them as both their birthdays were 9-21. It is a beautiful site, near a fountain and flowers. On the way back we saw the Iwo Jima Memorial, went by the Women's Memorial and the Vietnam Memorial. Afterwards we went to Barb and Ed's home for dinner and were fortunate enough to see a large fox come into their back yard.

The next day, Barb and Ed took us to Wash D.C. where we went to the WW II Memorial. (Dedicated May 2004) It is located in a straight line between the Lincoln Memorial and the Washington Monument with tide pools all around. One can see the Jefferson Memorial on one side of the tide pool as well. This is where the cherry trees are located which bloom in the spring. Many people come here to sit on the benches and meditate. The fountains and walls of water pouring into pools lend to the quiet meditative atmosphere.

From there we went to the FDR Memorial (Dedicated May 1997) I have always admired FDR for his courage and optimism in the face of his own physical challenge as well as how he led our country after the depression, through the war with a vision that not only united us but gave each person the same courage and optimism to live by.

This memorial is truly great with its shade trees, waterfalls, statuary and quiet alcoves, which create the feeling of a secluded garden. It is divided into four outdoor areas, one for each of FDR's terms in office. (1933-1945) The areas have walls of red granite (with FDR's famous quotations carved in them) and ornamental plantings. These areas have scenes sculpted with things that happened during that particular term of office, depicting such things as the New Deal programs providing immediate relief, creating jobs and fostering economic recovery, reforms in civil rights, labor relations, banking and civil service, as well as creating the Social Security Administration in 1935 and his historic meeting with Churchill and Stalin in 1945 in Yalta. Water cascades and pools are present throughout the memorial.

There are sculptures of FDR in his wheelchair, FDR sitting wearing his cape with his dog Fala by his side and of course a sculpture of Eleanor who spoke out so well for human rights when she was a UN representative. Most famous of his words were, "Freedom of Speech, Freedom of Worship, Freedom from Want and Freedom from Fear" and "THE ONLY THING WE HAVE TO FEAR IS FEAR ITSELF". (Interestingly enough the phrase most often mentioned in the Bible is, "Be not afraid"). I will always remember sitting with my parents by the radio listening to his fireside chats.

He had the ability to succinctly put profound messages into short phrases and sentences." More than 50 years after Roosevelt's death, his own words call out from the walls of his memorial as if he were somehow present."

On the way back we saw the Capital, the back of the White House, (people are prohibited from parking in front of the White House due to 9/11), and other important D.C. buildings. We also saw the areas set aside for protests, as there were several that occurred that weekend.

WEST VIRGINIA, KENTUCKY, INDIANA and ILLINOIS

We left Virginia and turned westward for the trip back home. It was a cloudy and rainy day as we traveled through the VA Appalachians and crossed the West Virginia border into the Allegheny Mtns.

Traveling through West Virginia we saw lots of brilliant color in the trees...reds, oranges, yellow and shades of green. Everything was fine until we got close to Kentucky where a lot of road construction was being done. All of a sudden 2 lanes became one and before we knew it a big truck almost took off the right side of our motor home and could have demolished us. I still shake thinking about it. I uttered a short prayer out loud for God to help us and by a miracle the truck missed us by inches. Everything fell on the floor as Tom put on his brakes and Tao's water bowl spilled all over.... but we are safe!!!

We left Kentucky, crossing the Indiana border over the Ohio River. We stayed in the Lynnville Park for the night. We had T-storms and rain within an hour of arrival.

Traveled through Indiana into Illinois and across border. We spent the night just outside of St. Louis, Mo in Eureka.

298

MISSOURI

Went from top of Missouri into Springfield for weekend visit with friends, Darlene & Bob Wilson. Darlene was my Matron of Honor. It is just good to hang out and visit after a week of very steady driving. Bob fixed us a delicious brunch of homemade tomato juice with a bit of hot sauce in it...ummmmm good with fluffy scrambled eggs, ham, sausage, potatoes, gravy, and homemade tender biscuits.

OKLAHOMA and TEXAS

We left Springfield, Mo. and ended up in the state "where the wind comes sweeping down the plains".
We are in a campground on a Native American reservation, but more than the wind there is a lot of humidity and temps into the high 80's like we had in Springfield yesterday. Billowy T-clouds surround us. Traveling on I-44, we passed Tulsa and tomorrow we go through Oklahoma City.

Around Oklahoma City we caught I-40. Today we are having those famous winds.... Tom really does a fabulous job of holding our motor home on the road. We stopped for gas and with the motor home stopped I could really feel the pull and roll from the winds. This is Cherokee country and the soil is really red...we went past a river appropriately named the red river. You can see why the Native Americans were able to mix the soil with liquid and come up with red paint. Since we had trouble finding campgrounds in western OK or Eastern Texas, we drove all the way to Amarillo before stopping for the night.

NEW MEXICO

We left Amarillo, Texas, traveling on I-40 west, which parallels most of the legendary Route 66. We saw remnants of what used to be restaurants, gas stations, motels, and swinging entertainment lounges of a bygone era. It was fun to let my imagination wander about that time (in the 50's) when the Route was widely traveled and publicized by the song and TV show, "Route 66" with Martin Milner and George Chakaris, I believe (I remember watching it). We traveled 305 miles, getting into Albuquerque during the commute, only to find most RV parks full as the Hot Air Balloon Festival was in full swing.

We found a site at the Enchanted Trails RV Park. The advertised (for 3 days) cold front finally hit us and the temp at night went into the low 40's. Wouldn't you know our heater gave out on us and Tom packed me with heating pads and needless to say we didn't get much sleep. However today (Thurs. 10-6) a mobile RV repair came to our rescue and fixed the problem. This eve. We went out to a great Mexican dinner in Old Town with friend Marie Stockton, saw her new apartment and had a wonderful visit.

Barb (Chu-teh Killian, PLHS) & Larry Germaine came by for us and took us to The Albuquerque Museum where Picasso, Spanish and New Mexico art was on display...what a fantastic afternoon!

We met Emily, Larry's caretaker, who is delightful! Best of all was seeing how much Larry has improved. He had his stroke in 2000, two months after we visited here last time. Docs gave him very little hope but that doesn't keep a good man down. We saw Larry again at our high school 50th reunion in 2003 and he had come a long way but nothing like what has happened in the last 2 years. He is talking, moving around, doing some walking and even dancing with Barb On outings he uses a wheelchair but his overall health improvement is a miracle.

We left Albuquerque late as 2 tires were low and we had to find out what the problem was. Finally had the valve extender pulled out and that seemed to take care of it. Going past Gallup on I-40 we saw the beautiful formations of mesas and rocks formed by the wind. We drove into Arizona with T-storms, wind and rains. We camped for the night at the Zuni Indian Reservation (alongside Route 66 again) and they had some petrified wood for sale so we picked up some.

ARIZONA and NAVADA

We took Highway 93 over Hoover Dam and Lake Meade to Las Vegas. It is a very interesting and pretty drive. On the way there was a Homeland Security checkpoint at Hoover Dam and we had our motor home inspected (we passed the test). In Las Vegas, Friends Virginia and Bob Anderson came by and we went to the buffet lunch at Boulder Station (yummy). We celebrated Virginia's birthday early, which is next week. We had a wonderful visit. Now back to California. We arrived back home in San Diego on October 12, 2005.

2006 TRAVEL

We left San Diego Wednesday, March 8, 2006 for Arizona. In Yuma we had visits from Kathie (Miller-PLHS '54) & Tom King, who introduced us to friends Shirley & Bob. They were over there for a Classic Car Show & parade. On the evening news I saw Kathie with their 32 Chevy. The next day Judy Planck, friends we met in Rexhall group & her friend Bobbie visited us. Judy & Ron spend the fall and winter (from Oct to end of March) in Arizona every year. Tom & I absorbed the warm sun & I was able to get out & practice my walking.... had to use walker as there were gravel roads. I also started doing my morning exercises, which I had been restricted from doing until my 6-week checkup The exercises have really helped give me strength in my Left leg and my Homeopathic Doctor gave me a remedy, which after 2 weeks has released the excruciating pain I was having from the bone grafts. Thanks be to God!!!!

We are now here in Mesa at Mesa Spirit Campground with asphalt & concrete pad. For 1st time outside, I was able to walk by myself (with Tom close by of course.) Thanks be to God!!!!! Tonight we are going out to dinner with Pat Barrett (PLHS-51) and Thurs. we will be with Lori White (Jan Brooks PLHS-'53) and hubby Jon.

Must tell you about our delightful experience with Jan and Jon. We went to Monti's La Casa Vieja for dinner (best King Cut

301

prime rib ever per Tom & delicious salmon per Nancy), plus great company with Jon & Jan, and wonderful ambience. Leonard Monti, after whom restaurant is named, was Arizona Sen. Carl Hayden's home (built in 1871 by Hayden's father in the hacienda style with adobe architecture) and is now a restaurant but they kept the historical significance as well as the authenticity intact and is designated as an historical landmark. It has lots of historical memorabilia and can seat 725 people. If any of you get to the Phoenix area, you must take this place in. It is actually located in Tempe.

CALIFORNIA

Well, the best made plans of mice & men...
Due to the change in weather, we re-evaluated our plans to go to Prescott, AZ & we are glad we did as we have heard snow packed the area, but were sorry we missed seeing friends Carol & Jerry Mumford. Carol is co-pastor of First United Methodist Church in Prescott & we had planned on hearing Carol give the service.

We are now in Palm Desert California and it is warm although there is snow in the mountains around us. We got a beautiful picture as the palm trees in the front make a beautiful contrast to the snow in the mountains, serving as a background. There is a lot to do here with all the entertainment at the Casinos and Theatres as well as just "hanging out and relaxing". The roads are flat asphalt so it is good walking here.

We couldn't get a site at Thousand Trails until yesterday, so we were told to go to Spotlight 29 Casino Parking Lot for free overnight parking.... no hookups but lots of room in a gigantic asphalt parking lot & good food in the Casino (prime rib buffet at $8.95). Since there were about 100 motorhomes parked there we felt quite comfortable.

The next day we moved to the Thousand Trails Campground. Tao loves it here as he has buddies all over the place, including a baby Shi Tzu 3 sites down (cute!!!!!!). The motor home folks next to us are from Lebanon, OR, close to Sweet Home, where we go to the country jamborees, so we have a lot in common with them.

We will rent a car since we will be here for over a week and will take in the local activities as well as relaxing here at the campgrounds. We were able to get tickets for the Suzanne Summers show at the McCollum Theatre this Fri night so are looking forward to that.

My! The area around Palm Springs has certainly grown! Indio, La Quinta, Indian Wells, Palm Desert, Cathedral City, Desert Hot Springs, Rancho Mirage and Palm Springs are all "blooming" with date palms, lawns, flowers, new condos, buildings, malls and lots more construction.

Thursday, our managers had home made cinnamon rolls for us...ummmm! Then we went to the annual La Quinta Arts Festival which people are saying rivals Laguna Arts Festival and is rated one of the 10 best in the U.S. Picture this...green lawns with a sidewalk meandering around a man made lake which curves around an island with food and music. Cabanas or awnings are installed throughout to protect some of the exhibits, while the sculpture and other collections shine in the bright sun. It is a display of fine craft, sculpture, jewelry, printmaking, drawings, photography, paintings, textile design of fascinating colors, etc. The warm sun is interspersed with balmy breezes waving through the palm trees with the snow-capped mountains of San Jacinto in the background as the mellow sounds of jazz float through the air.

Friday night we went to the McCollum Theatre to see Suzane Sommers. The theatre is fairly new and quite nice with a spouting tall fountain out front. Suzanne's "one woman show" is terrific. A comedienne, singer, dancer, author of books, including her best seller story of her life and also of poetry, has given much of her time to humanitarian causes. She has got to be 60+ but you would never know it from her legs and figure. She danced, sang and told her story through 90 minutes without a single break. Now back home to San Diego.

GODS LOVE HELP AND SUPPORT WILL GUIDE US

In the last 10 Months, Nancy has had 3 major surgeries and 3 minor ones. She has had the step bacteria since April and it is still with her. She is very weak and can't get around much. She is under hospice care and I have hired a nurse to be with her for about 60 hr a week.

I will out line the operations below:
Left Knee replaced December 05
Left hip replaced and bone graft Feb. 06
Strep bacteria April 06
Abdominal surgery, In Oregon, Aug. 06
Cancer growth removed from right temple Sept. 06
Left hip drained and drainage bag put in Sept. 06
Right shoulder drained October 13, 2006.

Still to go after she gets stronger will be her right shoulder replacement and bone graft and removal of remaining cancer from face.

With all this you would think that a person faith is challenged. Not Nancy's. Not once did she blame GOD or others she remains a strong believer in Christ and is very proud of What she has done with her life.

How does one deal with all this? Well you don't play "the what if game". You deal with what ever is there and take it one step at a time and most of all trust that GOD will give you the guidance that is needed.
Nancy as you all know is a fighter and I expect that she will be back to her normal self some time before year end.

After we returned home, Nancy went in to see her doctor since her left knee and hip were hurting her. The X-rays showed that both knee and hip needed replacement. So in November 2005, Nancy went in the hospital for left knee replacement and in January 2006, Nancy had her left hip replaced. The knee replacement was a wonder since it gave Nancy back her mobility.

It was a better knee than the last one and rehabilitation was faster and Nancy was all smiles. We where so impressed with the mobility, that we bought stock in the company. The Hip was no picnic, but it went well. Big problem was that she was to be first that morning but ended up last and the nurse gave her a pain shot in the operating room and than another nurse gave her another pain shot a few min later in the recovery room, she had another near death experience. A fast acting nurse quickly gave her the antidote that brought her back.

The wounds just would not heal and her doctor ran blood test in April 2006 and found out that she had a streptococcus pneumonia bacteria.

Our worse nightmare returned. She was placed into the hands of San Diego Hospice on 4/20/06 and we prayed to God every minute from that day on.

The bacteria had opened soars on her ankles, knee and foot as well as her arthritis nodule on her tailbone. Bandages are changed twice a day with antibiotic ointment added to the wound on top of oral antibiotic and homoeopathic remedies, herbs, and flower essences as needed.

Each night we would rub her down with oils or essences that would ease the pain of the arthritis and each morning Nancy would spend 45 minutes doing exercises to keep her limbs strong and working.

That summer we went up to Oregon to the country and western Jamboree in Sweet Home. Nancy didn't feel good on the last day but felt it was maybe a cold or bad food. We left for Detroit Lake the next day and got our site. Nancy felt weak and couldn't eat that night, so we left the next Morning for Salem Oregon and took her to the hospital.

X-rays showed that her small intestines got pushed into a cavity left over from her Hysterectomy back in the 70's. Into the operating room and they straighten them out without having to cut any part out. The doctor once again prescribed a strong pain medication and Nancy went in to convolutions. The antidote was given and she came out of it, but once again she was so near death with her weaken condition from the operation and the streptococcus pneumonia bacteria, which we are still treating. She spent Three days in the hospital and I brought her sister Charlotte to see her. After leaving the hospital we stayed 4 more days in the Salem campground so her doctor would be able to see her again before we left for San Diego.

We stopped at our property in Murphy Oregon so Nancy could see it for the last time. Nancy loved this property so much because it gave her the sense of being out in nature and close to God.

Back in San Diego it was back to her Doctors and more blood test. San Diego Hospice reenrolled her into the program since we had to revoke her Hospice benefits when we went to Oregon. A little PR for San Diego Hospice, The Nurses and Doctors that came to our house, from San Diego Hospice are very Kind and professional in their duty and it was always a Joy to see them and relived the stress on Nancy and me just to have someone reassure us that we are doing the correct thing. San Diego Hospice has a volunteer group of people with different backgrounds. They found for Nancy, a woman that does reiki and she would come over once a week as a volunteer, Nancy loved it and it always left her with far more energy.

It was about this time that my feet and legs became so painful that we needed a Nurse to care for Nancy. I could no longer stand or walk for long periods of time. So we hired the Susan Dominguez agency to come in at night to get Nancy dressed and undressed and help her to the pot during the night. We had put a hospital bed in the front room for Nancy when we first placed her under Hospice care back in April.

Nancy's right shoulder which X-Rays shown to have disintegrated from the osteoporosis needed draining as well as her left hip so we ended up with 4 more minor surgeries and a bag was attached to her left hip which had to be drained each day and a week later it was removed. During the following months the results of Nancy blood test had shown she had a staff infection Staphylococcus aureus bacteria "MRSA" The antibiotics that was used to treat her caused a fungus in her mouth and she had a return of the shingles twice during this period.

I had 24 hour nursing care for Nancy now, Susan would stay the night and Beth would come during the day. Both are Gods children who are dedicated to Nancy's comfort and care.

NANCY WENT TO BE WITH THE LORD ON JUNE 17TH 2007
NANCY'S LAST WORDS TO ME WAS (WHAT CAN I DO)

I CRYED

OH GOD I WENT TO CLOSE ON THE HAPPY NOTE KNOWING THAT NANCY IS THERE WITH YOU, FREE OF ALL THE PAIN AND SUFFERING THAT SHE SO LONG ENDURED,

THANK YOU GOD

APPENDIX A

MISSED OPPORTUNITIES

I wanted to share love, joy and peace,
The conflict caused my sharing to cease.
My message was lost in divisive talk,
All I wanted t do was get up and walk.

We could have enjoyed so much more,
Instead you choose to ignore
What I wanted to say and share,
I felt that you didn't really care.

For my part I had many regrets,
So I asked God to forgive me my debts,
And as I forgave my debtors I found I could cope,
My faith gave me unlimited strength, love and hope.

How we say things is as important as what we say,
Let's try it over again another day.
Then perhaps we both will bring
Opportunities to grow and learn many a positive thing.

NANCY T. BURK, M.A., Msc.D.

THINK BEFORE WE SPEAK

If we think before we speak
Will others think that we are weak?
We want to appear forceful and strong,
We never want to show we can be wrong.

We want to control the conversation,
But when we do it leads to devastation.
Will we ever learn not to make the same mistakes?
I hope so for goodness sakes.

Yes, we need to think before we speak,
It is better to be humble and meek,
Rather than talk without respecting others' feelings,
Because people can be hurt and it clips their wings.

When we take time to do the listening,
We will learn many things we could be missing.
We'll find our friends will increase,
And good conversation will never cease.

NANCY T. BURK, M.A., Msc.D.

STEP BY STEP-A DREAM

I was standing in front of a big thicket with thorns and big thistles all over. Across from the thicket was a beautiful meadow and behind it was a forest and mountains. I knew I had to get across the thicket but I was paralyzed with fear and couldn't move. I didn't know how I was going to make it across. I decided to put out my left foot and see how far it would go. Suddenly a path opened up in front of my left foot. I was amazed! Then I put out my right foot and a path appeared in front of it. Each time I took a step the path opened up in front of me but it extended only about two feet in front of me. As I walked faster and faster, the path spread faster. About half way through, I stopped to look around and the path stopped. Then I started again step by step, and again the path opened up. I was able to gain confidence and move faster and faster. I reached the other side and It was beautiful. There was a stream in the meadow and I could see animals in front of the trees ahead. The birds were singing and I gave thanks to God. I had reached my destination. It was like the promised land.

NANCY T. BURK, M.A., Msc.D.

LOVING YOU

Loving you means my day begins with a smile,
Loving you means disappointments last only a short while.
Loving you makes me grin from ear to ear,
Loving you casts out all my doubt and fear.

Loving you brings sunshine and song to my heart,
Loving you is knowing we'll never part.
Loving you brings healing to my body and mind,
Loving you gives me everything I could ever find.

Loving you means I can achieve without threatening your
masculinity,
Loving you means our closeness will never destroy our
individuality.
Loving you is knowing you accept me for being me,
Loving you means I allow you to be all that you can be.

Loving you brings forgiveness its release,
Loving you gives me joy, harmony and peace.
Loving you means your happiness is my life,
Every day I thank God I'm your wife.

Thank God you feel the same way about me too,
Thank you for loving me as much as I love you.

NANCY T. BURK, M.A., Msc.D.

GOOD NIGHT MY LOVE

Good night my love, good night,
I bid you sleep in love and light.

Our love has lasted o'er the years
Because before we slept we dried our tears
Coming from anything we did or said each day,
As God guided us along the way.

We were committed to each other from the start,
Knowing nothing could ever break us apart.
We've prayed, talked, hugged, and admitted our mistakes,
We're only human, for goodness sakes!

Even so, we know the best is yet to come,
I treasure each day with you, from dawn to setting sun.
And now I treasure our closeness as night sets in,
I'll see you in my dreams as they begin.

So now, good night my love, good night,
I bid you sleep in love and light.

NANCY T. BURK, M.A., Msc.D.

REFLECTIONS OF ONENESS

AS I STAND HERE UNDER THIS MAJESTICTREE, I FEEL
THE VIBRATIONS OFMILUONS OF YEARS OF BEING
ONE-WITH NATURE AND WITH THEE.

MY LIFE IS ENTWINED WITH ALL LIVING THINGS
BEFORE ME, ALL
LIVING THINGS IN THE PRESENT AND THOSE IN THE
FUTURE, AS THE
ROOTS OF THIS TREE ARE ENTWINED WITH THE
TRUNKS AND ROOTS OF OTHER TREES AND VINES.

I LOOK TO FIND THE TOP OF THE TREE AND FIND IT IS
SO HIGH IT HAS
BECOME ONE WITH THE SKY. I LOSE AI-L SENSE OF
PROPORTION AND
DIMENSION TO MY BODY AS I MELT INTO THE WONDER
OF THIS MOMENT.

I HEAR THE BIRDS, THE SOUNDS OF OTHER ANIMALS
AND THE WATER
GUSHING OVER THE ROCKS. THE SCENT OF FLOWERS
AND LEAVES
AFTER THE RECENT DOWNPOUR OF RAIN SURROUNDS
MY BEING WITH CLEANSING AND FRESHNESS.

I REALIZE I AM ONE WITH ALL AND THEE, AND WE ARE
ALL ONE IN THEE-REFLECTIONS OF ONE ANOTHER AND
REFLECTIONS OF THEE,
AS IS THIS MAJESTIC TREE.

By Nancy T. Burk, M.A., Msc.D.

APPENDIX B

BIBLIOGRAPHY/REFERENCES

The Holy Bible: Old and New Testaments, KJV. , (Nashville, TN: Thomas N. Nelson, 1953)

The Holy Bible: Old and New Testaments, New International Version, (Grand Rapids, Mich: Zondervan, 1986).

Halley, Henry H., *Bible Handbook,* (Chicago, Ill.: Henry H. Haley,1955). 20th Edition

Webster's Collegiate Dictionary, Ed. Robert B. Posner (New York: Random House, 1995).

Chapter 2

Borg, Marcus J., *The Heart of Christianity,* (San Francisco: Harper, 2003).

Lewis, C. S., *Mere Christianity,* (New York: The MacMillan Co.,1987).

Munger, Robert Boyd,*What Jesus Says,* (Westwood, New Jersey: Fleming H. Revell Co.,1955).

Ogilvie, Lloyd John, *Discovering God's Will in Your Life,* (Eugene, Or.: Harvest House, 1982)

Warren, Rick, *The Purpose Driven Life,* (Grand Rapids, Mich.: Zondervan, 2002)

Wilkinson, Bruce, *Secrets of the Vine,* (Sisters, Or., Multnomah Pub., 2001).

Chapter 3

Dossey, Larry, M.D., *Prayer is Good Medicine,* (New York: Harper Collins)

Chapter 4

Piper, Watty, *The Little Engine That Could*, (Retold from *The Pony Engine,* By Mabel C. Bragg, Copy Right by George H. Doran & Co.), (N.Y.:The Platt & Munk Co. Inc.,1930).

Chapter 5

Dossey, Larry, M.D., *Healing Words: The Power of Prayer and the Practice of Medicine,* (New York: Harper Collins, 1993).

Gregg-Schroeder, Susan, *Prayers for a Sojournming People,* (San Dego, CA: Educational Ministries, 1997).

Parker, Dr. William, and St. Johns, Elaine, *Prayer Can Change Your Life,* (Englewood Cliiffs, N. J., Prentice Hall Inc., 1957).

Puryear, Meredith Ann, *Healing Through Meditation and Prayer,* (Virginia Beach, Va.: A.R.E. Press,1978).

Chapter 8

Buscaglia, Leo, *Love*, ((New York: Fawcett Crest, 1982)

Dunham, Maxie and Reisman, Kimberly Dunham, *The Workbook on the 7 Deadly Sins,*, (Nashville, TN: Upper Room Books, 1997).

Gibran, Kahlil, *The Prophet,* (New York: Alfred A. Knopf, 1969).

James, Muriel and Jongeward, Dorothy, *Born to Win,* (Reading, Mass: Addison-Wesley Pub., 1971).

Jampulsky, Gerald G., M.D.,, *Love is Letting Go of Fear,* (New York: Bantam Books, 1981)

Siegel, Bernie, M.D., *Peace, Love and Healing,* (N.Y.: Harper-Perennial, 1990).

Stearn, Jess, *Edger Cayce: The Sleeping Prophet,* (New York: Bantam Books, 1980)

Trueblood, Elton, *The Common Ventures of Life,* (New York: Harper Brothers, 1957).

Chapter 9

Benson, Herbert, M.D., *Timeless Healing-The Power and Biology of Belief,* (New York: Fireside, 1996)

Borysenko, Joan, *Minding the Body, Mending the Mind,* (N.Y.: Bantam Books,1988)
.
Epsein, Gerald, M.D.,*Healing Visualizations-Creating Health Through Imagery,*(New York: Bantam Books, 1989).

Gawain, Shakti, *Creative Visualization,* (New York:Bantam Books, 1978)

Hill, Napoleon and Stone, W. Clement, *Success Through a Positive Mental Attitude,,* (New York: Pocket Books, 1977)..

Peale, Norman Vincent, *The Power of Positive Thinking*, (N.Y.:Prentice Hall,1955).

Schuller, Robert, *The Greatest Power Thinker Who Ever Lived,* Garden Grove, CA, Crystal Cathedral Ministeries, 1984).

Schuller, Robert, *Power Thoughts,* (New York: Harper Collins, 1993)..

Shealy, C. Norman, M.D., Ph.D.,*90 Days to Self-Health,* (Missouri: Brindabella Books, 1987).

Chapter 10

Ansari, Masud, *Modern Hypnosis: Theory and Practice* (Washington: D.C., Mass Press, 1991).

Bach, Edward, *Heal Thyself: An Explanaion of the Real Cause and Cure of Disease*, (London: C. W. Daniel, 1974) and *The Twelve Healers   and Other Remedies (London: C. W. Daniel, 1975)*

Beveridge, Dr. Irving C., *Hypnotherapy: Its Christian Aspects,* (Columbus, Georgia: Brentwood Christian Press, 1992).

Boericke, William, M.D., *Pocket Manual of Homeopathic Materia Medica & Repertory*, (New Delhi: B. Jain Pub, Pvt. Ltd. 1990 Ed)

Brennan, Barbara Ann, *Hands of Light,* (New York: Bantam Books, 1987).

Chips, Dr. Allen S., *Clinical Hypnotherapy: A Transpersonal Approach,*   (Goshen, VA: EIH Pub., 1999).

Chopra, Deepak, M.D. *Quantum Healing,* (New York: Bantam Books,   1990).

Cousins, Norman, *Anatomy of an Illness*

Dooley, Timothy R., N.D., M.D., *Homeopathy: Beyond Flat Earth Medicine,* (San Diego: Timing Publications, 1995)

Engle, Beverly, *The Power of Apology,* (John Wiley and Sons)

Gerber, Richard, M.D.,*Vibrational Medicine,* (Santa Fe, New Mexico: Bear & Co., 1988).

Gordon, Marilyn, *Extraordinary Healing,* (Oakland, CA: Wiseword Pub.,   2000).

Gregg-Schroeder, Susan, *In the Shadow of God's Wings,* (Nashville,TN: Upper Room Books, 1997).

Hyman, M., M.D. and Liponis, Mark, M.D., *Ultraprevention: The 6 Week Plan That Will Make You Healthy for Life,* (Scribner)

Jeffers, Susan, Ph.D., *Feel the Fear and Do it Anyway,,* (New York: Fawcett Columbine, 1988)

Larson, Bruce, *There's a Lot More to Health Than Being Sick,* (Garden   Grove, CA: The Cathedral Press, 1991)

Lewis, Roger, *Color and the Cayce Readings,* (Virginia Beach: A.R.E.   Press,1973)

Lingerman, Hal A., *The Healing Energies of Music,* (Wheaton, Ill.: The   Theosophical Pub. House, 1983).

McGarey,William A., M.D., *Healing Miracles: Using Your Body Energies,*   (San Francisco: Harper and Row, 1988)

Mein, Eric, M.D., *Keys to Health:The Promise and Challenge of Holism,*   (San Francisco: Harper and Row, 1989)

Shealy, C. Norman, M.D., Ph.D. and Myss, Caroline M., M.A, *The Creation of Health,* (New Hampshire: Stillpoint Pub., 1988).

Wapnick, Kenneth, *Forgiveness and Jesus,*(Crompond, N.Y.: Foundation for "A Course in Miracles",1983).

Ward, Milton, *The Brilliant Function of Pain,* (Lakemont, Georgia: CSA   Printing and Bindery, 1977).

Weil, Andrew, M. D., *Health and Healing,* (Boston: Houghton Mifflin Co.   1988)

Weil, Andrews, M.D., *Eight Weeks to Optimum Health*

TAPES/CD'S
Weil, Andrew, M.D. & Arem, Kimba, *Self-Healing With Sound & Music,*   (Boulder, Co.: Sounds True, 2004) 800-333-9185-2 CD'S

Chapter 14

Halverson, Richard,*Christian Maturity,* (L:os Angeles, CA: Cowman   Pub., 1952).

Chapter 15

Chittister, Joan, *Called to Question,* (New York: Sheed & Ward, 2004)

Marshall, Ellen Ott, Dr., *Choosing Peace Through Daily Practices,* (Pilgrim Press, April, 2005)

Tillich, Paul, *Love, Power and Justice,* (New York: Oxford Univ. Press,   1954).